D0621215

POOR PEOPLE'S KNOWLEDGE

*Promoting Intellectual Property
in Developing Countries*

About the Cover

In the main market in the capital city of Dakar, Senegal, a customer hands over money to a stall owner to purchase a music CD. In late 2001 the government of Senegal instituted a mandatory "banderole" system—shown as the square hologram sticker affixed on each CD or tape in the photo—to help combat illegal copying of music compositions. This system aims to ensure that artists receive their due income for their creations. *Cover photo by Monique Thormann, August 2002.*

Background photo: Woman weaving, Bhutan. *Curt Carnemark*

POOR PEOPLE'S KNOWLEDGE

*Promoting Intellectual Property
in Developing Countries*

*Edited by J. Michael Finger
and Philip Schuler*

A copublication of the World Bank
and Oxford University Press

© 2004 The International Bank for Reconstruction and Development / The World Bank
1818 H Street, NW
Washington, DC 20433

All rights reserved.

1 2 3 4   06 05 04

A copublication of the World Bank and Oxford University Press.

The findings, interpretations, and conclusions expressed here are those of the author(s) and do not necessarily reflect the views of the Board of Executive Directors of the World Bank or the governments they represent.

The World Bank cannot guarantee the accuracy of the data included in this work. The boundaries, colors, denominations, and other information shown on any map in this work do not imply on the part of the World Bank any judgment of the legal status of any territory or the endorsement or acceptance of such boundaries.

Rights and Permissions

The material in this work is copyrighted. No part of this work may be reproduced or transmitted in any form or by any means, electronic or mechanical, including photocopying, recording, or inclusion in any information storage and retrieval system, without the prior written permission of the World Bank. The World Bank encourages dissemination of its work and will normally grant permission promptly.

For permission to photocopy or reprint, please send a request with complete information to the Copyright Clearance Center, Inc., 222 Rosewood Drive, Danvers, MA 01923, USA, telephone 978-750-8400, fax 978-750-4470, www.copyright.com.

All other queries on rights and licenses, including subsidiary rights, should be addressed to the Office of the Publisher, World Bank, 1818 H Street NW, Washington, DC 20433, fax 202-522-2422, e-mail pubrights@worldbank.org.

Research for this book was funded by the Bank-Netherlands Partnership Program.

ISBN 0-8213-5487-6

Library of Congress Cataloging-in-Publication Data

Poor people's knowledge : promoting intellectual property in developing countries / edited
    by J. Michael Finger, Philip Schuler
        p. cm.—(Trade and development series)
        Includes bibliographical references and index.
        ISBN 0-8213-5487-6
            1. Intellectual property—Developing countries. 2. Intellectual property (International law).
    I. Finger, J. M. II. Schuler, Philip. III. Series.

K1401.P66 2003
346'.12408—dc22   2003061376

CONTENTS

Contributors   vii

Acronyms and Abbreviations   ix

Introduction and Overview   1
J. Michael Finger

1   Kuyujani Originario: The Yekuana Road
to the Overall Protection of Their
Rights as a People   37
Nelly Arvelo-Jiménez

2   Handmade in India: Traditional Craft
Skills in a Changing World   53
Maureen Liebl and Tirthankar Roy

3   Enhancing Intellectual Property
Exports through Fair Trade   75
Ron Layton

4   The Africa Music Project   95
*Frank J. Penna, Monique Thormann,
and J. Michael Finger*

5   Preventing Counterfeit Craft Designs   113
Betsy J. Fowler

6   Bioprospecting Agreements
and Benefit Sharing with
Local Communities   133
Kerry ten Kate and Sarah A. Laird

7   Biopiracy and Commercialization
of Ethnobotanical Knowledge   159
Philip Schuler

8   Prevention of Misappropriation
        of Intangible Cultural Heritage
        through Intellectual Property Laws   183
        Daniel Wüger

9   Making Intellectual Property Laws Work
        for Traditional Knowledge   207
        Coenraad J. Visser

        Index   241

CONTRIBUTORS

Nelly Arvelo-Jiménez, emeritus professor of anthropology at Instituto Venezolano de Investigaciones Científicas, director of Asocación Otro Futuro

J. Michael Finger, resident scholar, American Enterprise Institute

Betsy J. Fowler, international development policy consultant

Sarah A. Laird, Department of Anthropology, University College, London

Ron Layton, president, LightYears IP, Washington, D.C.

Maureen Liebl, museum and craft development consultant

Frank J. Penna, managing director, The Policy Sciences Center

Tirthankar Roy, professor, Gokhale Institute of Politics and Economics, Pune, India

Philip Schuler, Development Research Group, World Bank

Kerry ten Kate, director, Investor Responsibility, Insight Investment

Monique Thormann, private consultant

Coenraad J. Visser, professor of intellectual property law at the University of South Africa, Pretoria, and the head of that university's Department of Mercantile Law and its Center for Business Law

Daniel Wüger, Institute of International Economic Law, Georgetown University Law Center

ACRONYMS AND ABBREVIATIONS

ACAA	Asociación Cubana de Artesanos Artistas (artists' association in Cuba)
AIPO	Australian Intellectual Property Organization
ATO	Alternative trading organization
ATSIC	Australian Institute of Aboriginal and Torres Strait Islander Commission
BNPP	Bank-Netherlands Partnership Program
BSDA	Bureau Senegalais du Droits d'Auteur (Senegal agency responsible for collecting royalties for artists)
CAS	Country Assistance Strategy
CBD	Convention on Biological Diversity
CD	Compact disc
CIAC	Council for Indigenous Arts and Culture (U.S.)
CIAP	Central Interregional de Artesanos del Peru
CIAT	International Center for Tropical Agriculture, Cali, Colombia
CIEL	Center for International Environmental Law
CMW	Composite minimum wage
COICA	Coordinadora de las Organizaciones Indígenas de la Cuenca Amazónica (Coordinating Body of Indigenous Organizations of the Amazon Basin)
CONIVE	Consejo Nacional Indio de Venezuela (national organization representing indigenous villages and organizations of Venezuela)
CSIR	Council for Scientific and Industrial Research, South Africa or India
EFTA	European Fair Trade Association
EPA	Environmental Protection Agency (U.S.)
EPO	European Patent Office
EU	European Union
FLO	Fairtrade Labelling Organizations International

FOB	Free on board
GATT	General Agreement on Tariffs and Trade
GBS	Global biocollecting society
GDP	Gross domestic product
IACA	Indian Arts and Crafts Association (U.S.)
ICBG	International Cooperative Biodiversity Group
ICC	Inuit Circumpolar Conference
IDB	International Development Bank
IFOAM	International Federation of Organic Agriculture Movements
ILO	International Labour Organization
INAC	Indian and Northern Affairs Canada
INBio	Instituto Nacional de Biodiversidad, Costa Rica
IP	Intellectual property
IPR	Intellectual property rights
ISM&H	Indian Systems of Medicine & Homeopathy
IT	International Treaty on Plant Genetic Resources for Food and Agriculture
ITC	International Trade Centre
KIRTADS	Kerala Institute for Research, Training and Development of Scheduled Castes and Scheduled Tribes
NGO	Nongovernmental organization
NIAAA	National Indigenous Arts Advocacy Association, Australia
NISCOM	National Institute of Science Communication
PSC	Policy Sciences Center, Inc.
PSD	Private sector development
SCP	Standing Committee on the Law of Patents
SEWA	Self-Employed Women's Association
TBGRI	Tropical Botanical Garden and Research Institute
TKDL	Traditional knowledge digital library
TRIPS	Trade-related aspects of intellectual property rights
UNCTAD	United Nations Conference on Trade and Development
UNESCO	United Nations Educational, Scientific, and Cultural Organization
UNIDO	United Nations Industrial Development Organization
USDA	U.S. Department of Agriculture
USPTO	U.S. Patent and Trademark Office
WCT	WIPO Copyright Treaty
WIPO	World Intellectual Property Organization
WIPO-IGC	WIPO Intergovernmental Committee on Intellectual Property and Genetic Resources, Traditional Knowledge and Folklore
WPPT	WIPO Performances and Phonograms Treaty
WTO	World Trade Organization

INTRODUCTION AND OVERVIEW

J. Michael Finger

How can we help poor people to earn more from their knowledge—rather than from their sweat and their muscle? This book is about promoting the innovation, knowledge, and creative skills of poor people in poor countries, and particularly about improving the earnings of poor people from such knowledge and skills.

Since the agreements reached at the Uruguay Round came into effect in 1995, the World Trade Organization (WTO) Agreement on the Trade-Related Aspects of Intellectual Property Rights (TRIPS) has more or less defined the discussion of intellectual property (IP) and development. This agreement, as I explain below, is about knowledge that exists in *developed* countries, about developing countries' access to that knowledge, and particularly about developing countries paying for that access. This book is about knowledge that exists or might be created in *developing* countries.

To the extent that the international community has paid attention to knowledge in developing countries, it has focused on two issues:

- The defense of "traditional knowledge" against misappropriation by industrial country interests.
- The policing of "biopiracy" on the part of industrial country interests, that is, exploitation of the biodiversity that exists in developing countries to develop agricultural products, healthcare products, and so forth, without proper compensation to the "traditional communities" that first discovered the usefulness of such genetic material.

1

This book aims to expand the international discourse by:

- Calling attention to a broader range of knowledge that has commercial potential in developing countries.
- Bringing an economic dimension into the discussion of traditional knowledge, where legal analysis has thus far been at the forefront.
- Bringing out the incentives for and concerns of poor people—which may be different from those of corporate research, Northern nongovernmental organizations (NGOs), or already successful entertainment stars.
- Demonstrating that the best answer is sometimes a commercial one, for example, providing musicians basic training in small business management or reform of regulations that burden small businesses, rather than obtaining formal patent or copyright protection.
- Calling attention to the many income-earning (rather than the income-using) dimensions of culture—to dispel the notion that culture and commerce are necessarily in opposition.
- Bringing out instances in which more or less standard legal approaches have been effective as an antidote to the general sense of conflict between traditional knowledge and normal legal conceptions so as to identify the problems in which legal innovation—beyond diligent application—is really needed.
- Imbuing into the discourse a sense of the legal and commercial tasks needed to solve a developmental problem—away from "knowledge" as an isolated legal issue.

Scope of the Work

"Life is more than making a living, economic development is in the end about enjoying life," noted Amartya Sen (2000) during the opening of a workshop on the economics of music in Africa. With all the political, medical, social, and economic problems the Africans face, their enthusiasm for music still brings smiles to many faces and joy to many lives.

Maureen Liebl and Tirthankar Roy (2000, p. 199) provide an anecdote that expresses a similar feeling. When an Indian historian, Dr. Shobita Punja, was asked to comment on his role in economic development, he replied: "Others may be concerned with making sure that every Indian has potatoes to eat. My concern is to preserve the part of our culture that has resulted in a thousand different recipes for potatoes."

In chapter 2 of this book, Liebl and Roy begin by reminding us that handicraft in India has value beyond its capacity to generate income. But, they continue, it is also a source of income for large numbers of poor people. In India almost 10 million people earn more than US$3 billion per year from handicrafts. Though Liebl and Roy's motivation is to maintain the art of Indian crafts and to improve the situation of talented artists living in poverty, they recognize that in the natural evolution of things it is neither possible nor desirable to preserve every single piece of the past. Except in a museum setting, they point out, no traditional craft skill can live on unless it has a viable market. The other authors who have contributed chapters to this volume share this orientation: they are value driven and market accepting.

Many of the authors give examples about enhancing the commercial value of poor people's knowledge in which there are no worries about this use being culturally offensive to members of the community or about this use undermining the traditional culture of the community. Ron Layton, for example, is working with Congolese artisans who have offered a product for sale in the U.S. market. There is no issue of unethical use; the artisans are in the market to make money. Other chapters examine instances in which the community considers social and cultural concerns more important than commercial possibilities. Daniel Wüger, for example, explains how the people of the Santo Domingo Pueblo thought it sacrilegious for pictures of a traditional dance to be displayed outside the community and demonstrates that in this instance intellectual property (IP) law might not have prevented the abuse. However, legal instruments that protect privacy did prove useful.

With one exception, the authors describe attempts to help poor people get along in the modern world—to use modern instruments for managing the ownership of knowledge either to collect on the commercial value of that knowledge or to prevent its use in a way that its owners consider inappropriate.

Nelly Arvelo-Jiménez is the exception. Her chapter is not about modern instruments. Her premise is that the traditional knowledge of the Yekuana people of the Amazon and Orinoco Basins is a body of knowledge for an alternative conception of all the dimensions of life—those introduced to the Yekuana people from outside their territory as well as those they have dealt with for a long time. Her concern is not to deal with poor people's knowledge within the legal and commercial conceptions of modern society. Instead, it is to find the Yekuana spirit in outside things, to find a way to bring outside things into the Yekuana world rather than to help the Yekuana take on the conceptions of the outside world.

Intellectual Property in the WTO: The Development Dimension and the Developed Dimension

The WTO agreement on TRIPS requires that all member countries provide minimum standards for legal recognition of intellectual property rights (IPRs) and for enforcement of the rights of holders, both foreigners and nationals. The level of protection required is more or less the level in place in the most advanced countries.

Industrial country enterprises were the force behind this agreement. If the level of IP protection was as high in developing countries as in industrial countries, then developing country users would have to pay royalties on the IP that their national laws had allowed them to copy for free. A lot of money was at stake—the obligation the developing countries took on comes to about US$60 billion per year.[1]

There would be benefits for developing countries from this arrangement, industrial country negotiators contended. If developing countries enforced IPRs as the TRIPS Agreement specifies, they would attract considerable foreign investment. Furthermore, industrial country companies would have an incentive to create products aimed at problems, such as tropical diseases, that were of particular concern to developing countries. The agreement also promised assistance to put the new rules in place.

As to the WTO legalities, to pass and enforce the laws that create the US$60 billion a year obligation is a bound obligation; however, the implementation assistance and the impact on investment and innovation are not. In short, TRIPS identifies an opportunity that industrial country enterprises saw in developing countries and provides a way for them to collect on this opportunity—through the WTO legal mechanism. Meanwhile, it provides no mechanism to ensure the benefits for developing countries that the negotiators alleged would follow.

For developing countries, the IP issue that TRIPS brings forward is how to pay the US$60 billion a year and how to ensure that they, the developing countries, derive the maximum of foreign investment, technology transfer, and so forth, in response. This is less a capturing of the development dimension of IP than it is the make-do part of the *developed* dimension.

The other component of the IP issue for developing countries is to identify what problems their citizens face in earning a living from the knowledge they create or apply, and to work out solutions for their problems. This task has not yet been taken on. It is the unwritten half of the TRIPS Agreement—and within this lies the development dimension of IP.

This book is a modest attempt to look at the issue from the perspective of the economic value of poor people's knowledge. It is about the knowledge poor people own, create, and sell rather than about what they buy. It is a collection of stories of attempts to increase poor people's earnings from their knowledge.

The authors were selected because they have been actively involved in helping poor people earn more from their knowledge, including through marketing ethnobotanical knowledge and creating new opportunities for music composers and performers in Africa.

Chapter Summaries

Nelly Arvelo-Jiménez: Kuyujani Originario: The Yekuana
Road to the Overall Protection of Their Rights As a People

Carib-speaking peoples, such as the Yekuana, have inhabited the tropical forest of the Amazon and the Orinoco Basins for the past 4,000 years. The Yekuana share most of the behavioral patterns that characterize tropical forest cultures, particularly those related to the knowledge, understanding, and sustainable management of the tropical forest ecosystems.

Ms. Arvelo-Jiménez's essay builds from the premise that the traditional knowledge of the Yekuana is a reserve of knowledge for alternative economic and social modes of living and ways of life. It reports an effort, in which she has been actively involved, to manage the interaction between the Yekuana and modern society in a way that preserves the indigenous culture—to conceptualize elements of modern society within traditional conceptions of life rather than to take on the perceptions and values of modern culture. Hers is the only chapter in this volume that does not deal with poor people's IP within the legal and commercial conceptions of modern society; instead, it is about finding the Yekuana spirit in modern things rather than the modern spirit in Yekuana things.

Ms. Arvelo-Jiménez outlines the major incursions of modern society, some associated with attempts to exploit natural resources through large-scale mining and rubber plantations, and others with Christian evangelization. As the people attempted to avoid being impressed as plantation or mining labor, Yekuana settlements became widely dispersed. Furthermore, four decades of evangelization had provoked ideological differences between and sometimes within family groups. Takeover of their territory was an increasing threat, and the Yekuana had little capacity to resist.

Even so, 15 Yekuana villages were able to convene in three successive general assemblies and agree on the primacy of their Yekuana ethnocultural identity. They further agreed that beliefs that question this primacy were inimical to the defense of Yekuana territorial rights. In 1993, with technical support recruited by the Asociación Otro Futuro, the Yekuana started a program to bring their lives—in particular their dealings with the modern world—into closer harmony with their traditional view of the order of things. The program was informally named Esperando a Kuyujani. Kuyujani is their cultural hero, who at the beginning of time demarcated the lands which He left in trust to the Yekuana people. Once Kuyujani's teachings were assimilated by the Yekuana people, Kuyujani vanished. He left with His people the prophecy of His return. The program was registered as an Asociación Civil (nonprofit civil organization) in November 2001 under the name Kuyujani Originario.

In modern terms, the element that brought the Yekuana back together was the defense of territorial rights. The skill of the leaders to build the program on the traditional conception of the origins of their space and knowledge was a key factor in using this motivation to restore the traditional culture rather than to move further into the modern. Through oral history, the Yekuana were able to reconstruct all of Kuyujani's steps, taken when He was carrying out the original demarcation of Yekuana lands. From this oral history they carried out the physical demarcation of the borders of Yekuana ancestral territory, and by 2001 had completed a map that not only identified their borders but also included cultural data, topographic features, historical and sacred monuments, and natural resources.

A parallel effort put together an archive of Yekuana visual images, crafts, medical knowledge, and so forth. This written and photographic record of Yekuana cultural heritage has become an important pedagogic tool in the Aramare schools that the Yekuana established. The schools emphasize the teaching of religion, ceremonies, dances and sacred music, playing of musical instruments, and oral history. Just as Yekuana culture and traditional knowledge were becoming an incomplete chapter in the lives of younger generations, the schools became the center for their revitalization. The teachers there are wise old specialists in oral history, religion, and the ancient ways. Their role in the schools is helping to restore the status that elders and wise men once had in Yekuana society. Within the context of Yekuana culture, the schools also offer workshops in modern matters, such as ecotourism and indigenous rights, as provided for in the constitutions of several South American countries.

The archives are also a base for defending Yekuana IP in the modern world, although Ms. Arvelo-Jiménez deals minimally with this dimension. Though many contacts between the traditional and modern worlds have engendered apathy and even disdain for traditional ways, the Yekuana have assimilated knowledge of the external world through the Kuyujani Originario program in a way that has strengthened their appreciation for their own cultural heritage. The program has become a model that many other Amazonian indigenous peoples are trying to adapt to their particular geographical, social, and cultural realities.

Ms. Arvelo-Jiménez notes that when the political and economic interface between modern and traditional is handled by persons drawn from the modern world (government agencies or NGOs) they often operate within the modern rather than the Yekuana perception. The situation improves markedly as people from traditional societies take up these responsibilities, for example, as they did through an organization called the Coordinating Body of Indigenous Organizations of the Amazon Basin or Coordinadora de las Organizaciones Indígenas de la Cuenca Amazónica (COICA). She identifies two tensions that remain, however. First, dealing with outside economic and political agents requires unity among traditional peoples, but indigenous political systems in the interfluvial areas are decentralized and resistant to the delegation of local power to a centralized agency. Leadership in traditional communities has more the spirit of continuing customary modes of life than adapting to new ones. Second, even leaders drawn from traditional peoples—particularly when working within an organization responsible for several traditional communities—sometimes "seem to lean more on the national and non-Indigenous axis of power" (Ms. Arvelo-Jiménez's phrase). They work within the modern conception of their responsibilities, and they see their status and ambitions as their modern colleagues see theirs—in the modern rather than in the traditional world. They fail to communicate the link to the modern world in a way that enables the indigenous peoples to be active participants in shaping the link.

Lessons   Several lessons emerge from this experience. One is that creating a record of the Yekuana's property that will serve them in their dealings with the modern world can be done in a way that strengthens rather than weakens indigenous culture. A complementary lesson is the need for an active program to maintain and to build on indigenous culture. The momentum of the interface is more toward the modern world, but the Yekuana experience demonstrates that, when creatively managed, the dynamic of the indigenous culture can be maintained.

Maureen Liebl and Tirthankar Roy: Handmade in India: Traditional Craft Skills in a Changing World

Handicrafts provide a modest livelihood to large numbers of poor people in India, particularly to the rural poor. Currently, about 9.6 million people earn about US$3.3 billion a year, or just under US$400 per person. The part-time rural nature of much crafts activity complements the lifestyles of many craft workers and provides supplementary income to seasonal agricultural workers and part-time income to women. Engaging in this type of work often provides the means for people to remain in their traditional villages rather than migrate to the city.

Handicrafts have value beyond their capacity to generate income. India's myriad craft traditions and living craft skills are rare and irreplaceable resources, generally acknowledged as living links to the past and a means of preserving cultural meaning into the future. Both within India and without, large numbers of connoisseurs avidly collect examples of specific craft genre. Numerous scholarly treatises and expensive coffee-table books have been written on various craft forms.

Though the authors' motivation is to maintain and advance such art and to improve the situation of talented artists living in poverty, they recognize that in the natural evolution of societies it is neither possible nor desirable to preserve every single piece of the past. Except in a museum setting, no traditional craft skill can live on unless it has a viable market.

The study looks into two possible ways to improve the situation for artisans:

- To increase the income of crafts producers. The prerequisites are adaptation of skills and products to meet new market requirements and improvement in market access and supply.
- To sustain the traditional skill base and to protect the artisans' traditional knowledge resources. The priority in this area is development of appropriate IPR legislation and implementation.

Artisans in India face the same IP problems as in other developing countries: cheap knockoffs, extensive copying among artisans, artisans who pass along (and sometimes sell) designs belonging to a client, and buyers who have a sample designed and produced in India, then manufactured in bulk somewhere else.

People in the crafts business are pessimistic about obtaining design and process protection through enforcement of patent and copyright laws by the Indian government. The authors interviewed many dealers, manufacturers, and exporters on the matter, and not one expressed optimism. The entire system of legal enforcement in India has problems, and these problems are unlikely to be overcome for the sole purpose of protecting crafts ownership.

Problems with enforcing ownership are particularly complex given what the artisans themselves accept as norms of behavior. Copying among artisans is a long-established tradition. Artists acquire their skills by copying.

Among successful artisans, maintaining secrecy is the first option for protection. Most cope by guarding every stage of the process as closely as possible, prohibiting photography, and avoiding such things as catalogs and extensive web displays. Some crafts communities go so far as to guard the processes from daughters in their families. As one artisan explained, "The girls get married and leave us. We cannot take the chance that they will take our secrets with them."

Adapting skills and products to new market conditions offers real possibilities, but commercial realities do not paint an optimistic picture for all artisans. Take, for example, weavers of everyday garments. In the past, wrapped, unstitched cloth was the basic mode of dress (the woman's *sari* and the man's *dhoti*) throughout the country. The local weaver was thus an important member of the community, and his economic well-being was assured. Many women today prefer the brilliant chemical colors, novel synthetic texture, and low price of machine-made *saris*, and many are shifting to tailored clothing. Throughout India, women still prefer *saris* for formal and ritual occasions, and there will always be a market for the exclusive (and often expensive) high-end woven *saris*. But the livelihood of the multitude of local weavers has disappeared.

Upscale markets offer more optimistic examples, one of which is the designer Ritu Kumar. In the 1970s, she revived a traditional form of embroidery done with silver and gold wire to create fine evening and bridal outfits. In time she expanded into other traditional crafts, such as other forms of embroidery, mirror work, and handblocked prints. At first she incorporated these into traditional Indian outfits, but she has since moved into fusion and Western clothing, as well as into accessories and home decoratives. Today, Ritu Kumar has boutiques throughout India as well as in London, and she is an international presence.

Ritu Kumar has been the inspiration and model for a new generation of designers who see traditional craft skills as the foundation for a contemporary Indian design aesthetic. One group is working with traditional palm-leaf manuscript painters from the eastern state of Orissa, teaching them carpentry and opening their eyes to the ways in which their paintings can be incorporated into fine furniture. In the southern Indian state of Kerala, sensitive development of "backwaters tourism" has saved the *kettuvallom* and its makers. The *kettuvallom* is a type of boat that was originally used for cargo transport and is now used as a private floating hotel. They have become fashionable with high-end international tourists.

At the same time, many producer groups have failed, unable to overcome the factionalism, patronage, nepotism, and corruption that are also traditional.

As for the distribution of benefits between artisans and the designer/entrepreneur, many of the designers see the artisan as a partner, regard their work with some idealism, and accept responsibility for equitable sharing of returns. Others do not. The most committed try to work with artisans in their traditional settings, but the demands of economic survival often require artisans to edge into the modern world, for example, to relocate to centralized workshops in cities.

Perhaps the identifying characteristic of the successful operations is leadership, often from an individual who combines mastery of modern commercial skills with respect and affection for traditional artistry and traditional artists.

Lessons   Many people engaged in commercial activities that will help developing country artisans earn more from their artistry are motivated by their love for the art and their concern for the artists, as well as by the opportunity to profit from their work. The effective ones are market accepting; they realize that except in a museum setting, no traditional craft skill can be sustained unless it has a viable market.

Finding commercial applications of traditional artistry in clothing, furnishings, and so forth is a critical form of entrepreneurship.

The lack of enforcement of IPRs in the domestic economy orients activity toward foreign markets, where such protection is available, or toward the high end of the home market. Here, the artist is protected from unauthorized copying by the uniqueness of his or her skill and the appreciation of his or her customers for the objects that skill can render.

Ron Layton: Enhancing Intellectual Property Exports through Fair Trade

A cloth doll that would bring no more than 25 cents if sold in the Andean village where it was sewn might bring US$20 in a shop in New York. The fair trade movement was sparked by concerns that when such products are sold in industrial country markets the Andean seamstress receives no more than 25 cents, and the difference is absorbed by traders and retailers. Fair trade importers (known as alternative trading organizations, particularly "Northern ATOs") are intended to operate at sufficient profit levels to sustain themselves while sharing with poor producers the rents implicit in the differential between market prices in rich and poor countries. Two such organizations, Ten Thousand Villages (U.S.) and SERRV International (U.S.), began in the 1940s and remain viable, demonstrating long-term business sustainability.

Northern ATOs partner with Southern ATOs, which are generally organizations of growers or artisans. Northern ATOs contract with developing country ATOs that meet criteria such as transparency in financial operations, efficient management for reasonable profits, fair returns for individual producers, and fair working conditions. The key element of fair trade is the development of respectful, long-term relationships with marginalized producers. These relationships include in various combinations contracts for annual supply, fair prices, advances against future production, training for producer skill development, and provision of market information. Paul Myers, chief executive officer of Ten Thousand Villages, considers sustained purchasing from poor producers to be a larger factor in poverty reduction than the higher prices paid by Northern ATOs. The longer-term relationships with the ATOs allow poor producers to manage their family life more effectively, for example, to budget to send children to school. Fair traders attempt to set a standard that suppliers might also demand from conventional businesses and to demonstrate that a business that abides by such a standard can be economically viable.

Taking advantage of opportunities in the market for IP (in the "content industry") involves skills different from those necessary for the production and marketing of commodities—products that embody minimal IP value. Often, a handicraft product that sells well when introduced by Ten Thousand Villages or SERRV is quickly followed by a machine-made copy distributed by a mass retailer. As a consequence, the ATO has only one opportunity to address the market: when the product is first exposed.

The Korean animation industry provides an example of a developing country industry that has not succeeded in IP markets. Over the past 30 years, Korean animation companies, through subcontract production for foreign companies, have built up a world-class production capability and excellent design skills. As production companies, they earned recognition as among the best and most reliable in the world. In the more recent past several Korean subcontractors created their own products, aiming to capture the rents available in international markets from ownership of successful animated shows. The quality and creativity in these speculative productions were high, but the Korean companies had no success in placing them with major worldwide animation buyers such as Warner Brothers, Canal Plus, and the Cartoon Network. The Korean animation industry remains a "manufacturer" of content industry inputs and is now subject to fierce price competition from manufacturers in China and India.

In the content industry, legal and commercial skills are closely intertwined. The work done by agents, brand specialists, and so forth is more one-off in nature than the production and even the marketing of commodities. LightYears IP is an ATO set up to specialize in the marketing of developing country IP. This marketing aimed initially at industrial country markets, where IP instruments already exist. Moreover, that is where the big money is, and industrial country markets are open, with few tariff or nontariff barriers to IP exports. Existing fair trade importers support the project, because they recognize that they have found it difficult to manage the IP elements in their marketing of handicrafts, including the patenting of designs, brand development, and design and style recognition.

LightYears IP will utilize initially a group of IP lawyers who have agreed to provide pro bono services to fair trade producers and their Northern ATO partners. As Layton's article points out, a sustainable solution will require that such services be paid from revenue generated. Like earlier ATOs, LightYears IP's success should provide an example to creative groups in developing countries as to how they can operate in industrial country markets, as well as an example for industrial country buyers of their ideas.

An ongoing project to market Congolese-made toy autos in the United States illustrates how LightYears IP will work. In February 2002, representatives of Volkswagen (VW) that America approached Ten Thousand Villages in relation to a toy VW "Beetle" that Ten Thousand Villages was importing and selling in the United States. The scale models of the Beetle were produced by a group of Congolese handicrafters. VW claimed certain rights in the design of the toy, as they are derived from

VW's design of the actual car. VW asked Ten Thousand Villages to stop marketing the product, as it was not authorized by VW. In time, Ten Thousand Villages negotiated a limited license that allowed it to sell out its inventory after payment of a small license fee.

The Congolese artisans had been making distinctive toys made entirely from strands of wire. The Congolese artisans were from a tribe that traditionally has made articles from wire; their jewelry and women's accessories are perhaps their most familiar product. Just as VW has rights to the design of the automobile, a designer who creates his or her own interpretation of the automobile as a model or toy has rights under IP law. Legal enforcement is equally available in the United States to the interpreter as it is to VW.

Armed with this knowledge, Layton's group, LightYears IP, obtained advice from a branding specialist to look into the potential for a large order from VW for a design from the Congolese group. Perhaps VW America might use the Congolese models in its promotions, building both on the artistic value of the interpretation and on publicizing the business the order would create for a design group in a poor country.

The capacity of the Congolese group is basically their design capacity. Their production to now has been by hand in small lots. If they obtain a large order, they would need assistance to arrange for production to be handled by third parties and to ensure that they were compensated for their design elements. With a view to the long run, such an order might be a step toward building a market awareness of their design style and thus lead to further earnings from design.

Lessons   The first lesson is that people who know knowledge-based industries see considerable potential in poor people's knowledge. A second important lesson is that IP is a commercial as well as a legal skill. Having the appropriate laws and police in place is insufficient. Artisans not familiar with the use of *commercial* tools, such as brand names, trademarks, and copyrights, to manage the knowledge value of their product often find their successful products copied by large-scale producers who can make a living simply from the commodity value. However, command of the commercial skills to collect the value of their knowledge embedded in their products is within reach of the Congolese, and it will make a difference.

This and other chapters illustrate the important role of good intentions. The fair trade organizations are market-accepting organizations; they accept that over the longer term commercial viability is necessary. At the same time they allocate returns beyond their costs to developing country suppliers, even when these suppliers do not have the market power or the market knowledge to command these returns in the marketplace. The fair trade organizations aim to provide a transition from artistry to commercial viability, and the effect will be to build a successful business community in the supplying country.

Frank J. Penna, Monique Thormann, and J. Michael Finger:
The Africa Music Project

African music has significant business potential. It currently makes up about half of the fast-growing "world music" segment of recorded music, and music industry experts suggest that African music today may be at the jumping-off point where country music and rock and roll were in the United States in the 1950s.

At the initiation of this work, Paul Collier, director of the World Bank's Development Research Group, pointed to an important psychological element. To maintain its own resolve to push forward and to prevent its more dynamic young people from going off to Europe or America, Africa has to see itself as succeeding in activities that have some glamour. The music industry has the potential to be an important symbol, as well as a substantive element in bringing a poor society forward.

The scheme to support development of the music industry in Africa actually stems from the Bank's work to help developing countries make more effective use of the WTO. Spurred by increasing concern that WTO obligations on IP, standards, and other behind-the-border parts of economic regulation were not consistent with good development policy, a small group set out to find "real development projects" that would involve these policy areas.

The immediate objective of the work was project design, to help African musicians identify problems and bottlenecks and to prepare plans and proposals for investments, policy and legal reform, and so forth, to take on these problems. This information would provide lessons on the usefulness of the WTO obligation on IP to generate increased earnings by local musicians—which we interpret as the development dimension of the issue. The work reported in the chapter was financed by a small grant from the Bank-Netherlands Partnership Program (BNPP).

The intent is to include a half-dozen or so countries. Work has begun in Senegal, and a diagnostic study in Mali began in spring 2003 that will involve some of the people who have contributed in Senegal. Frank J. Penna, managing director of the Policy Sciences Center, Inc., has organized the work. We refer to the contributors informally as the WB–PSC team.

The work program on African music took to heart the new (when the work began) Bank emphasis on local ownership and empowerment of local stakeholders. As soon as the relevant government ministries had approved development of a strategy for the music industry, the WB–PSC team held meetings in Dakar with local musicians to invite them to explain their problems and to suggest solutions.

The musicians came forward with a long list of complaints. A few of those listed in the chapter are repeated here:

- Most Senegalese musicians make their living from the local market. Of some 30,000 musicians, perhaps a dozen derive income from foreign sales.
- Piracy of local music is rampant. Cassettes sold locally are quickly counterfeited, and radio stations play the music without paying royalties. Most musicians are unaware that there are laws to combat such piracy, they do not know how to use the laws, and they do not have the resources to engage lawyers to represent them.
- The local collection agency is ineffectual. Pirates have more resources at their disposal and better connections with influential politicians than does the collection agency.
- The tax burden is disproportionate; for example, as imports, musical instruments are treated as consumer goods rather than as producer goods, and the rate of collection of taxes on concerts/performances is higher than the rate on economic activity elsewhere in the economy.
- There is little business infrastructure—there are few managers or administrators in the music field. The few recording studios are able to charge monopoly prices.
- Live performances are a major source of income but performance venues are expensive. Because musical instruments and sound equipment are expensive, they often belong to the hotel, bar, or concert hall. Musicians must kick back a significant part of their earnings for use of the instruments and equipment.
- Musicians who enjoy success in the international market produce and record their music in foreign studios; thus, their success does not provide jobs for sound technicians in Africa.

"Big fish eat little fish" is how Africans describe the economic structure of the music industry. Financial institutions in Africa will not lend to the music industry, and rampant piracy and weak collection societies make the collection of royalties problematic. Elite musicians or otherwise capitalized individuals who have their own recording studios pay local composers and performers on a work-for-hire basis. When the workday is done the output belongs to the hirer, as with working in a factory or contributing a chapter to this book. (Usually a contributor to a scholarly book receives an honorarium upon delivery of his or her contribution, while the copyright for the book rests with the publisher.) Because the collection societies that are supposed to collect royalties for performers and composers rarely do so, the little fish hardly have an alternative to selling their songs to a publisher/recording company for a single up-front payment. The big fish then sells the song on the international market through his or her own record labels or through foreign multinational record companies.

The Senegal Musicians' Association already had on its drawing board a development plan for the industry. The plan follows closely the problems outlined above. From the initial BNPP funding, the team provided technical support to develop operational proposals for the various elements in the plan. The initial BNPP grant also provided legal expertise to support the association's input into the government's reform of copyright regulations and of the collection society. Spurred by the government's interest and by the activities of the Musicians' Association, the collection society has become more dynamic. It has taken legal action to force radio stations to pay royalties; it has also initiated a system to combat local piracy by providing difficult-to-counterfeit stickers to attach to cassettes and discs on which royalties have been paid. The sticker system will help to identify counterfeit products; its success, of course, depends on the rigor of the police and the courts to enforce the law.

The government of Senegal is now preparing with the Bank components for a tourism industry project loan that will address some of the investment and training elements in the music industry development plan, as well as provide additional support for legal and institutional reform. Embedding this work in a tourism industry project will help to keep it focused on providing facilities in Senegal—to deepen the music industry to include the behind-the-stage infrastructure that will multiply the number of jobs provided. As the local music industry develops, more Senegalese artists should gain international recognition, but the persons responsible for the project realize that one cannot pick the winners ahead of time. Even if the development of "stars" was the objective, the program would have to provide broad support to succeed.

The most forward-looking element in the overall plan is for an Internet-based distribution system for African music. An African musician plays a song in an African studio. Computerized equipment records the song, creates the records for his or her copyright, and mounts the song into an encrypted dot.com facility that listeners around the world can access. As a listener downloads or plays the song, his or her bank or credit card account is automatically debited, and the musician's account is automatically credited. Such a system, experts insist, is within the bounds of present technology.

Lessons   A poor country will not find the development dimension of IP in its TRIPS. All but a dozen or so of Senegal's 30,000 musicians earn a living in the domestic economy. TRIPS could be the basis for foreign music companies (through their governments) to press the Senegalese government to more rigorously defend their interests in Senegal, but the benefits from this effort would not spill over to local musicians.

As a related lesson, the development dimension of the music industry is much broader than the legal dimension. The scope of problems the musicians identified and the scope of the development program they outlined make the point. Even within the legal dimension, the reforms TRIPS requires will not by themselves undo the "big fish eat little fish" structure of the industry, nor will they provide musicians the commercial skills needed to manage the IP dimensions of their business.

Empowerment of the poor musicians—getting the government to recognize them as a political force—is part of the remedy. Attention to ownership of reform by local stakeholders has been productive. A dynamic program of reform and development has been initiated for a minimal amount of money. Another part of the plan is to create alternative opportunities in the local economy. An important dimension is the positive impact on African morale that additional success in music will bring—further enhancing the sense of "can do" that Africans have for this work.

Betsy I. Fowler: Preventing Counterfeit Craft Designs

In many poor countries, crafts production is a source of income as well as a vehicle to preserve indigenous art and culture. Artisan handicrafts represent an estimated US$30 billion worldwide market. With globalization, industrialized counterfeiting is common and often displaces the livelihood of artisans. For example, products that mimic southwestern Native American basketry are manufactured in Pakistan, and companies in Romania manufacture and sell knockoffs of Taiwanese knockoffs of Native American jewelry. Artisans cannot make a living selling at the prices at which machine-made articles can be sold.

Standard legal mechanisms do not always protect artisans. For example, some European designers toured Peru and subsequently used traditional Peruvian designs in their jewelry collections. The Europeans registered the designs in Europe and on that basis prevented certain sales of Peruvian-made jewelry in Europe.

The Fowler chapter, however, spends more time with the positive side of the story. Ms. Fowler warns that abuse is rampant, but she presents several examples in which standard IP mechanisms have helped to protect artisans.

Australia   The use of reproductions of traditional aboriginal designs to decorate mundane products for the tourist trade, such as key rings, T-shirts, and drink coasters, is a matter of increasing concern to aboriginal peoples. Aboriginal customary law provides for collective ownership of paintings and other artistic works, but that collective ownership does not carry over into Australian law. Even so, Australian courts have found ways to defend aboriginal artistic creations against exploitation from outside the aboriginal community while at the same time recognizing the spiritual and sacred significance of the images and respecting the community's sense of communal ownership.

Ms. Fowler reviews a case that involved the importation of carpets that reproduced without authorization designs from aboriginal artists. The court recognized the aboriginal artists as owners of the designs under Australian law but made a collective award of damages rather than awards to individual artists. This left the aboriginal community to distribute or otherwise use the award as it considered appropriate. Furthermore, in its awarding of damages the court took into account the culturally inappropriate use of the designs.

Another informative case involved a picture titled *Magpie Geese and Water Lilies at the Waterhole,* painted by John Bulun Bulun, an aboriginal artist. The R&T Textile Company reproduced the picture on a T-shirt and offered it for general sale. The court in this case recognized Mr. Bulun Bulun as the owner of the design under Australian law but in addition ruled that Mr. Bulun Bulun bore a fiduciary duty to his aboriginal community (a) to guard against infringements of copyright that would misuse the ritual knowledge depicted in the painting and (b) to consult with other traditional owners in doing so. Mr. Bulun Bulun had in this case taken what the court considered appropriate action, and the court did not explore further the characteristics of the fiduciary relationship.

A strong NGO, the Australian Institute of Aboriginal and Torres Strait Islander Commission (ATSIC), is another factor contributing to the successes that the aboriginal communities have achieved.

Native Americans   The Native American community in the United States has been active in establishing both state and federal legislation to protect their arts and crafts. U.S. law requires Indian-style imported products to be indelibly labeled with the country of origin and imposes penalties for marketing non-Indian-made goods as Indian made.

Even so, many devices are employed to evade the law. A simple one is to paste the seller's label over the mark of origin. In a more sophisticated scheme, ingenious people set up a town named "Zuni" in the Philippines, then stamped goods with the label "Made in Zuni." (The Zuni are a North American tribe whose crafts are highly valued.) Ms. Fowler also reports cases in which Native Americans are employed for final assembly of foreign-made parts that are then sold as "Indian made."

The U.S. Patent and Trademark Office (USPTO) advises tribes to draw up and register lists of tribal symbols. The registration helps to prevent use by nonmembers, and it is a tool to push for cancellation of existing trademarks that incorporate Native American symbols.

NGOs, often in cooperation with tribal or artisans' associations, have been active in the United States and Canada to combat deceptions. They have lobbied extensively and have helped Native American tribes to develop certificates of authenticity. The impact of such certification depends, of course, on buyers being aware that such a system exists, and also on their concern to purchase only authentic items. Canvassings by NGOs have found widespread lack of awareness of both the laws and certification systems to protect Indian-made articles—both among buyers and among Indian artists.

Latin America   Constitutions in several Latin American countries mandate the protection of the rights of indigenous cultural communities and indigenous peoples. These regulations aim to prevent outsiders from registering patents and copyrights based on indigenous people's ancestral knowledge and genetic resources, while at the same providing these people protection within their communal conception of ownership. Panama, for example, has set up a Department of Collective Rights and Forms of Folkloric Expression to grant and administer collective ownership copyrights for indigenous groups and to prevent registration by any outside party. The National Crafts Department of the Ministry of Commerce administers a system of authenticity stamps, and Panamanian law prohibits the importation of any products that resemble indigenous crafts without the permission of the indigenous community. This legislation is the result of efforts by and on behalf of the Kuna people to stop the sale by outsiders of copies of *molas*. The Kuna are a Panamanian indigenous community, and the *mola* is a traditional dress that has proved popular with tourists.

Ms. Fowler reports on efforts by government agencies, NGOs, and artisans' groups in Peru, Bolivia, Colombia, and Venezuela to develop national registries of crafts and to advance the use of marks of authenticity.

Bobbo Ahiagble in Ghana   Ghanaian law provides for the registration of certain textile designs and hence their protection through standard IP mechanisms. *Kente,* however, and several other well-known designs of a particularly communal nature cannot be registered. There was no legal recourse then for the Ghanaian *Kente* artist, Gilbert "Bobbo" Ahiagble when J.C. Penney reproduced his designs on bedsheets and marketed them to the American public.

Louise Meyer, who founded Africancrafts, a nonprofit organization to help preserve the tradition of *Kente* cloth weaving, has closely followed Bobbo's career. According to her, Bobbo worried years back about copies, but as he realized that his weavings are of higher artistry and technical quality, he concluded that his identity is his protection against copies. He uses unique labels to distinguish his creations, and his status is such that all of his weavings are produced and sold to special order. Any buyer in the secondary market can consult his records on questions of authenticity.

Lessons   In her conclusions, Ms. Fowler points to the importance of combined efforts of networks of indigenous populations to bring the counterfeiting problem to the forefront. Networks and associations have proved to be effective tools for pooling resources for lobbying, awareness training, and enforcement. She notes that artisans need training on IP tools and how to use them. The cost of using these tools, however, is high relative to the incomes of artisans, and unless such tools are provided on a pro bono basis, they are not likely to be attainable.

Kerry ten Kate and Sarah A. Laird: Bioprospecting Agreements and Benefit Sharing with Local Communities

Global sales of pharmaceuticals derived from genetic resources exceed US$75 billion a year. Add in other healthcare products, agriculture, horticulture, and biotechnology products and the total comes to more than US$500 billion a year. Many of these products link back to knowledge that traditional communities possess on how to use natural materials as medicines, foods, and preservatives, yet these communities have received minimal revenues from such sales.

The past quarter-century has witnessed considerable political action to help traditional communities obtain a better deal from the commercial application of their knowledge and of genetic material found in the areas they occupy. (The following is an example to explain the meaning of traditional knowledge and genetic material: the San [bushmen] of the African Kalahari have long used the Hoodia plant to stave off hunger and thirst on hunting trips. The Hoodia plant is genetic material; to use it and how to use it are traditional knowledge.) Preserving global biodiversity has been a complementary objective of many of these reforms.

The movement has brought forward three basic principles on commercial access to genetic materials and traditional knowledge: prior informed consent, mutually agreed terms, and benefit sharing. The principles have found expression in a number of political outputs, ranging from international agreements such as the Convention on Biological Diversity (CBD) to declarations and statements of demands from indigenous people's organizations.

A number of agencies have done extensive work to devise ways to apply these principles. For example, extensive study at the World Intellectual Property Organization (WIPO) has led to several concrete programs, such as one to set up an electronic database of clauses for contracts on use of genetic resources. Researchers have developed a number of codes of ethics and research guidelines through professional societies such as the International Society of Ethnobiology. A number of bioscience companies have developed corporate policies that set out their approach to dealing with traditional knowledge and particularly with how they will comply with the CBD.

The product Jeevani, which is based on the traditional knowledge of the Kani in India, illustrates the commercial as well as the scientific results that people involved in this work hope to achieve.

The Kani are an ethnic group of some 16,000 people who live in southwestern India. Working primarily with three Kani consultants, the Tropical Botanical Garden and Research Institute (TBGRI) of India learned of the antifatigue properties of a wild plant. From this plant the TBGRI developed the drug Jeevani. When the TBGRI transferred manufacturing rights to Aryavaidya Pharmacy Coimbatore Ltd., TBGRI agreed to share 50-50 the license and royalty income with the Kani. It took a while for the various Kani clans to agree, but in time they established the Kerala Kani Samudaya Kshema Trust to manage this income.

Through 2001, the Trust Society—fully managed by Kani—has received 1,350,000 Indian rupees (about US$30,000) of royalties and fees. This income has been invested in an interest-bearing account, and only the interest from the account is expended.

The Trust Society has funded various self-employment schemes for unemployed Kani youth and has provided special financial assistance of IRs 25,000 for the welfare of two tribal children whose mother was killed by a wild elephant. It also paid IRs 50,000 to the three Kani consultants who initially provided the knowledge to TBGRI.

As sales of Jeevani have grown, so has demand for the raw material. The Forest Department has now agreed to permit the Kani to cultivate the plant and sell the raw drugs in semiprocessed form to the manufacturer. This cultivation project, coordinated by the Trust Society, will provide additional income to the Kani.

The traditional knowledge of the Kanis would not have been suitable for a patent. The TBGRI research team isolated the active ingredient in the plant, developed an herbal formulation suitable for medicinal application, and patented this discovery. As India did not have legislation that protected the tribe's knowledge, the tribe would have had no legal means to claim a share in the revenues from the patent. TBGRI—established to support bioprospecting and to look out for the interests of indigenous communities—provides an alternative model to the strictly legal approach followed in the West.

There are few other examples of such commercial success. Through the International Cooperative Biodiversity Group's (ICBG) first five-year cycle ending in 1997, the group had screened more than 7,000 natural samples and from these had identified about 35 priority leads. The ICBG also produced and circulated a number of scientific reports and created several new databases and software programs for accessing and utilizing these databases. The ICBG's activities have provided extensive research experience and training for people from the host developing countries as well as the sponsoring industrial countries, but the final report on this cycle indicates no commercial earnings from any of the discoveries. Through its second cycle, the ICBG has produced two patents relating to the tropical diseases leishmaniasis and malaria. In the opinion of ICBG's management, these patents are not likely to generate financial benefits.

In recognition of the long odds against discovery of a profitable product, and because getting a new product to the market often requires 10 to 15 years of development and testing, the ICBG programs emphasize income derived by local people from the process of exploration and discovery rather than on the promise of huge royalties that may never materialize.

Though companies continue to use ethnobotanical knowledge as part of discovery programs, scientific and technological developments in recent decades have shifted demand toward other inputs. New scientific technologies synthetically generate numbers of first-stage compounds, computerization provides faster ways to screen out the ones that merit further development, and new techniques provide better ways to transform the new compounds into effective products. In healthcare, research dollars are moving toward approaches that focus largely on human material; drug design then employs synthetic chemistry to reverse-engineer from the human material. In this environment, natural products are often too slow, costly, and problematic.

Product discovery programs use traditional knowledge to help identify natural products that have potential; thus, interest in traditional knowledge depends on interest in natural products as first-stage inputs. Much traditional knowledge, however, is already in the public domain and can be sourced through publications. It is rarely sourced from interviews with local and indigenous communities themselves in such a way as to require prior informed consent and to trigger benefit-sharing negotiations.

Lessons A growing number of national laws and international guidelines require the acquisition of prior informed consent and the sharing of benefits with local communities when researchers seek access to genetic resources on their land or to their traditional knowledge about those resources. The scientific and the business communities have put in place programs to identify promising genetic resources in developing countries and to ensure that the communities from whose land the resources originated share in any commercial rewards that might result. The scientific output has been significant, the developing countries have obtained valuable scientific and business experience, and a number of people in developing countries have been employed in the field and in laboratories. But commercial returns from new products have been modest—far short of making the programs self-sustaining on commercial grounds.

Philip Schuler: Biopiracy and Commercialization of Ethnobotanical Knowledge

Schuler takes up the concern that poor people are somehow "shorted" by companies that register patents based on traditional knowledge and thereby collect revenues that should go to the poorer communities. He reviews several recent incidents that are often cited as illustrative of the problem, identifies their key dimensions, and from this analysis suggests possible reforms.

Biopesticides from the Neem Tree   The neem tree is mentioned in Indian texts written more than 2,000 years ago. Products made from it have many uses, including for human and veterinary medicines, cosmetics, insect repellent, and fungicide. There are many patents on neem products, in India as well as in the United States and Europe.

The present controversy focuses on U.S. and European patents on pesticides made from neem seeds held by the specialty chemicals company W.R. Grace. The major element of novelty of the patented pesticide was that it has a shelf life of several years. In contrast, Indian farmers traditionally soak neem seeds in water and alcohol, and the resulting emulsion begins to biodegrade immediately—it must be used within a few days or it is no longer potent. Defenders of the patent also pointed out that it does not prevent Indian farmers from producing and using their traditional extracts.

In 1993, P.J. Margo Private Ltd. (W.R. Grace's Indian partner) began producing and marketing stabilized neem biopesticides in India. Public demonstrations broke out against this joint venture, and a collection of advocacy groups joined together in 1995 to challenge the European and U.S. patents on the grounds that the product/process was not novel—Indians had been using neem products in the same fashion for centuries. The European Patent Office revoked the patent in Europe, but the U.S. patent remains valid.

Schuler's key finding is that the plethora of patents on neem products do not prevent Indian farmers from producing and distributing traditional extracts, nor do they prevent Indian chemical companies from producing and selling stabilized extracts. Several Indian companies sell neem-based products in world markets, and several have distribution facilities or production subsidiaries in the United States. Indian farmers have also benefited. With the burgeoning use of neem products, the price of neem seeds has risen over the past 20 years from IRs 300/ton to more than IRs 8,000/ton.

Turmeric   Turmeric has long been used in Asia and elsewhere as a spice and coloring agent. It also has medicinal uses. In traditional Indian Ayurvedic medicine, for example, it is used to treat a variety of ailments.

In 1995, Suma K. Das and Har P. Choly, two scientists working at the University of Mississippi Medical Center, were granted a U.S. patent for the use of turmeric in treating wounds. The New Delhi–based Council for Scientific and Industrial

Research (CSIR) challenged the patent, citing Ayurvedic texts as evidence that it was not novel. The USPTO eventually ruled against the inventors. As in the neem example, Schuler finds that there are many U.S. patents, including several patents for medical uses, that to a nonexpert appear similar to traditional uses. The patent holders are in large part Indian scientists, some working in the United States, some in India. Schuler cites a stated objective of an Indian organization to pursue foreign patents on traditional Indian knowledge. The major lesson he draws from the story is that developing country inventors can use industrial country patents as a commercial instrument. According to newspaper accounts, CSIR challenged the turmeric patent partly for symbolic reasons and partly to acquire experience with U.S. patent reexamination procedures.

Basmati Rice   Since the 1950s, the governments of India and Pakistan have been supporting work to develop improved strains of basmati rice and have taken steps to protect the reputation of basmati by limiting commercial use of the name to certain varieties cultivated in certain areas.

In the 1980s, RiceTec, a U.S. company wholly owned by a European, began work to develop basmati strains that would grow profitably in the United States—traditional strains would not. The company applied for a broad patent on basmati varieties, and the Indian government objected. In the end the USPTO granted a patent only on the three new varieties RiceTec had developed. RiceTec's U.S. patents cannot block South Asian cultivation of traditional strains or strains they have developed. Nor does it prevent Asian researchers from developing additional varieties. Indian researchers have since developed the world's first hybrid strain of basmati rice.

A patent is only one element in commercialization and not always a necessary one. The California Basmati Rice Company has neither patent nor trademark protection on its Calmati strain of rice.

A second controversy arose over the use of the words "basmati" or "jasmine" to market rice. In response to a petition in the United Kingdom, the U.K. Food Standards agency issued labeling regulations limiting "basmati" to those varieties/locations that the Indian and Pakistani authorities recognize as basmati. The U.S. Federal Trade Commission has ruled that U.S. regulations treat these terms as descriptions of aromatic rice, wherever it is grown. The WTO agreement on IP provides extensive protection to geographic indicators for wines and spirits, and extending similar protection to developing country products is on the table at current WTO negotiations.

Yellow Beans   The controversy over yellow beans involves a Mexican strain, "Mayacoba," and a U.S. strain, "Enola." Mexican farmers have been growing yellow beans at least since the time of the Aztecs. More recently, Mexican agronomists developed a variety of yellow bean that they registered in 1978 as "Mayacoba."

There is a substantial market for such beans in the United States, principally but not exclusively among Mexican immigrants. Mexican farmers and U.S. importers have made substantial investments in these beans to serve the U.S. market.

In 1999, a Colorado agricultural company obtained a certificate of patent and plant variety protection for the Enola variety, one the company had developed from beans originally from Mexico. The Colorado company has since licensed Enola bean production to a number of U.S. growers and processors. It has also initiated legal action against several importers, alleging that Mexican farmers have been raising Enola beans and selling them as Mayacoba. Countersuits have been filed, and the legal dispute has considerably slowed Mexican exports. U.S. Customs officials stop bean shipments from Mexico to search for Enola beans. Superficially, it is difficult to distinguish one variety from another. The International Center for Tropical Agriculture (CIAT) in Cali, Colombia, claims that it maintains some 260 bean samples with yellow seeds, and six are substantially identical to claims made in the Colorado company's patent.

It is possible that the Enola variety is superior to the Mayacoba and that Mexican farmers have been using it without authorization. If so, the normal justification for IP protection applies—to encourage innovation. The social justification depends, of course, on the Enola variety being substantially better in some nutritional or economic way, for example, greater yield per liter of irrigation water. A distinctive color might satisfy the legal standard for novelty without satisfying the social standard for improvement.

Even if the Enola variety turns out in the end not to be sufficiently novel to merit IP protection, the legal process itself is a powerful commercial instrument that the Colorado company has used to gain advantage over its competitors.

Lessons   In industrial countries discipline over the granting of patents depends more and more on challenges from other producers rather than on careful examination by the patent-granting authority. This tends to leave consumer interests underrepresented because registering a patent is too easy. (The explanation is the familiar concentration of producer interests relative to consumer interests that helps to explain import protection.) As to remedy, encouraging increased action by NGOs may be more effective than attempting to provide additional resources and additional authority to regulatory agencies.

Daniel Wüger: Prevention of Misappropriation of Intangible Cultural Heritage through Intellectual Property Laws

In this era of globalization, indigenous communities find themselves face to face with alternative cultures in increasing frequency and intensity. While some communities welcome this development, others do not. Uses of their music, drawings, and other cultural expressions outside of their community might be offensive to them and they might completely oppose outside use—regardless of the compensation offered by outsiders. While other chapters pay attention to the use of modern IP instruments to manage the commercialization of cultural property, Wüger's chapter pays particular attention to the issue of preserving cultural value, either by barring or by imposing conditions on outside use.

In traditional communities it is difficult to separate "art" from "technology." Household articles, tools, weapons, and medicines have cultural as well as technical meanings. Wüger analyzes a number of cases to examine the use of IP law as well as other laws to protect cultural property.

The *Pueblo of Santo Domingo* case involved a newspaper photographer who flew over the Pueblo of Santo Domingo in the southwestern United States and photographed a ceremonial dance. According to the Pueblo's customary laws, the dance was sacred and had to be kept secret from outsiders. The photos, however, were published. The Pueblo filed suit, alleging trespass, violation of the Pueblo ban on photography, and invasion of privacy. Members of the Pueblo believed that the intrinsic value of the dance had been diminished—that it had been used as "nothing more than commercial entertainment for the white man." Though the loss could not be restored by postinjury remedies, the Pueblo stopped further use of the pictures.

In this instance, Wüger reasons, it would have been difficult to apply IP law. The choreography of the dance was not fixed, nor was an author identifiable; hence, for copyright purposes the dance is part of the public domain. Furthermore, the people of the Pueblo could not seek protection as performers; in general, U.S. copyright laws do not afford protection to performers of uncopyrighted works.

Registration of such cultural expressions would make modern IP law more useful to protect them, but registration includes disclosure—exactly what the Pueblo wanted to avoid. Where secrecy is not an issue, registration can be useful. Wüger describes the Cultural Goods Registry provided by Guatemala's Cultural Heritage Protection Law.

Protection of cultural values becomes particularly troublesome when the proposed commercial use of traditional knowledge is in a country different from where the indigenous community is located. A patent on a variety of the Ayahuasca plant granted by the USPTO raised a controversy over patenting a product that had major spiritual significance for a foreign community. Ayahuasca is a South American vine with hallucinogenic properties. It is used in traditional Amazonian rituals to produce a ceremonial drink; the drink is used to treat sicknesses, to contact spirits, and to foresee the future. The preparation and administration of the drink are strictly regulated by customary law, and the drink may be prepared only under the guidance of a shaman.

The patent holder obtained in the Amazon samples of a particular variety, brought it back to the United States, and claimed a patent on it as a newly discovered plant. The COICA opposed the patent on grounds that the plant was widely known in scientific literature (nonnovelty) and that the patent would violate the religious beliefs of South American indigenous peoples (nonutility). In response, the USPTO first revoked the patent but later reinstated it, on grounds that the variety discovered by the patent holder is not identical to specimens of Ayahuasca found in U.S. herbarium collections. U.S. patent law excludes the consideration of unpublished foreign sources when determining novelty. The USPTO did not address the question of whether the vine being a sacred religious symbol precluded its patentability. The patent does not, however, limit the traditional use of the vine.

Ethiopian practice illustrates another approach to protecting folklore. Ethiopia requires prior authorization by the Ministries of Culture and Information and payment of a fee for any reproduction or adaptation of folklore. The ministry has authorized the Musicians' Association as the agent to license the use of folklore music. Wüger explains a case in which one musician obtained permission from the Ethiopian Musicians' Association to use several songs—the Musicians' Association claiming authority on grounds that the songs were part of Ethiopian folklore. Another musician claimed that he had written the songs; however, the court denied him copyright protection. In making its determination, the court did not consider whether the adaptations that the second musician made of the traditional folklore songs constituted derivative works protected under copyright laws. The novelty value of the songs was captured by the regulatory authority rather than by the composer. The tradeoff here, Wüger points out, is that artists who are unable to protect their works will be unable to live from their profession—the same complaint brought forward by many Senegalese musicians in the chapter on the Africa Music Project.

In several other countries, as well as in Ethiopia, the protection of cultural property is assigned to a central agency. Wüger points out that legislation could assign authority directly to indigenous communities, provided that the communities have corporate or NGO status or otherwise have standing in the legal system.

The Arogyapacha incident, also described in the chapter by ten Kate and Laird, brings out a problem that can arise when protection of cultural property revolves on a community decision. In this example, the TBGRI learned from the Kani people of the antifatigue properties of a wild plant and from the plant developed the drug Jeevani. The TBGRI obtained a patent in India and helped the Kani people to set up a trust fund to which a substantial share of the royalties from the patent were assigned.

As to respecting the cultural values of the community, the Kanis do not constitute a cohesive community. Their families are scattered over a wide area, and the

TBGRI interacted primarily with one group of them. Within that group, younger members of the tribe eagerly took part in the TBGRI project while the older generation regarded the knowledge as sacred and looked unfavorably on commercial use. A group of nine medicine men wrote to the chief minister of the district, objecting to the sale of their knowledge to outside companies.

The example illustrates not only a clash of culture, represented by young versus old, but it also illustrates differences in who could step forward as owners or custodians of the knowledge: family versus family and medicine men versus the community at large.

The traditional knowledge of the Kanis would not have been suitable for a patent. A TBGRI research team isolated the active ingredient in the plant, developed an herbal formulation suitable for medicinal application, and patented that discovery. TBGRI was under no obligation under Indian IP law to share the benefits with the Kanis or to seek formal consent before starting its research project. The agency was, however, created to conduct research on possible applications of traditional biogenetic material and charged to look out for the interests of the indigenous communities where the material was found. This is thus an alternative way to advance the interests of poor people.

Wüger points out that legislation requiring prior informed consent of holders of traditional knowledge before it can be used by third parties would be a useful instrument in such situations.

Lessons   Wüger concludes that many modern instruments can be used to protect the cultural values of indigenous communities, but the results will not always be satisfactory to all members of a community. He warns, however, against overprotection to the detriment of other cultural, social, or economic interests. As do Liebl and Roy, he concludes that an intangible cultural asset will be preserved only if the lifestyle embodying it provides reasonable economic prospects. In this regard, commercialization of certain aspects of intangible cultural property can contribute to the preservation of cultural heritage as a whole. Countries have to consider a holistic approach that combines the provision of legal tools with support initiatives.

Coenraad J. Visser: Making Intellectual Property Laws Work for Traditional Knowledge

Visser reviews how modern legal instruments, such as patent and copyright, might be used to protect traditional knowledge. He begins by offering an intuitive sense of what we mean by the term "traditional knowledge." Drawing mainly on WIPO usage, he explains that the category includes traditional and tradition-based cultural expressions in forms such as stories, music, dance, artworks, and crafts, including symbols, marks, and other recurring expressions of traditional concepts. It also covers similarly traditional agricultural, medical, and technical knowledge.

Before going further, Visser offers a caution: Poorer countries are net importers of IP, and raising the level of protection they provide on *all* IP (as the WTO IP agreement requires) would mean a net outflow of hard currency.

Visser identifies two motives for protecting traditional knowledge. People in traditional communities, like people in modern communities, want protection that will help them to benefit from the gainful use of their knowledge. In addition, members of these communities often want to prevent use that is offensive to the cultural or spiritual meaning of the knowledge. Modern communities, too, object to demeaning use of social or religious symbols, but the line between the cultural/spiritual and the commercial/scientific is less clearly and perhaps less often drawn in traditional than in modern communities; hence, the cultural/spiritual motive may have more weight in traditional communities.

Patents   As to gainful use, Visser reports several instances in which industrial country patent offices have refused or revoked patents demonstrated to be based on traditional knowledge from a developing country. Many uses, however, do slip through the screen. He also reports a UN estimate that developing countries lose about US$5 billion a year in royalties from unauthorized use of traditional knowledge.

The screening of patent applications for traditional knowledge might be improved in several ways. One suggestion is a consent requirement for patentability. When it appears that an invention for which a patent is sought is based on the biological or genetic heritage of a traditional community, a copy of the contract affording access to the biological resources of the country of origin must be shown.

Databases of traditional knowledge can help to protect them from unauthorized use. WIPO has set up the WIPO Portal of Traditional Knowledge to help users find and use such knowledge. Such databases facilitate demonstration that an alleged invention is not new. Professor Peter Drahos has suggested a further step, that a global collection society be established, perhaps under the World Bank. A collection society would be a repository for communities' databases and would facilitate contacts between companies and groups over the use of such information.

Visser also reviews the possible use of several other legal devices (such as trade secrets law) that might be used to protect traditional knowledge that has possible commercial application.

Many patent laws allow patent applications to be screened for uses that are culturally offensive. In New Zealand, for example, the Intellectual Property Office has guidelines for patents based on indigenous flora, fauna, and nonorganic materials that direct patent examiners to consider if the application is likely to have cultural or spiritual significance for the Maori. Where such application might be offensive to the Maori, applicants must be advised accordingly and given the opportunity to obtain the consent of the competent Maori authority.

Patents, however, are granted country by country, and the screening or consent requirement imposed in the country in which the traditional knowledge originated (for example, screening in New Zealand against Maori concerns) does not automatically carry over to patent applications in other countries.

Copyright   Legal protection has been sought for a variety of cultural expressions: paintings and traditional designs reproduced on carpets or T-shirts, music and stories transcribed or recorded, designs from handwoven textiles incorporated into mass-produced clothing, and many others. Such cultural expressions were sometimes photographed, transcribed, or recorded and then published for ethnographic purposes; the availability of such publications and recordings has facilitated unauthorized application.

The strongest advantage of copyright protection is that it transcends national borders. An expression protected in one country is protected by all signatories to the Berne Convention. Copyright normally requires a novel expression and an identifiable author, but problems of outside exploitation often involve existing knowledge that is shared by many people. Even so, copyright law often has been effectively applied. Visser outlines a set of Model Provisions developed by a United Nations Educational, Scientific, and Cultural Organization (UNESCO)-WIPO experts group to protect such expressions. Many developing countries have in place laws that take advantage of a Berne Convention special provision that allows for protection of expressions whose individual author cannot be identified.

Visser cautions, however, that with such protection the public domain shrinks, and further evolution of the art or craft is retarded. Other chapters (Wüger, Fowler) provide examples of the application of mainstream copyright law to expressions within the traditional style that are different enough from preexisting expressions that they satisfy the standards for novelty of mainstream law.

The Digital Environment: The WIPO Copyright Treaty   The emergence of global information networks and electronic commerce raises a number of key issues in the field of copyright. Digitization expands exponentially possibilities for transmission, and also for unauthorized copying. In principle, an author has the same rights over use and distribution of his or her work through the digital media as through older media, but to protect works in this environment requires not only adaptation of legal structures but also new technical devices such as encryption and software that limit copying. Visser reviews the guidelines for relevant legal structures provided by the WIPO Copyright Treaty of 1996.

Trademarks and Labels of Authenticity   Several countries use marks that designate products as coming from a particular community as an effective technique to protect against the manufacture and sale of indigenous artifacts by nonindigenous people at the expense of indigenous communities. An Australian NGO, for example, has registered with the government marks that identify traditional crafts from the aboriginal community. Distinctive packaging likewise can qualify for trademark protection and serve as a means to identify articles from a particular community. Such marks will help to raise the profile of genuine articles and will aid buyers so inclined to avoid buying counterfeit articles. Trademark law serves to prevent the use of the labels on nonauthentic articles; however, such marks do not make illegal the production or sale of counterfeit articles.

Trademark law can also prohibit the registration as trademarks of signs or symbols traditionally used by or distinctive of indigenous communities. Legislation proposed in New Zealand would allow the trademark office to refuse to register a trademark when such use would likely offend a significant section of the community, including the Maori. A law already in effect in the United States empowers the USPTO to refuse registration of a mark that would bring into contempt or falsely suggest association with persons, institutions, beliefs, or national symbols. Native American tribes and other indigenous communities are protected by this law. The USPTO has set up a searchable database of official insignia of Native American tribes—the intent of the database is to prevent registration of marks confusingly similar to such insignia.

Visser concludes with a list of recommendations on the elements of a legal structure that facilitates protection of traditional knowledge.

Traditional Knowledge, Modern Knowledge, and Poor People's Knowledge

In chapter 9, Coenraad Visser provides an intuitive sense of what the term traditional knowledge usually covers. The category includes traditional and tradition-based cultural expressions in forms such as stories, music, dance, artworks, and crafts, including symbols, marks, and other recurring expressions of traditional concepts. It also covers traditional agricultural, medical, and technical knowledge. "Indigenous knowledge" and "traditional knowledge" are more or less synonyms.

One characteristic is that such knowledge is handed down from generation to generation, usually as part of an oral tradition. Another is that its use is interwoven in a net of customary obligations and rights of the individuals and the community.

Within indigenous communities, the practical and the spiritual/ceremonial dimensions of life overlap perhaps more than they do in modern communities. In addition, traditional knowledge suggests a sense of common or community ownership.

At the extreme, one might imagine a simple analytical model in which people in modern society and in a traditional community each view the origin and ownership of knowledge in a manner parallel with how they view the origin and ownership of tangible property. Consider a stereotypical community of hunter-gatherers. People in such a community are aware that many unseen plants and animals are alive in the wild. Provisioning oneself is a matter of acquiring these rather than of creating them. They conceptualize knowledge in a similar way. People in modern society perceive innovation or creativity as access to and drawing from a hidden stock of knowledge—or, to use perhaps an overly sophisticated phrase, drawing from a divinely inspired subconscious.

Modern intellectual property law recognizes "common knowledge" as the property of all—the "public domain." No one can obtain a patent or copyright for it. However, individuals can own *new* knowledge. The conception here is that knowledge, like cars or carrots, is *produced* through the efforts of people rather than taken from a stock that nature provides. The basic elements needed to claim a copyright or a patent include a creative step, an identified creator, and a basis to demonstrate that the claimant *is* the creator. In short, to gain ownership of knowledge, it has to be novel and it has to be yours.

The requirements for patents and copyrights are different. The law presumes that if you write a new story or compose a new song, it is yours. If it comes down to defending your ownership in court, there are standards for what "new" means. To demonstrate that the song or story is yours, it is useful to have a written copy, particularly one with a verifiable date on it. It is even better if you had deposited a copy with someone the law will trust, such as the copyright office. Registration makes it easier to prove that the property is yours.

You apply for a patent. If you demonstrate that your idea is novel, that it is yours, and that it has industrial application, you *receive* a patent from the government.[2]

From society's perspective, the rationale for allowing temporary individual ownership of new knowledge is that in time all members of society will gain. IP protection provides an incentive for creative acts and for progress. It adds "the fuel of interest to the fire of genius," said Abraham Lincoln.

Traditional knowledge can be a useful analytical concept, but Visser warns against overdrawing the distinction between it and modern knowledge. The cases presented in this book suggest that the warning merits serious attention.

An obvious part of this warning is a straightforward point: no one's life is entirely traditional, and no one's life is entirely modern. Traditional versus modern is better thought of as opposite ends of a scale rather than as a clean sorting.

Each community fits somewhere along the scale, in some combination of modern and traditional. Along this scale, many people who are members of more traditional communities are relatively poor, but many poor people live in the modern world. Traditional knowledge is only a part of poor people's knowledge—one should not slip into thinking that developing countries' commercial interests lie only in collecting on traditional knowledge.

Respecting Collective and Individual Ownership

Respecting the collective ownership that some indigenous communities value is a complicated matter. The problem is not, however, that modern conceptions of IP cannot handle collective ownership. Any collectivity that law recognizes as a legal entity can own IP: a corporation, a nonprofit organization, and so forth. In chapter 9, Coenraad Visser reviews suggestions for novel forms.

In chapter 1, however, Nelly Arvelo-Jiménez points out that it is difficult to create such organizations in a way that blends with a traditional community's sense of organization and leadership. The indigenous political systems of the Yekuana are decentralized and resistant to the surrender of diffused authority to a central agency. Furthermore, leadership is often based on seniority and has more the spirit of continuing customary modes of life than adapting to new ones. The TBGRI in India did establish a trust fund for the Kani people to administer royalties from patents taken on their ethnobotanical knowledge, but in chapter 8 Wüger points out that there were significant differences among the Kanis as to the wisdom of the venture.

Recognition of collective ownership raises questions about where to draw the line between the traditional knowledge that belongs to everyone and the innovations produced by individual members of the community. Moving the line too far toward protecting traditional knowledge can have negative consequences for the culture or art of poor people as well as for the earnings they enjoy from its commercial use.

To illustrate the point, we compare the development of country music as a major source of income for what was once an impoverished part of the United States with two of the cases in developing countries.

In the United States, the country music business developed in the first half of the 20th century from a rich tradition of indigenous music in the southeastern states.[3] The story of this development is warmly told in a book by Mark Zwonitzer with Charles Hirshberg (2002) that relates the experiences of the Carter family of western Virginia.[4] From the beginning, the entrepreneurs who sought out Appalachian artists looked for music in the Appalachian tradition that was sufficiently novel to copyright. Ralph Peer was one of the early entrepreneurs in country music. From time to time he would set up a temporary recording studio in Bristol, on the Virginia-Tennessee border, and word would circulate that he was in town paying for music.

Most of the acts racing toward Bristol would go back home to obscurity, with nothing. Many of the mountain acts Peer saw repeated the same songs: hymns, centuries-old ballads, or popular standards that had been recorded already. Peer needed material he could copyright and cash in on, so he needed musicians who could write their own songs, or at least restitch the traditional songs enough that he could 'put them over as new' (Zwonitzer with Hirshberg, pp. 94–95).

Within a static conception of knowledge/culture, this might sound like parsing out the common domain—all traditional music would pass into private ownership and the community tradition of music would disappear.

In fact, the opposite happened. Many commercially successful artists now enjoy playing and recording more traditional forms, and with the income they earn from their more commercial products they can afford to do more traditional things simply for the pleasure of it. Furthermore, commercially successful music tends to liven the cultural tradition rather than stifle it. Baaba Maal and other successful Senegalese artists' music is now part of the Senegalese musical tradition. Carter family music has become part of the Appalachian tradition. It is celebrated at festivals from Australia to the upper reaches of Canada, in Europe and in Asia, and from Newport, Rhode Island, to Alaska. Moreover, as music evolves away from its roots there are commercial opportunities to turn back. Baaba Maal's 2002 album is traditional music performed on African acoustic instruments. In U.S. country music, Willie Nelson and the "outlaws" who split away from the Nashville version are another example of going back to the roots without sacrificing commercial potential.

Arrangements more focused on protection of folklore sometimes backfire. Rather than collecting rents *for* a traditional community, an organization with authority over the community's musical or artistic tradition may find an incentive to collect rents *from* the community.

In chapter 8 Daniel Wüger explains that the government of Ethiopia authorized the Ethiopian Musicians' Association as the agent to license the use of folkloric music. The association interpreted its authority as extending into popular music that had roots in folkloric music. In doing so the association was able to claim royalties for itself that would otherwise have gone to individual composers. Wüger warns that if artists are not able to claim ownership of their works they will not be able to make a living from their profession—and there will be no music in Ethiopia.

John Collins (2000), professor of musicology at the University of Ghana and a leading figure in the music business there, has provided a more detailed description of a similar experience in Ghana.

Musicians in Ghana created the first distinct form of acculturated African popular music—the brass-band Adaha variety of highlife—in the 1880s. When Ghana became independent in 1957, its leader, Kwame Nkrumah, endorsed highlife and encouraged local popular entertainment. By the mid-1970s Ghana was perhaps the liveliest center in Africa for popular music: recording studios, record pressing plants, scores of nightclubs, 20 top highlife dance bands, dozens of Afro-rock fusion bands, 70 or so highlife guitar bands, and "concert parties," which are a local form of comic highlife opera.

In 1991 the government created the National Folklore Board of Trustees, ostensibly to make a register of Ghanaian folklore and to monitor its use outside the Third World. The Folklore Board interpreted its charter to give it the authority to regulate commercial use by Ghanaians as well, and it interpreted "folklore" to include the entirety of Ghanaian popular music. The board imposed a special tax and licensing arrangement on the use of folklore; the tax and arrangement in fact were applied to all commercial popular music.[5]

Today there is no popular music business in Ghana except for techno-pop. Techno-pop is computer-generated music that uses no musicians or musical instruments. According to Professor Collins, the folkloric tax and regulation by the Folkloric Board were a major cause of the disappearance of the music business—and popular culture—in Ghana.

Liebl and Roy, in chapter 2 of this volume, report a similar concern about Indian crafts. Dr. Jyotindra Jain, dean of the Faculty of Arts and Aesthetics at Jawaharlal Nehru University, initially supported creation of a regulatory agency. From his experience with it, he has since concluded that any regulatory machinery imposed on the crafts community will ultimately end up hurting, rather than helping, those who need protection most.

The lesson here is that maintaining the liveliness of the culture as well as taking advantage of economic opportunity lies in expanding the dynamics of poor people's knowledge much more than in defending a static stock of knowledge from outside exploitation. Culture in a bottle soon becomes an empty bottle.

The Development Dimension

Justification for protecting traditional knowledge can be found in noneconomic motives. There is sometimes value in preserving a culture, a way of life, from disappearing. In chapter 1, Nelly Arvelo-Jiménez makes the case for the Yekuana in Venezuela. In another example, in some poor communities, craft sales by women have provided them cash income. This income elevates them toward equality in their situation vis-à-vis men in the family and community.[6]

There is no need, however, to choose between cultural and commercial objectives for or uses of poor people's knowledge. On the whole, economic and noneconomic uses are complements, not substitutes. The positive side of this aspect, as Liebl and Roy point out, is that the culture they want to preserve evolved because it had economic support. The negative side, as Wüger's, Liebl and Roy's, and John Collins' findings caution, is that regulation that attempts to limit commercial use can end up destroying rather than supporting culture.

Perhaps the key point here is that novelty is not foreign to poor people's knowledge. In many cases that the book explores, poor people's knowledge meets the standard of novelty that modern IP law demands. Recall the cases that involve paintings and designs from Australian aboriginal artists in the chapters by Fowler and by Wüger. The art satisfied legal standards for novelty. The complex dimensions of the cases related to the interplay of individual ownership on which Australian law is based and the aboriginal community's traditional law concept of collective ownership. Meanwhile, for the Congolese model of the VW Beetle, and the songs of the Senegalese composers and performers, the commercial problem was not that they lacked novelty; rather it was the capacity to use the commercial tools of knowledge or "content" management. In Senegal there was also the ineffectiveness of the local enforcement mechanism. Indeed, in few of the cases taken up in this book is lack of novelty the characteristic that reduces earnings.[7]

The development dimension lies in helping poor people to master the commercial/legal tools needed to collect the value of their novelty. This is about entrepreneurship, about finding clever ways to repackage traditional knowledge into products useful for consumers in mass markets, and about developing the capacity to produce and deliver these products in sufficient quantity and quality as to satisfy such markets. It is also about building local business infrastructures, overcoming corruption, and overcoming disproportionate tax burdens.

The legal strategy should follow from the commercial strategies of local business, not the other way around. B. Zorina Khan (2002), in her examination of IP in the development of the U.S. and European economies, points out that the level and form of IP protection provided were what, at the time, best supported their own knowledge-based industries. People who figured out how to make some money out of new ideas then lobbied for new laws that solidified their property rights in the face of competition from imitators. Birds build birds' nests, not the other way around. Or perhaps the lesson is more existential: birds' nests are something birds build as they carry on what birds do.

Notes

1. The argument in this and the following paragraphs is elaborated and documented in Finger 2002.

2. Wüger and Visser provide more technical explanations of the requirements for a patent, a copyright, and other legal instruments.

3. This music had evolved in significant part from the music that the people who settled in Appalachia brought with them from Scotland and England.

4. The authors are cultural historians, not economists.

5. The Folklore Board and folkloric tax originated from a recommendation of the WIPO, although the WIPO recommendation was to apply the tax only to use of Third-World traditional knowledge outside of the Third World.

6. In this instance we suggest that an element of a traditional way of life be changed. We refrain from adding that improved status for women often has a positive economic development impact. The point stands on its noneconomic value.

7. A secondary point, the commercial value of the *stock* of traditional knowledge is perhaps less than proponents of defending it might hope. Ten Kate and Laird report a good faith effort by the scientific and business communities to ensure that local people got a share of the revenues based on the genetic materials from their homelands. Over 10 years the program has generated no patent royalties. The local people have, however, received scientific training and have earned from employment in discovery programs. (Perhaps everything of value was stolen in the past, but shaming the thieves into making retribution is not likely a reliable basis for funding economic development.) From Philip Schuler in chapter 7 we learn that the patented version of a pesticide made from neem seeds has a storage life of two years, while the traditional version biodegrades in a few days. One is a viable commercial product; the other is not. Development is about acquiring the capacity to come up with a commercially viable product. That is certainly not out of the reach of poor countries. The neem pesticide patent is registered in the United States to Indian owners, and its value has been captured by Indian companies that have set up affiliates in the United States.

References

Collins, John. 2000. "The Ghanaian Experience." Presentation at the World Bank–Policy Sciences Center, Inc. Workshop on the Development of the Music Industry in Africa, Washington, D.C., June 20–21, 2000. Available at http://www.worldbank.org/research/trade/africa_music2.htm.

Finger, J. Michael. 2002. "The Doha Agenda and Development: A View from the Uruguay Round." Asian Development Bank, Manila. Available at http://www.adb.org/Economics/pdf/doha/Finger_paper.pdf.

Khan, B. Zorina. 2002. "Intellectual Property and Economic Development: Lessons from American and European History." United Kingdom Commission on Intellectual Property Rights Study Paper 1a, London.

Liebl, Maureen, and Tirthankar Roy. 2000. "Handmade in India: Preliminary Analysis of Crafts Producers and Crafts Production in India; Issues, Initiatives, Interventions." Report prepared for the Policy Sciences Center, Inc. Available at the website of the World Bank–Policy Sciences Center, Inc. Crafts Workshop: India at http://lnweb18.worldbank.org/essd/essd.nsf/Culture/CW-Agenda.

Sen, Amartya. 2000. "What's the Use of Music? The Role of the Music Industry in Africa." Prepared for the World Bank–Policy Sciences Center, Inc. Workshop on the Development of the Music Industry in Africa, Washington, D.C., June 20–21, 2000. Available at http://www.worldbank.org/research/trade/africa_music2.htm.

Zwonitzer, Mark, with Charles Hirshberg. 2002. *Will You Miss Me When I'm Gone? A History of the Carter Family and Their Legacy in American Life.* New York: Simon and Schuster.

KUYUJANI ORIGINARIO: THE YEKUANA ROAD TO THE OVERALL PROTECTION OF THEIR RIGHTS AS A PEOPLE

Nelly Arvelo-Jiménez

Yekuana Culture

The Yekuana people are speakers of a Carib family language with origins in the highlands of the Guyana Shield (Durbin 1977). According to researchers in historical linguistics, Carib-speaking peoples have inhabited the tropical forests of the Orinoco Basin for at least the past 4,000 years (Durbin 1977; Villalón 1987). The Yekuana share most of the behavioral patterns that characterize tropical forest cultures. These patterns relate to the understanding and sustainable management of the tropical forest ecosystems of the Amazon and Orinoco Basins.

As has been the case for many indigenous groups, incursions from the modern world have challenged traditional Yekuana ways. The mineral and biological richness of Yekuana territory has brought outsiders in; the variety of things available in the modern world has attracted the Yekuana out. Ecologists and environmentalists have referred to indigenous ancestral lands in the Amazon and Orinoco Basins as biological hot spots, regions with many biological assets that have untapped potential for commercial application in the modern world.

This chapter describes how the Yekuana people have managed the juncture of their world and the modern world so as to benefit from the value of their physical and intellectual property in the modern world and at the same time preserve their own society. The premise of their approach is that it is possible to conceptualize elements of modern society within their traditional conceptions—and it is not necessary to take on the perceptions and values of modern culture.

The chapter describes Yekuana society and how it has come into contact with the modern world. It explains how the Yekuana organized themselves to maintain their own way of life, preserving their own cultural and natural assets while at the same time benefiting from the value of these assets in the modern world. The chapter provides an example of adapting commerce to traditional culture rather than adapting culture to commerce.

During the second half of the 20th century, the Yekuana opened the symbolic gates of their lands and culture to Christian missionaries. The real reasons for such a warm welcome to foreigners and to a foreign religion have not been thoroughly researched. What we know for sure is that colonial literature reports that the Yekuana, since the moment of their first contact with European colonizers and Spanish explorers, displayed a fierce resistance to being subjugated. We also know that in the late 18th century the Yekuana were among the most important leaders of an interethnic revolt against European missionaries. Their oral history reports that during the 19th and early 20th centuries, many Yekuana chose to commit suicide rather than fall prey to gangs recruiting laborers for rubber plantations. Capture by these gangs would have meant enslavement in the rubber barracks, so the Yekuana split their villages into tiny settlements that relocated in remote areas (Arvelo-Jiménez 1974). Unfortunately, many Yekuana were captured by these gangs and went through all the horrors and hardships so vividly described in the literature on working and living conditions during the rubber boom (Taussig 1986).

Rubber exploitation left Yekuana society culturally weakened and demographically decimated. At this juncture, evangelical Christian missionaries from the United States showed up with their powerful technology of planes, shortwave radios, and Western medicine. All of these seemed to offer the Yekuana a better world.

It took several decades for the Yekuana to realize that the benefits of converting to Christianity were to be enjoyed not in this world but perhaps in an afterlife. At the beginning of the evangelical missionary period, however, the Yekuana were very much impressed by Christian beliefs. Being religious and spiritually oriented, they were astounded by the similarities between their beliefs and some of the Christian teachings that were translated into Yekuana. The first Yekuana interpreters taught their language to the missionaries and jointly with them translated the Bible into Yekuana. Given protection and special privileges by the missionaries, the translators became the first Yekuana elite group created and sustained by an external political power. The people in the elite group were mainly teachers and assistant nurses; all had adopted the Christian faith of the evangelicals and were dutifully loyal to the demands of the powerful outsiders.

Three consecutive waves of external, neocolonial social change washed over Yekuana culture during the first 60 years of the 20th century:

- The rubber exploitation in the Orinoco and Amazon Basins described above.
- The conquest of new frontiers after World War II by the United States as the emerging Western power (Davis 1977).The beachhead of this political and geographical incursion was established by the Christian missionaries (Beidelman 1982). The impact of those neocolonial processes forcefully changed Yekuana society, altering Yekuana settlement patterns and disrupting their social organization and intraethnic political stability.
- The implementation of a government economic and geopolitical program known as the Conquest of the South, which brought change to indigenous societies in several ways. It triggered theft of indigenous ancestral lands by individuals and corporations. As part of its plan for infrastructure expansion to facilitate the exploitation of the region's resources, the government of República Bolivariana de Venezuela established airports, roads, and radio stations. The government's program also established public services, lay educational programs, and Western health services. It included several microeconomic development programs intended to support the emergence of small businesses among indigenous people as well as among the modern people who might be attracted to the region.

These three major waves of cultural change constitute the beginning of the geopolitical conditions that now encapsulate most indigenous peoples living in the south of Venezuela, including the Yekuana. Throughout the past three decades I have been a witness to and in a way a chronicler of the trajectory followed by the Yekuana while they acquired the political consciousness and wit to fight back against encroachments and violations of their rights, most of all by the Venezuelan government and by international economic and geopolitical interests.

The Coveted Natural Resources of the Amazon Basin

My work with and for native Amazonian peoples is a good means of articulating the currently fashionable trend of protecting the collective intellectual property rights of indigenous peoples' traditional knowledge.

I started working with the Yekuana 35 years ago. At that time the value of natural resources was not openly discussed, and the importance of indigenous traditional knowledge in sustainable management of these resources was discussed even less. None of those issues were present in the economic and political agendas of public development plans. However, the then Amazon Territory of Venezuela had already been infiltrated by foreign agencies. Since the end of World War II, the Amazon Basin has been viewed by outsiders as a frontier of resources to be conquered and exploited.

The Yekuana's first contemporary experience with land invasion took place in the 1970s. The impact of this phenomenon on their culture revitalized memories of the horrors of the rubber exploitation and aroused their political awareness. Land invasion forced the Yekuana to take a new road to defend their territorial rights and to gain useful knowledge about the rules of the game prevailing outside Yekuana society. To retain their ancestral lands, the Yekuana have endured many difficult changes, transitions, and hardships.

The Yekuana's political engagement since the early 1970s has taught them hard lessons. One lesson is an understanding that the invaders of their lands have a different worldview, one that uses vivisection and segmentation to divide knowledge and the whole sociocultural world into alienable fragments, each fragment with a market value. Recognizing this enabled the Yekuana people to perceive themselves in historical opposition to, and in economic confrontation with, the intruders into their culture and their lands. It also provided the Yekuana with an acute awareness of the place that their ancestral lands have within the Venezuelan geography, the place of their society within Venezuela's social organization, their place within the Amazon Basin, and the meaning for the world economy of the Amazonian forest and its natural resources. It was a learning process that had to deal with ever-widening spatial contexts and fields of action.

The transition made by the Yekuana people implied a change in ethnic and cosmological consciousness. Like many other indigenous peoples, they considered themselves to be at the center of the cosmos. Thrown involuntarily into competition for resources with other peoples with different social philosophies, they acquired a historical consciousness through which they now realize their actual place in the field of geopolitical and economic forces prevailing in the Amazonian world. They have thus become acutely aware of the challenges to their survival. The dynamics of frontier expansion accelerated the transition that took place in the last three decades of the 20th century.

The Yekuana also learned the implications of the sharp difference in worldviews. Year after year, many of the Yekuana's wisest and most knowledgeable elders have served as sources of information for agronomists, explorers, botanists, zoologists, geographers, ecologists, historians, and anthropologists. The Yekuana hoped that their cooperation with scientists would bear fruits for the benefit of humanity and, by way of reciprocity, a degree of certainty about indigenous territorial rights and cultural survival. Their hopes, however, proved to be futile.

They recognized the knowledge available in the Western world through science and technology, ecological and environmental studies, and socioecological analyses. In their view, however, this knowledge brought no real improvement to their quality of life.

From their political activism the Yekuana have acquired invaluable experience on how to organize and fight for their territorial rights, cultural rights, freedom of religion, and the right to speak and learn in their own mother tongue. While doing so they became connected to other indigenous groups of the Americas, especially those of the Amazon Basin. Yekuana leaders have been invited to indigenous rights workshops as part of international agendas carried out by the United Nations, the International Labour Organization, and other human rights organizations.

Between 1993 and 1998 a government agency in Venezuela known as Prodesur launched a new Conquest of the South program. Its principal feature was the enforcement of a public policy favoring large-scale mining and the exploitation of forest resources. These new policies were in direct contradiction with a conservationist trend that had been developed and enforced over the preceding decades. Mineral and natural resources of the South had been "frozen" in protected areas known locally as ABRAE.[1]

In the administration preceding the Chavez government, mining and forest exploitation in protected areas became hot political issues. Indigenous peoples of Bolivar and Delta States joined the campaign against the new policies when large-scale mining came to indigenous territories and threatened to disrupt the precarious equilibrium of the tropical forest environment. The incursion also endangered the lives and physical survival of indigenous peoples, as attested by the Haximou genocide against the Yanomami (Mariz Maia 2001).

Threatened by growing mining activities encroaching upon indigenous ancestral lands, the Yekuana took a more proactive step toward securing their territorial rights. They made the decision to demarcate the lands they hold—the lands that provide the axis of their worldview and lifestyle.

In 1993, with technical support recruited by the Asociación Otro Futuro, the Yekuana established a long-term program to deal with the outside world in a way that would defend and extend their own culture. They developed a holistic approach and methodology that was in close harmony with their view of the order of things on Earth. The program was named Esperando a Kuyujani to honor Kuyujani, their cultural hero who, at the beginning of time, demarcated the lands which He left in trust with the Yekuana people. Once Kuyujani's teachings regarding the use and care of the land were assimilated by the Yekuana people, Kuyujani vanished, but not before leaving His People with the prophecy of His comeback. Therefore, the program was informally named Esperando a Kuyujani (1993–2001). Its name was changed to Kuyujani Originario in November 2001 when the Yekuana organization that created and managed it was registered as a nonprofit civil association (Asociación Civil), giving it juridical status.

Kuyujani Originario

Kuyujani Originario first emerged as a project to legally secure Yekuana ancestral lands. It also was intended to demonstrate to other segments of Venezuelan society that the Yekuana are a people socially, politically, and environmentally capable of managing their lands, their natural resources, and their culture. Their first step, taken in order to prove their command of those capacities, was to reintroduce healing mechanisms that would rebuild the intraethnic solidarity eroded by decades of evangelization. In fact, four decades of evangelization had provoked an ideological abyss that pitted members of sibling groups and extended families one against the other.

Fifteen Yekuana villages were able to convene in three successive general assemblies during which they agreed on two main issues:

- Yekuanness ethnocultural identity is a premise that transcends political and religious differences. Beliefs inconsistent with this premise foster nonadaptive political strategies inimical to the defense of Yekuana territorial rights.
- Oral history has to be put into writing so that the latter could be used in laying the historical and cultural foundations of the lands claim.

These two basic agreements allowed the people of the 15 villages to work together as one mind. Through oral history the Yekuana were able to track down and reconstruct all the steps Kuyujani had taken when He carried out the first and original demarcation of Yekuana lands. Following oral history, they were able to physically mark the borders of Yekuana ancestral territory. They constructed two maps, one in 1995 and an expanded version of the first one in 2001. The latter includes cultural data, topographic features and toponymy, historical and sacred monuments, and natural resources.

The construction and initiation of activities in the first Aramare school were a solid step toward restoring Yekuana culture. That school and the others that have been constructed since provide for the teaching of Yekuana religious beliefs, ceremonies, dances, and sacred music. They provide training in the playing of traditional musical instruments and in the oral history of the Yekuana people. The Aramare schools also provide instruction in knowledge and technologies useful for dealing with the outside world, for example, as ecotourism workshops, legal workshops on indigenous rights within the new Venezuelan constitution (discussed below), workshops on indigenism, and the geopolitics of biodiversity conservation.

The schools also serve as the anchor for the build-up of databases on local fauna and flora as well as Yekuana culture. The work is done in large part by Yekuana students at the Aramare schools. The codification of Yekuana cultural heritage began in 2000 with a catalog identifying Yekuana crafts; it also includes a recorded compact disc of photographs that provide an archive of Yekuana visual images. The catalog and the archive of visual images were put together first as a pedagogic tool to be used for teaching purposes in the Aramare schools. As a consequence of the schools' academic activities, a Yekuana atlas was prepared and published in December 2001. Producing the atlas was a joint effort between Yekuana historians and anthropologists working with Otro Futuro.

The Yekuana Kuyujani Originario program has become a model that many other Amazonian indigenous peoples are following and adapting to their particular geographical, social, and cultural realities. The program has created opportunities for young people inside Yekuana society to become better acquainted with the wealth and expanse of their ancestral lands. This experience has aroused pride in their cultural heritage. Prior to Kuyujani Originario this pride was absent. Younger generations showed indifference to learning the ways of the old and skepticism about the value and meaning of traditional knowledge.

The program has brought back close cooperation among all members of society: village with village, family with family, younger generation with older, male with female. Though such cooperation was present in earlier times, it had been diminished by the Yekuana's contact with the modern world. Evangelization and the emergence of an elite of converted Yekuana people produced a division in two main segments. The "backward" people followed traditional knowledge and religion, resisted cultural change, and located themselves in remote areas of Yekuana land. The "modern," "progress-oriented," Christians monopolized the new positions within the Venezuelan bureaucracy.

The new Bolivarian Constitution of 1999 includes a chapter on indigenous rights. This chapter has provided significant support for the Yekuana's Kuyujani Originario political and cultural strategies. The chapter allows an indigenous people to organize and to apply its political influence without fear of political repression. As a result of such constitutional changes in several countries, the indigenous world has become more lively, proactive, and dynamic.

However, participatory struggles such as the Kuyujani Originario program are not the same as concrete results and substantive changes within Venezuelan society. The majority of the nonindigenous peoples in Venezuela still find themselves in conflict with the so-called *criollo* segment of Venezuelan society. Many in *criollo* society are reluctant to accept the rights granted to indigenous peoples, alleging that creating such special status for indigenous peoples will have adverse economic and political consequences for the whole country. The debate over adoption of the new constitution included heatedly voiced objections to the chapter on indigenous peoples' rights. Only because President Chavez' political faction had the majority of votes in the National Assembly and the President himself was in favor of recognizing indigenous peoples' rights, was the chapter approved. The Chavez government, however, has not been able to achieve political stability, and its loss of influence could mean a great political loss for indigenous peoples. The road to overall protection of indigenous rights in Venezuela is long, and we have only begun to move ahead.

Fractionalization in the Protection of Rights: The Position of Some Indigenous Ethnopolitical Movements

In the early 1970s indigenous peoples in Latin America achieved considerable political visibility through ethnopolitical movements. Some countries, such as Peru and Ecuador, seemed to be better prepared to lead the way and set an example of goals to be accomplished through ethnopolitical mobilization. The Coordinating Body of Indigenous Organizations of the Amazon Basin (Coordinadora de las Organizaciones Indígenas de la Cuenca Amazónica [COICA]) has acquired from positive and negative experiences the knowledge to manage the relationship between indigenous groups and the North. Leaders of COICA and the national organizations that COICA coordinates have developed a better understanding of the motivations of the human and cultural rights organizations of the outside world. They have learned to behave cautiously when choosing allies from Northern groups that want to support indigenous peoples. They know now to insist that they, the indigenous people, set the agenda rather than have it determined by the outside groups. They also know that they must establish a clear position on issues of representation, mediation, alliances, and so forth. They also have learned how to deal with the presence of corruption within their own organizations.

COICA has launched a campaign against the paternalistic attitude that was often displayed by the staff of government indianist agencies, by anthropologists who work with indigenous people, by nongovernmental organizations (NGOs), and by funding agencies. COICA members have argued forcefully that too many intermediaries speak about rather than on behalf of indigenous peoples. They drown Indian voices, and they absorb with their organizational activities the larger part of the funds allocated to indigenous peoples by European, U.S. and Canadian agencies. Funds that did reach the indigenous communities were used to pursue the priorities of the sponsoring organizations rather than those of the indigenous communities.

COICA has worked to put the indigenous people themselves into direct negotiations with international funding agencies. COICA's campaigns against non-indigenous middlemen were intended to liberate indigenous struggles from the colonial heritage of paternalism and mediation, a paradigm that regards indigenous peoples as unable to make rational decisions, to solve problems, and to responsibly account for the money granted to them. COICA has been successful in clearing the ground of parasites and weeds in the international human rights and economic development funding agencies and in building its own space from which COICA is now able to let the world know its agenda and its priorities.

If COICA should be criticized, it is perhaps because it sometimes falls into the trap of addressing different issues as if indigenous worlds were fragments and not whole systems, not *complete* alternative ways of life. Several of its documents exhibit this attitude, for example: "Amazon Indians Seal Alliance of Equals with Environmentalists," "A la Coordinadora ante las Financiadoras del Desarrollo Amazonico: Nuestra Agenda" (To the Coordinator of Amazonian Development: Our Agenda) or "A la Comunidad de Ambientalistas. Nuestra Plataforma" (To the Community of Environmentalists: Our Platform). These documents provide partial reactions to different and fragmented Western stimuli.

Nevertheless, COICA's achievements and the political maturity it has developed have far greater political value than the mistakes it has made along the way. An example of its good work is COICA'S edited volume on *Biodiversidad, Derechos Colectivos y Regimen Sui Generis de Propiedad Intelectual* (1999) (Biodiversity, Collective Rights, and Sui Generis Regimes of Intellectual Property). In this volume, indigenous peoples propose an overall and sui generis system for the protection of their rights. In so doing Indians are telling Western experts that Western assumptions and juridical machinery are the wrong way to initiate a dialog with indigenous peoples. They are wrong to presume that indigenous worlds are collections of unattached parts that can be approached with a piecemeal methodology. On the contrary, indigenous worlds are integrated systems. Gender relations, the rights of indigenous women, linguistic rights, the right to learn and speak the mother tongue, rights to ancestral lands, and so on must be approached within a holistic conception of life, earth, and society that is respectful of existing indigenous conceptions.

COICA has established itself as a vertically integrated ethnopolitical movement in the Amazon Basin. In this role COICA's support for the Consejo Nacional Indio de Venezuela (CONIVE)[2] proved highly influential to reinforce the status of CONIVE before Venezuelan government agencies responsible for indigenous issues. Once consolidated as the coordinating entity of ethnopolitical movements in Venezuela, CONIVE became COICA's protégé. CONIVE grew through almost three decades and in 1998 was recognized by the Consejo Supremo Electoral as the legitimate convener and host of the first primary elections celebrated by indigenous peoples to choose their representatives to the National Assembly.

A word of caution is in order regarding both COICA and CONIVE. There is a risk that their leaders might monopolize the political power and direction of the human and material resources that the government and other agencies provide. This sort of thing has happened in the past; corrupt elites emerge who see their status with the modern world and who become blind to the interests, needs, expectations, and trust of the people who are their social and political base.

While COICA's actions attest to the political sophistication that indigenous leaders and organizations have acquired over the past three decades, COICA has had only limited success in sharing that knowledge with grassroots communities. Many indigenous communities remain permeated by colonial ideologies 500 years old, and not one of the indigenous groups of the Amazon and Orinoco Basins has been untouched by the contaminating spirit of colonialism. The leaders have enjoyed the privileged experience of access to readings and exchange of ideas at international meetings, and from this experience have developed an expanded worldview and a sophistication to deal with the outside. The persistence at the grass roots of the colonial mental rubble indicates, however, that lessons learned by the leaders have not been put to use for the benefit of the many. The persistence of this colonial perception is a strong deterrence to achieving liberation and self-determination for each local group. The gap of knowledge and absence of fluidity of communication between the leadership and the communities may result in an increasing separation of political goals between the two.

Both COICA and CONIVE have been successful in their relations with outsiders and are at present powerful influences in international politics and in the acquisition of economic resources. However, counterbalancing forces that might keep their actions more closely tied to the priorities of the local communities they claim to represent have not evolved. That is a principal reason why the Yekuana members of the Kuyujani Originario organization oppose the reinforcement and strengthening of centralized political elites and vertically integrated ethnopolitical movements.

At the beginning of the process of empowerment of local indigenous groups, the influence of the groups was strengthened by a political process known as *communitas*. *Communitas* was a horizontal sharing of power, a sharing that helped the indigenous groups to achieve political visibility and credibility in the national arena. Once in power, however, the empowered elites have shown signs of following the rationale of a typical bureaucracy sensitive only to its survival and unconcerned with the hopes and faithful trust given to them by local, regional, and grassroots communities of indigenous peoples.

If the most politically powerful indigenous leadership consolidates into a centralized bureaucracy, the basic principles of traditional political systems in lowland South America will be contravened. These systems reject the delegation of local power to a centralized authority. Centralized bureaucracy is a catalytic force bringing about a loss in cultural and political autonomy and brings with it the danger of political subjugation at the village level. Though indigenous peoples have accepted during the past three decades the need to have strong and visible national and international leadership, they are nevertheless distrustful of power invested in a few leaders who come to lean more and more on the nonindigenous axis of power for identity and authority. Indian leadership, when it takes on the attitudes and behavioral patterns of the leaders of the dominant system, becomes co-opted by it. They thus contribute to the extinction of cultural diversity and to the reinforcement of socioeconomic inequities.

The dilution or reduction of cultural diversity is an old colonial strategy. When and if the indigenous leadership goes along—aware or unaware of this strategy— that leadership is responsible for reinforcing a political handicap comparable to the splitting of the indigenous worldview systems into tiny particles. In the past, that approach has proved powerless to defend indigenous rights. It treats indigenous peoples not as members of a viable alternative system but as relics of an almost vanished world.

In short, indigenous peoples are open to dialog, to adaptation, and to changes provided they are recognized as sovereign people with a meaningful worldview that guides their lives. They must, however, be given the opportunity to make agreements on their own, and their institutions must be accepted on an equal footing with Western political and juridical institutions.

A key message from the preceding point is that to protect the rights of indigenous peoples is not a simple matter of changing one element of social structure (their customary collective rights) and replacing it with another (Western intellectual property rights). In the following paragraphs I use the specificity of Yekuana culture to illustrate the range of pressures for cultural change applied over the past three decades to indigenous people. This analysis demonstrates Yekuana willingness to continue the trajectory of cultural change provided certain basic premises are respected.

The Yekuana know of the origins of the pressures for change, that is, major transnational geopolitical and economic interests that compete for the exploitation of Amazonian natural resources. The agenda, however, has to be established by both parties involved. I also take up the strategies followed by ethnopolitical movements of the Amazon Basin that have struggled to resist the piecemeal pressures put to them by Western political and juridical systems. These pressures have tended to fragment and destroy indigenous thought and knowledge systems, and the indigenous political movements have achieved limited success in resisting such efforts. Indeed, a significant failing of many indigenous political movements was that they addressed each issue as an independent phenomenon, be it territorial rights, the right for direct political visibility, and so forth. The indigenous world is still immersed in a difficult learning process on how to deal with the modern world without being overwhelmed by it.

The disparity of sophistication in knowledge and expertise between the indigenous leadership elites and the multitude of indigenous people remains a significant problem. While the leadership has shown sophistication in how to fight for the "indigenous peoples' overall rights," its capacity to deal with generic issues at the level of written documents and position papers exceeds its practical knowledge—its capacity to inform grassroots communities of what is going on and to involve them in developing solutions.

While working with grassroots communities, any concerned outside analyst grasps immediately the existence of deeply ingrained and centuries-old colonial behaviors and attitudes as, for example, the persistence of paternalism and subservience in the relationship between the indigenous and the outside world. It means those sophisticated and powerful indigenous elites have failed in their pedagogic strategy to communicate and inform their accumulated knowledge to the vast majorities of indigenous communities. The seemingly wise and sharp statements of some indigenous organizations stand out in stark contrast to the persistence of colonial institutions.

Accommodation between the indigenous and the outside worlds is not possible, because the nature of indigenous systems of thought is in direct confrontation with Western juridical and political systems. Through the indigenous systems one can apprehend the essence of cultural differences and cultural diversity. Indigenous systems, however, do provide workable *alternative* systems of thought. The different philosophies inherent in each indigenous worldview teach us that unity and cultural diversity are not mutually exclusive. Indigenous objections to the imposition by the West of one way to do things and one way to solve indigenous issues does not necessarily block the possibility of the emergence and full development of sui generis regimes to protect indigenous overall rights.

Kuyujani Originario on the Protection of Indigenous Rights

Kuyujani Originario was created by members of an Amazonian indigenous society and a culture that did not lose its dignity, its pride in its lifestyle, or its place in the world. The colonial and neocolonial conditions to which the Yekuana were submitted shattered some of their values, but in time they realized the blind road they were following and turned back toward their own goals. Though half of its population converted to evangelism between the 1950s and 1980s, the "old way" was rejuvenated when in the 1990s 15 villages launched the project Esperando a Kuyujani. Esperando a Kuyujani's first goal was to recover the borders of their ancestral lands; they achieved that goal by physically marking the most strategic places of their territory.

The next part of the Kuyujani Originario strategy was to fill the gaps of cultural knowledge that had materialized among Yekuana youth. Traditional education had lagged as the Yekuana community came to depend more and more on mission schools. The Yekuana are slowly rebuilding their heritage; the Aramare schools and their pedagogic agenda are the principal instrument.

The Aramare schools have also provided a means to take on another issue: to recover the prestigious status their elders and wise men and women once had within Yekuana society. The Aramare school teachers are wise old specialists in oral history, religion, and the ancient ways. Part of the cultural reinforcement that has come through the Aramare schools is that each young Yekuana can now explain within his or her own worldview the basis for the Yekuana's claims to ancestral lands.

The Yekuana have been outstanding leaders of many political battles held in Amazonas State for land rights, for intercultural bilingual education, for freedom of religion, and for other cultural and economic freedoms. However, access to national non-Indian power within the bureaucracy of the Venezuelan State has never been part of its agenda. The leaders in Yekuana society have not made the same mistakes as several other groups of indigenous people. The present leadership at the national level—in CONIVE and in the National Assembly—is drawn mostly from the Kariña, the Wayuu or Guajiro, and the Pemon peoples. People from these groups have been at the forefront of indigenous leadership for some two decades. To maintain their status vis-à-vis others on the national and international scene, they have been forced to take up political agendas that are not their own and have little to do with indigenous issues.

During the past three decades, the international system to protect human and cultural rights has gone through radical changes. This system has been helpful to turn back the violations of the human rights of indigenous peoples. However, the international system for human rights was not developed specifically to protect indigenous interests per se. Many indigenous advocates have invoked the human rights system to protect indigenous peoples, and they have been useful. A shortcoming, however, is that there are no universal values or universal human rights. The so-called universal nature of international law was created by Western philosophers and politicians when Western colonial powers launched their conquest of the rest of the world in the 16th century. Nowadays, many intellectuals of the colonized world are highly critical of the premises and values of Western thought and political and juridical systems that are being imposed through globalization.

In this context, the Yekuana have learned to deal with the external world without committing themselves to any scheme that could prove detrimental to their own physical and cultural survival. For this same reason there are issues and values of the Western world that they are reluctant to adopt, such as the merchandise approach to intellectual property that allocates a market value to each human and cultural creation or system of thought and knowledge. The Yekuana have rejected to now Western juridical systems for the protection of traditional knowledge as if it were merchandise to be sold in the market. They demand the right to go slowly and with great caution in the discussion within their society about the market value that the West allocates to their traditional knowledge. For the time being, the Yekuana prefer to continue in the process of reflection until they are able to produce a formula to protect traditional knowledge. In the meantime, as a temporary tactic, the Yekuana will register the intellectual property of each of their products and continue working to create an overall sui generis scheme for their protection.

Notes

1. The term stands for "areas abajo regimen de administracion especial." These are natural resource conservation areas defined by government decrees and include national parks, forest reserves, biosphere reserves, sanctuaries, and so forth.

2. CONIVE is the national organization representing indigenous villages and organizations of Venezuela. It, like COICA, is a nonprofit NGO without religious or political creed.

Bibliography

Abya Yala. 2002. "Mandato Desde los Pueblos Indígenas de Abya Yala. Pueblos Indígenas: Otra integración posible ante el ALCA."

Albites, B. J. 2002. "La Protección de los Conocimientos Tradicionales en los Foros Internacionales. Informe sobre la situación Actual." Ms. preparado para el Ministerio de Ciencia y Tecnología de Venezuela.

Arvelo-Jiménez, Nelly. 1974. "Relaciones Políticas en una Sociedad Tribal: Estudio de los Yekuana, Indígenas del Amazonas Venezolano." México, Instituto Indigenista Interamericono. Ediciones especiales No. 68.

_____. 2000. "Three Crises in the History of Yekuana Cultural Continuity." Ethnohistory 47(3-4): 731–46.

_____. 2001. "Movimientos Etnopolíticos Contemporáneos y sus Raíces Organizacionales en el Sistema de Interdependencia Regional del Orinoco." Brasilia, UNB, Série Antropologia No. 309.

Beidelman, T. O. 1982. Colonial Evangelism. Bloomington: Indiana University Press.

Cariño, J. 2001. "Los Pueblos Indígenas y la Cumbre para el Desarrollo Sostenible (WSSD) Copenhague, IWGIA." Grupo Internacional de Trabajo sobre Asuntos Indígenas, pp. 4–7.

COICA/OPIP/OMAERE. 1999. Biodiversidad, Derechos Colectivos y Régimen Sui Generis de Propiedad Intelectual.

Coronil, F. 2000. "Naturaleza del Postcolonialismo: del Eurocentrismo al Globocentrismo." En E. Lander, ed., La Colonialidad del Saber: Eurocentrismo y ciencias Sociales. Perspectivas Latinoamericanas. Caracas: FACES/UNESCO, pp. 119–54.

Davis, S. 1977. "The Geological Imperative." Anthropology Resource Center, Boston, Mass.

Declaracion de Seattle de los Pueblos Indígenas. 1999. Available at http://www.dosemes.com/eco/Comunidades/seattle.htm.

Durbin, M. 1977. "A Survey of the Carib Language Family." In Ellen Basso, ed., *Carib-Speaking Indians: Culture, Society, and Language*. Tucson: The University of Arizona Press, pp. 23–38.

Dussel, E. 2000. "Europa, Modernidad y Eurocentrismo." En E. Lander, ed., *La Colonialidad del Saber: Eurocentrismo y Ciencias Sociales. Perspectivas Latinoamericanas*. Caracas: FACES/UNESCO, pp. 59–78.

Escobar, A. 2000. "El Lugar de la Naturaleza y la Naturaleza del Lugar: ¿Globalización o Postdesarrollo?" En E. Lander, ed., *La Colonialidad del Saber: Eurocentrismo y Ciencias Sociales. Perspectivas Latinoamericanas*. Caracas: FACES/UNESCO, pp. 155–200.

Gutiérrez, E. 2001a. "Sistema para la Protección de los Derechos de Propiedad Intelectual sobre los Conocimientos Tradicionales en Materia de Diversidad Biológica de los Pueblos Indígenas y Comunidades Locales." Informe Técnico para el Ministerio del Ambiente y los Recursos Naturales, Dirección de Acceso a los Recursos Genéticos.

———. 2001b. "Instructivo con el marco legal normativo y los mecanismos para concertar con los Pueblos y Comunidades Indígenas el CFP y la DJEB." Informe técnico preparado para la Dirección de Biodiversidad del Ministerio del Ambiente, Caracas, Venezuela.

Hernandez, F. 2002. "La Propiedad Intelectual Indígena."

Kuyujani Originario. 2001. Estatutos (foundational chart).

Lander, E. 2001. "Los Derechos de propiedad intelectual en la geopolítica del saber de la sociedad global."

———. 2002. "La utopía del mercado total y el poder imperial."

Mariz Maia, Luciano. 2001. "Haximu: Foi Genocidio! CCPY Pro Yanomami." Document No. 1.

Milton, K. 1993. "Environmentalism. The View from Anthropology." ASA Monograph 32. Routledge, London and New York.

Nandy, A. 1988. *Science, Hegemony and Violence. A Requiem for Modernity*. Delhi, Tokyo: The United Nations University. Oxford India Paperbacks.

Posey, D. A., and G. Dutfield. 1996. "Beyond Intellectual Property." International Development Research Center, Ottawa.

Quijano, A. 2000. "Colonialidad del Poder, Eurocentrismo y América Latina." En E. Lander, ed., *La Colonialidad del Saber: Eurocentrismo y Ciencias Sociales. Perspectivas Latinoamericanas*. Caracas: FACES/UNESCO, pp. 281–348.

———. 2001. "Colonialidad del Poder, Globalización y Democracia."

Rist, G. 1999. *The History of Development from Western Origins to Global Faith*. London: Zed Books, Development Studies.

Shiva, V. 1993. *Biodiversity. Social and Ecological Perspectives*. London: Zed Books and World Rainforest Movement.

———. 1995. *Monocultures of the Mind. Perspectives on Biodiversity and Biotechnology*. Zed Books and Third World Network.

Stavenhagen, R., ed. 1988. "Derecho Indígena y Derechos Humanos en América Latina." Instituto Interamericano de Derechos Humanos y el Colegio de México.

Stavenhagen, R., and D. Iturralde, eds. 1990. "Entre la Ley y la Costumbre. El Derecho Consuetudinario Indígena en América Latina." Instituto Indigenista Interamericano e Instituto Interamericano de Derechos Humanos, Mexico.

Taussig, M. 1986. *Shamanism, Colonialism and the Wild Man. A Study in Terror and Healing*. The University of Chicago Press.

Villalón, M. E. 1987. "Una Clasificación Tridimensional de Lenguas Caribes." *Antropológica* 68:23–47.

Vivas Eugui, D. 2002. "Análisis de Opciones Sui Géneris para la Protección del Conocimiento Tradicional y la Experiencia Venezolana en la Materia." Documento preparado para el Ministerio de Ciencia y Tecnología de Venezuela, Caracas.

2

HANDMADE IN INDIA: TRADITIONAL CRAFT SKILLS IN A CHANGING WORLD

Maureen Liebl and Tirthankar Roy

In a world that is becoming increasingly mechanized, increasingly homogenized, and almost completely exposed to the scrutiny of the Internet, it is logical to assume that the unique, the individual, and the culturally resonant will acquire ever more appeal and luster. A recent United Nations Educational, Scientific, and Cultural Organization (UNESCO) symposium, in fact, has concluded that "the industries of the imagination, content, knowledge, innovation and creation clearly are the industries of the future... they are also important contributory factors to employment and economic growth" (UNESCO 1999).

Try telling it to the weavers of Andhra Pradesh. In just one recent month, four skilled and talented traditional artisans in this southern Indian state died from starvation, and two more committed suicide (Gopinath Reddy 2002). They joined the several score more who have taken their own lives in recent years and the

---

"Handmade in India: Preliminary Analysis of Crafts Producers and Crafts Production in India; Issues, Initiatives, Interventions" is the title of a report that the authors of this chapter were commissioned to prepare by the Policy Sciences Center, Inc., under the direction of Frank W. Penna, in 1999. The study and the report were funded by the Development Grant Facility of the World Bank, and were expected to provide an analysis of the crafts sector in India that would be of use to the World Bank in planning future loan programs. The completed report was presented at a Bank workshop in Washington, D.C., in January 2001. Much of the information in the current chapter is quoted from the report or based on it. The full report and transcripts of the workshop sessions are available at lnweb18.worldbank.org/essd/essd.nsf/Culture/CW-Agenda.

uncounted thousands who have not yet been driven to this act of ultimate despair, but whose lives nevertheless have been devastated by financial ruin and by the hopelessness of a world in which their skills and their knowledge, once prized and respected, have become superfluous.

Their stories are harsh and tragic. "My husband begged master weavers for work," says one widow. "But they could not help us. He committed suicide." Another weaver gave up when the last in a long string of creditors demanded payment. "It was the last straw," comments one of his neighbors. "He collapsed, leaving his wife and children destitute." Still another hung himself the day after a major festival, during which his family could not eat (Gopinath Reddy 2002).

The Andhra Pradesh weavers represent the most extreme example of what can happen when possessors of traditional knowledge find that their specialized expertise is no longer economically viable. Relatively few of India's crafts producers, conservatively estimated to number more than 8 million, have actually been driven to suicide. The vast majority, however, must struggle to eke out a meager living and suffer from poverty, lack of access to social services, illiteracy, exploitation by middlemen, and extremely low social status.

Paradoxically, the products of these struggling artisans sustain rapidly growing export and domestic markets; the former is estimated at close to US$2 billion in 2000 and the latter at about US$1 billion during the same period (see table 2.1). The size of the markets enjoyed by the copies of their products that are churned out in China and Southeast Asia is unknown, but is substantial.

In India, crafts are one of the major industries of "the imagination" and of traditional knowledge and skill. India's myriad craft traditions and living craft skills

TABLE 2.1   Handicrafts in India: Basic Statistics

	1994–95	2000–2001 (estimated)
Number of employed	8.3 million	8.6 million
Value of output	US$4.6 billion	US$6.1 billion
Income	US$2.5 billion	US$3.3 billion
Exports	US$1.3–US$2 billion	US$1.9–US$2.4 billion
As percentage of manufacturing		
Employment	19.7	n.a.
Income	5.7	n.a.

n.a. Not available.

Source: National Sample Survey Organisation, Survey of Unorganized Manufacturing (45th and 51st Rounds), 1989–90 and 1994–5, New Delhi, India.

Note: 2000–2001 figures are estimated by assuming a constant growth rate of domestic demand, and constant real output-worker ratio, through the 1990s.

are rare and irreplaceable resources, generally acknowledged as living links to the past and as a means of preserving cultural meaning into the future. Both within India and without, large numbers of connoisseurs avidly collect examples of specific craft genre, and numerous scholarly treatises and expensive coffee-table books are written on various craft forms.

Handwoven Indian textiles appear on the ramps in Paris, handcrafted Indian jewelry is sold in the best stores in New York, and handmade Indian carpets cover some of the most elegant floors in the world. The craftsmen and craftswomen who create them often have learned their art as a hereditary profession and are taught from infancy. Some skills are so intricate and so specialized (such as the famous *thewa* gold filigree-on-glass jewelry or the grinding of local stones and minerals into paint pigments) that the manufacturing process is a secret still closely guarded by a small number of families. Others acquire their individual luster through lifelong apprenticeship and practice. Some are regional specialties, whose techniques, motifs, and materials make them instantly identifiable; others are found, with some variation, in communities throughout India. What all the many thousands of beautiful and unique craft expressions in India have in common, though, is that the weavers, potters, carvers, painters, embroiderers, goldsmiths, and others who create such beauty with consummate skill and knowledge enjoy few of the fruits of their labor.

Protecting and preserving these skills and knowledge is a major challenge; ensuring that they provide viable livelihoods for their owners is an even greater one. And the latter challenge is, of course, a necessary part of achieving the former.

The Case for Protection of Traditional Craft Skills

In any discussion of how to protect the inheritors of traditional skills and knowledge, one must of course face the question of whether traditions and expertise that are no longer naturally viable should, in fact, be preserved at all. All traditional knowledge developed in a context within which it was intrinsically viable. In the natural evolution of societies, it is neither possible, nor desirable, to preserve every single piece of the past. Some types of knowledge and skill, however, are clearly worth preserving. These would, minimally, include those that by virtue of their intrinsic beauty, cultural meaning, or value as a knowledge base represent a precious resource and also those that may have unrealized potential to generate viable income and to preserve traditional lifestyles.

Crafts form a special category of traditional knowledge, and many Indian craft forms fit into both of the above categories. The intrinsic beauty of many Indian craft traditions is obvious to even the casual observer, and their meaning and cultural resonance quickly become apparent to those with even a brief exposure to Indian history and society. The full potential of the role craft traditions can play in the development process, and specifically in the generation of income, however, has only recently begun to be appreciated.

In a global context, the International Trade Centre (ITC) points out that support to crafts has "become a must on the path towards poverty alleviation and environment protection, two topical and compelling concerns worldwide" (ITC 1999). The growing interest in the role that crafts can play in the development process has also led to increasing involvement in this area by a great many international organizations and agencies, among them the International Development Bank (IDB), the International Labour Organization (ILO), UNESCO, the United Nations Industrial Development Organization (UNIDO), the World Intellectual Property Organization (WIPO), and others. The World Bank has also begun to express new interest in the potential of cultural industries in the development process. In his foreword to a World Bank exhibition catalog, *Culture and Development at the Millennium*, World Bank President James D. Wolfensohn said that many individuals in developing countries "feel themselves increasingly powerless against the vast forces of global change" (Wolfensohn 1998). This is, in fact, an apt summation of the situation in which most of India's crafts producers find themselves.

Crafts show tremendous potential in terms of employment generation and poverty alleviation in India. Handicrafts provide a livelihood, albeit modest, to large numbers of poor people in India, and especially to the rural poor. Crafts producers often employ skills and complex knowledge systems that have evolved over long periods of time. Even as the products "globalize" (reaching an increasingly distant clientele via fairly sophisticated marketing systems), however, the skills and the knowledge systems remain largely informal, poorly protected, inadequately documented, socially and culturally disadvantaged, and imperfectly adaptive. The outcome is that return on skill remains low, and markets remain small and unstable. Weaknesses on the crafts producers' side limit quality of goods, innovation, intergenerational transfer and sustainability of skills, integration of traditional knowledge into the mainstream, and development of links between local traditions and the world market. These weaknesses all impinge on market prospects in the long term.

Craft industries form an important sector of the Indian economy, contributing substantially to manufacturing income, employment, and exports, and the scale of these contributions is increasing. The part-time, rural nature of much crafts activity also complements the lifestyles of many crafts workers, provides supplementary income to seasonal agricultural workers and part-time income to women, and provides craftspeople with the means to remain in their traditional villages, where alternative employment opportunities are limited. Many crafts-people themselves express the strong desire to remain in their traditional profession. And although many are highly talented and extremely skilled in their own craft form, most are poorly educated or illiterate and come from caste groups of low social status. Retraining is thus not a feasible option in most cases. The most viable means to improve their lives appears to be maximizing the high skill base they already possess.

There is a clear market for Indian handicrafts. If the crafts producers continue to reap so few rewards from it, however, more and more people will leave these traditional professions for other forms of employment, and the skills and knowledge will ultimately be lost.

The Paradox and the Problems: Changing Market Patterns and Supply-Side Constraints

The paradox of talented artisans living in unrelenting poverty while their products support a flourishing export trade is the result of the complex, diverse, and pervasive problems that affect the crafts sector in India. Some of the problems are related to the changing context of consumption; others to the social and economic problems of craft communities; and others to the basic character of the crafts sector, which is vast, dispersed throughout India, and totally unorganized.

There is no doubt about the fact that the share of the crafts producer in the thriving export market is minimal. It is impossible to determine the exact percentage of revenues that actually accrue to the artisan; this information is carefully guarded by the many levels of middlemen and dealers through whose hands the product must pass. The case study (see appendix) of the ratio of the artisan's price to final retail price in one particular case in Jodhpur may be illuminating in this regard.

The majority of India's artisans suffer from severe limitations in accessing and understanding viable new markets, as well as in adapting their products to those markets. In addition, they must deal with the fact that the markets themselves are in a state of transition.

Changing Market Patterns

There has been a lively international market for Indian crafts for millennia. India's textile traditions have been particularly well documented; these documents show the amazingly long history of many traditional skills as well as the immense fame that India's artisans once enjoyed.

This international market was, however, possible only because the domestic Indian market provided a vast and secure base of patronage. Ancient scriptural references in India give divine association to lengths of unstitched cloth; until recently, wrapped, unstitched cloth was the basic mode of dress throughout the country (the woman's *sari* and the man's *dhoti*). The local weaver was thus an important, indeed essential, member of the community, and his economic well-being was assured.

The importance of the *sari* as the national female costume in India is quite remarkable, and its many variations have inspired and sustained the world's most vibrant handloom weaving tradition. Now, however, patterns of life and clothing are changing, and in most urban (and even semiurban) areas, young women and working women are switching to variations of the *salwar-kameez* (an outfit consisting of trousers, a long tunic top, and a long scarf), or even to Western clothing. And even in areas where the *sari* still maintains its traditional importance, market forces have had a negative impact on the weaver. Local markets are now flooded with machine-made *saris* in synthetic fabrics. To the eye of the connoisseur, these *saris* are often gaudy and cheap, vastly inferior to the handloomed traditional cottons. To the local women, however, the brilliant chemical colors, novel synthetic texture, and low price are great advantages, and the livelihood of the local weavers has been destroyed.

Throughout India, women still prefer *saris* for formal and ritual occasions, and there will always be a market for the extremely exclusive (and often very expensive) high-end woven *saris*. For the many millions of weavers who depended on local markets, however, the scenario is grim.

The booming handicraft export market has also produced problems. It is true that it has generated new income for many crafts producers, but often at the cost of debasing their traditional skills. The major part of the handicraft export market revolves around mass-produced items destined for medium- to low-range "gift shop" buyers and moderately priced furniture and furnishings outlets. There is no lack of employment opportunity, to take just one example, for a traditional miniature painter living in Jodhpur, in the western state of Rajasthan. Handicraft dealers always need more painters who can sit on the floor in the factory and paint flowers and animals on several hundred wooden boxes, or several dozen liquor cabinets, each day. The challenge is to develop markets for the exquisite, finely burnished paintings that the artist is capable of making, or new products that will enable him to use his talent and highly developed skills. No handicraft dealer would be willing to invest the time or money that would allow an artist to hand-grind stones and minerals into subtle, glowing pigments, or to spend days painstakingly building up sheer layers of subtle, fine colors. The painted liquor cabinet may be pretty in a facile sort of way, and may indeed provide necessary income, but a true talent and hard-won skill base are being totally ignored.

We must of course acknowledge that the world's markets cannot and will not stand still to accommodate the holders of traditional skills and knowledge. If these resources are handled creatively, however, many of them can remain alive and greatly enrich our contemporary lives, as well as allow the possessors to survive. New markets are opening, both for new products made with traditional skills and for traditional products adapted to new needs. Understanding how to adapt to these markets can ensure the preservation of the traditional skill, as well as provide a viable income and lifestyle to the artist.

Supply-Side Constraints

It is extremely difficult to tackle the many problems of the crafts sector in any remotely comprehensive way because of its amorphous, unorganized nature. Indeed, the very nature of the problems can be quite different in different areas and for different types of crafts producers.

Nevertheless, some basic problems are common to all. The most important issues are as follows:

- Artisans generally lack knowledge of and access to means of increasing quality and productivity, especially in the areas of skill development, design input (to meet market requirements), and technical innovation (in such areas as labor-saving methodology, standardization, productivity enhancement, and environmental concerns and consumer safety).
- Crafts producers who have lost their traditional markets often are not aware of potential new markets for their products, in urban India and abroad. The low level of education and rural orientation of the majority of craftspeople leave them vulnerable to exploitation by all those middlemen who are their only means of access to distant markets. When they do have the opportunity to interact directly with a buyer, the problems multiply. The essentially agrarian, rural worldview of the producer does not mesh easily with the exacting demands of the international market, and experiments in direct market access often end in total failure.
- Crafts producers suffer greatly from lack of working capital and access to credit and loan facilities. The producer who receives a large order will often not be able to find the funds necessary to purchase raw material in bulk, or to support the family while the work is in process. And the irony is that the amounts that could make a real difference to the crafts producer are often extremely modest. Various credit schemes are available to craftspeople, primarily through government institutions, but it is difficult for the uneducated artisan to understand and access these programs, and it is often impossible for a poor craftsperson to manage the necessary collateral or funds for required bribes.

- A major disadvantage of life in the "unorganized sector" is the total lack of civic, professional, and social service infrastructure. The individual craftsperson suffers from all of these problems. Scarce and irregular electricity, lack of good roads, and absence of transportation facilities are professional problems as well as daily aggravations. Craft-specific professional infrastructure—worksheds, storage space, shipping and packing facilities—is totally lacking for most rural crafts producers. And social services infrastructure—insurance, pension plans, medical care—is something beyond hope.

In addition to these practical problems, the craftsperson in most cases gets little recognition or tangible reward for extraordinary skill or talent. This lack of professional respect is at least partially because crafts production in India is still linked to caste status, and crafts-producing communities, with very few exceptions, are at the lower levels of the social scale. This situation often presents tremendous contradictions. An artisan who has received the national Master Craftsman Award from the president of India may be barred from entering the lobby of a hotel in his own city.[1] A weaver whose textiles are being sold in Paris would seldom be invited to dinner in the home of his exporter in Delhi. The home of a nationally acclaimed master craftsman may be a virtual hovel, on whose otherwise bare walls will hang a carefully framed photograph of the artist being presented his plaque by a beaming president of his country. It is an ironic, and sad, state of affairs.

"Ownership" and Intellectual Property Issues for Indian Craftspeople[2]

In addition to the above problems, the crafts producer has little means of protecting individual creative innovations or traditional community knowledge. Copying is a way of life in India, and exploitation is pervasive at every level. Dealers and designers freely appropriate designs of traditional artisans. Crafts producers who specialize in unique, time-consuming processes suffer competition from cheap knockoffs in local markets. And craftspeople themselves often leak unique designs belonging to their clients to the highest bidder. On a larger scale, a recent trend has been for buyers to have samples designed and produced in India, but manufactured in bulk in China or Southeast Asia. The original producer, needless to say, benefits from this not at all.

Tackling these issues in the Indian context is extraordinarily difficult and more complex than it seems to be in many other countries. Many aspects of crafts production in India, as well as the very nature of the crafts traditions themselves, present unique problems in developing and implementing intellectual property rights (IPR) mechanisms for their protection. There are three primary areas of difficulty:

determining ownership, developing membership structures for owners, and establishing and maintaining enforcement procedures.

Ownership

Although the "stock" of design ideas tends to be collectively shared within a community of artisans, the legal regime does not usually recognize as intellectual property ideas that are already public in some form. Given this context, handicrafts can in principle receive two types of protection. Individual innovators can claim—under the copyright act in particular—rights to designs that they create, even when based on an existing stock of ideas. And artisan communities can claim rights to the original stocks of design ideas, to defend against poaching on traditional knowledge by nontraditional businesses. For protection of collective rights, however, the Geographical Indications Act offers perhaps the most promising means of protection at the moment.

In the case of both individuals and groups, however, establishing ownership is the initial problem, and the concept of ownership is complicated with Indian crafts because of certain cultural perspectives in India regarding creativity, and also because of the intrinsic nature of crafts communities.

Cultural Perspectives Regarding Creativity   Most traditional crafts in India follow classical traditions, many of which are hundreds, and even thousands, of years old. Aesthetic forms are often thought of as springing from a kind of universal, divinely inspired subconscious.

Probably because of this way of regarding aesthetic expression, in India the concept of "copying" has never had the pejorative connotations that it does in the West. Traditional Indian artists (and this includes musicians, dancers, vocalists, sculptors, painters, potters, metalworkers, poets, and many others) do not hold sacrosanct the notion of individual creativity. Rather, the most important task of the artist is seen to be the interpretation of a classic theme, rather than the creation of a new one. This is a real and easily observable cultural perspective, and one that has a profound impact on how one views ownership of creative expression, or, indeed, creativity itself.

At a less philosophical level—although perhaps partly because of this cultural perspective—design ownership is seldom recognized or respected at any point in the crafts industry. With traditional crafts, the line between copying and innovation can be thin, and it is important to note that copying is not always detrimental to the interests of the artisan or the community. If the copy is an improvement in quality or cost, it feeds into and increases the sustainability of the heritage for the entire community. In markets catering to elite urban consumers, design ideas sometimes borrow from traditional knowledge, and this can in some ways also help rather than hurt the interests of the producers by increasing the recognition of and the demand for that particular expression. But flagrant copying can also deny the original producers any share in the market rewards, as well as eventually result in dilution of standards.

The Nature of Craft Communities   The concept of ownership is further complicated by the fact that craft communities in India are seldom, if ever, frozen in time and space. Although most crafts are regional and caste based, they are not necessarily static. There are certain types of metalsmiths, to cite just one example, who move from village to village, setting up temporary camps until the clientele is exhausted. In the process, ideas, techniques, and forms travel with them (Jain 1989). And although upward mobility between castes has always been difficult, lateral mobility is not infrequent. A child in a jewelry family may show exceptional talent in *meenakari* (enamel work on gold) and be sent off to study with a miniature painter, where, it is believed, his talent may have greater economic return. An entire family of painters, faced with declining patronage, may switch over to stone carving. A woman from one craft community may marry into another, bringing her own group's traditional designs, which will be enthusiastically accepted, and used, in her new village.

Moreover, different communities may be involved in various stages of one craft. The famous handblock textile printers of Sanganer and Bagru, in Rajasthan, for instance, are all from one caste-based Hindu community. The wooden blocks they use for printing, however, are made by Muslim woodcarvers from the state of Uttar Pradesh. Designs are sometimes developed by the printer, sometimes by the block-carver, sometimes by the domestic or foreign buyer, or sometimes borrowed from those of rival silk screen-printers, who use designs done by artists from the neighboring state of Gujarat. Currently, there are numerous popular patterns and color combinations that obviously owe their inspiration to designs provided by Japanese buyers, although the local interpretations and modifications are now regarded by the artisans as "original." Identifying and attributing the individual strands that resulted in any particular design can be an almost impossible task.

Some isolated and tribal communities do possess distinctive designs and forms, and have a membership base that is fairly easy to delineate. These groups are very much in the minority, however.

Membership Structures for Owners

Even if ownership can be determined, the first step in developing any system of IPR is the formation of a structure that certifies its members as "owners" (such as collecting societies) and that serves as their representative. In India, this is another extremely difficult task. Although craftspeople may, in fact, see themselves as professionals, they are likely to give their first loyalty to other aspects of their self-identity, such as family or caste group. This, combined with the culture of patronage, nepotism, and corruption that has filtered down through all levels of Indian society, makes it extremely difficult to organize membership structures in India that do not, ultimately, work against rather than for the majority of members.

Dr. Jyotindra Jain, dean of the Faculty of Arts and Aesthetics at Jawaharlal Nehru University and until recently the senior director of Delhi's famous Crafts Museum, is a scholar who has devoted much thought (and much analysis for the government of India) to this subject. Although he formerly was a vigorous advocate of protective action, he says that he has come "full circle" and changed his mind on the entire issue. His fear, as he has thought through each proposed structural development to its logical conclusion, is that any regulatory machinery that is imposed on the crafts community will ultimately end up hurting, rather than helping, those who need protection most.

This issue cannot be dealt with in a facile manner. The success of some organizations that involve craftspeople (such as the Self-Employed Women's Association [SEWA] and the URMUL Rural Health Research and Development Trust)[3] seems to prove that it is possible to develop profession-based community organizational structures that do function fairly effectively. How these organizations have seemingly avoided the factionalism, patronage, and outright corruption that have swamped such organizations as, for instance, weavers' cooperatives, is a question whose answer would require informed and highly sensitive analysis. The obvious common element in URMUL, SEWA, and a few other successful organizations is that they were founded by, and are still under the wing of, individuals with extraordinary and selfless commitment. Whether or not this is the critical requirement is open to debate. If the essential elements contributing to the success of these organizations can be identified, however, they would serve as a useful basis for determining the types of ownership organizations that might work in other areas, such as IPR protection, as well.

Establishing and Maintaining Enforcement Procedures

India has a highly sophisticated legal system that is enforced in an extremely ad hoc manner. Although the system does sometimes function with extraordinary efficiency, many well-known criminals of all types escape legal action for long periods of time, if not forever, and ordinary citizens are often involved in civil court cases that have been initiated by their parents and grandparents. Crafts producers, asked about the possibility of obtaining redress from the courts for infringement of ownership rights on their products, will generally respond with a hearty laugh. Of the many dealers, manufacturers, and exporters we interviewed, not one expressed any optimism regarding the possibilities for legal enforcement of ownership rights. The problems affecting the entire system of legal enforcement in India are deep and widespread and are unlikely to be modified for the sole purpose of protecting crafts ownership.

In fact, well-developed legal resources are available for IPRs in India, and these are currently being modernized. They include patents, trademarks, copyrights, and industrial design acts. Generally speaking, the structure of these acts is regarded as adequate, but enforcement and the tardiness of the dispute settlement system as a whole minimize their utility. In addition, the system has so far not been designed to address, let alone meet, ownership concerns in respect to handicrafts.

That said, however, it is clear that efforts must be made to deal with the problems and to develop a way of addressing ownership concerns in the Indian context. As one expert in this field has pointed out, "copyrights are the currency" of the developing new global economy, and, in his opinion at least, India "with its vast cultural resources, will benefit more than any other nation from an effective copyright system."[4]

Existing Legislation

Protective legislation does exist, at least on paper, for various types of intellectual property protection. Two main acts are especially relevant to crafts.

The Copyright Act of 1957 was amended in 1994 to afford greater protection to original literary, dramatic, musical, and artistic works. The government is attempting to strengthen and enforce the protection afforded under this act. The Trade and Merchandise Marks Act of 1958 and the Design Act of 1911 have also been replaced. The new Trademarks Act, among others, amplifies the definition of trademarks to incorporate collective marks. This may have some relevance for protection of traditional knowledge.

More promising is a new piece of legislation, the Geographical Indications of Goods (Registration and Protection) Act of 1999. This is the first time that geographical indications have received any protection under Indian law. One of the first groups to take advantage of this new act has been the government of India's Tea Board, which has received certification for protection of Darjeeling tea. This act does hold promise for some of India's most famous region-based craft forms. The difficulty, of course, is that whereas Darjeeling tea leaves actually grow in Darjeeling ground, the provenance of a craft product has more ambiguous parameters. How does one decide, for instance, exactly when a piece of silk may be sold as "Kanjeevaram"? For a traditional weaver who lives in Kanjeevaram (in the southern state of Tamil Nadu) and who still uses the traditional techniques and designs of this famous type of weaving, the designation is straightforward. Unlike a Darjeeling tea bush, however, the weaver may very well move to another part of India. If he continues to use his traditional skill, design base, and process in a new location, is he no longer a Kanjeevaram weaver? And what happens when a weaver from another part of India moves to Kanjeevaram? Does physical location alone qualify him to use the name? What happens in case of a closely similar product that does not use the appellation of origin and yet threatens to compete with the original? These are simplistic hypothetical questions, but the realities can actually become quite complicated.

Still, this act holds great promise if it can be channeled properly. The two preconditions required for a fruitful and not overly restrictive application of geographical indication are a strong natural claim to a distinct locational identity and strong collective bodies at the local level. It is not yet clear how many and which handicraft clusters can answer to these two requirements for a successful claim to geographical distinctness. A commissioned survey-based study covering the major craft brands and clusters is urgently required in this area.

In analyzing existing framework and discussing needed new framework, one must take into account several different types of owners in the crafts sector of India who need protection:

- **Traditional craftspeople making traditional objects.** It is difficult to see any way in which to define and protect ownership of timeless expressions that occur and recur throughout the subcontinent. Certain region-based crafts may qualify for protection under the new Geographical Indications Act, but it will by no means apply to all traditional artists.
- **Craftspeople using their traditional skills, materials, and techniques to produce new products of their own design.** This is an area in which registration or ownership becomes more feasible, although still not without problems. In most craft communities, copying is a way of life; indeed, traditional artisans learn by copying. A "new" design will often be an interpretation of an older one, and deciding on the degree of innovation necessary to claim ownership could be a procedural nightmare. Since the traditional design base often spreads throughout a region, or even throughout the entire country, registering individual innovations of this traditional base becomes highly complex.

One Delhi-based nongovernmental organization (NGO) decided to concentrate on this area a few years ago. With the support (and funding) of the government's Development Commissioner of Handicrafts, the group worked with a community of printmakers in Rajasthan, with the stated intention of helping them to establish rights of ownership over their designs. Three thousand designs were registered and documented on compact disc (CD). The results have been unfortunate, as a bitter dispute resulted over ownership of the CD documentation itself. The NGO felt that *it* owned the CD documentation; this view was shared neither by the government sponsors nor by the print-makers themselves, who believe they have once again been exploited. Although we have not been able to verify it, one of the authors of this report has been told that copies of the CD are now being sold quite freely in the Jaipur markets. This incident illustrates some of the pitfalls of venturing into these areas in India, and also shows why many crafts producers believe that the only hope for design and process protection lies in maintaining as much secrecy as possible.

• **Designers and craftspeople who work together to create "fusion" products.** This is a category in which protection is feasible, since designs are likely to be extremely innovative and easily recognizable. The difficulty, however, is in deciding which party is the owner of the design.

• **Designers/manufacturers who provide designs to craftspeople or use crafts producers' skills in execution of particular designs.** Many of the most exciting and innovative new uses of traditional craft skills are being explored in this category. Many Indian designers are beginning to establish international reputations for this type of work. Some have been responsible for large-scale revitalization of particular crafts skills, and a number of them are working with government and NGO projects, as well as for their own business interests. They, too, however, are plagued by cheap copies, often manufactured by competitors who buy one sample piece, and then more or less openly manufacture cheap copies in quantity. One well-known fashion designer who has suffered greatly from this has initiated several court cases against such acts. Although it is extremely costly and time-consuming, she hopes that her action will establish a precedent and will instill some sense of caution in competitors.

In addition to protecting the human owners, one must ultimately look at the protection of the skill and knowledge base itself. There has been a recent new effort to do this in another area of traditional knowledge in India, that of medicinal plants. The Ministry of Health and Family Welfare, working in collaboration with the National Institute of Science Communication and the Indian Systems of Medicine and Homeopathy, has developed a traditional knowledge digital library to document traditional knowledge relating to disease prevention and treatment. By documenting this traditional knowledge, the government hopes to make it accessible to everyone, and also to protect it from "poaching" by international firms that obtain patents on traditional Indian substances. The officials involved explain that the project was first conceived after India managed to revoke the patents on neem and turmeric that had been granted by the U.S. Patent and Trademark Office. The first section of the library is available on a website as of September 2002 (*Indian Express* 2002). This effort will bear close watching; if it works, it may provide a model for similar documentation of certain types of traditional craft forms and processes as well.

Until such time as such innovative projects can be undertaken related to crafts, and until adequate legislation, structures, and enforcement procedures can be developed, most people in the crafts industry will have to continue to depend on their own wits to protect their products and designs. Most cope by guarding every stage of the process as closely as possible, prohibiting photography, and avoiding such things as catalogs and extensive web displays. Some craft communities go so far as to guard the processes from daughters in their families. As one artisan explained, "[T]he girls get married and leave us. We cannot take the chance that they will take our secrets with them. We could, of course," he added, "train our daughters in law, but by the time we get them, they are too old to learn properly."[5] Secrecy is not the most desirable form of IPR, admittedly, but in India it is still the most effective.

Possible Solutions

The spectacular variety of problems facing India's crafts producers requires myriad solutions. All presuppose, however, that there is a continuing market. Except in a museum setting, no traditional craft skill can be sustained unless it has a viable market. Two basic types of solution are required:

- To increase the income of crafts producers, the prerequisites are adaptation of skills and products to meet new market requirements and improvement in market access and supply.
- To sustain the traditional skill base and to protect the artisans' traditional knowledge resources, the priority is development and implementation of appropriate IPR legislation.

Given the difficulties of implementing IPR structures at this point, the market adaptation and access problems are more manageable.

The government of India, through the offices of the Development Commissioner for Handicrafts and the Development Commissioner for Handlooms (both under the Ministry of Textiles), contributes substantial funding to crafts intervention, as do numerous other government agencies. In the past, much of this funding was misdirected and ineffective. Current sophisticated and innovative programs are, however, changing the nature of government support. In the handicrafts area, especially, strongly focused programs are involving designers and technical experts in targeted cluster development programs. The results have been impressive, and products produced under these programs are gaining a strong new presence at a number of international trade events. The Ford Foundation and the European Union, among others, are also developing substantial new programs to tackle various market adaptation and access difficulties. A comprehensive study of all these new initiatives is needed, as is a comparative analysis of the ways in which they are addressing the problems. There is little, if any, central coordination among all the organizations and agencies involved, and few know much about what the others are doing.

Two promising ways to improve livelihoods while saving skills and knowledge are:

- Adapting traditional skills to new products for changing markets. This adaptation can be accomplished in many areas in India, including fashion, home furnishings design, and tourism.
- Repositioning skills and products for upscale markets that appreciate and are willing to pay premiums for handcrafted quality and character.

The potential of this type of adaptation and repositioning is demonstrated by many of the best fashion designers in India, who are increasingly using the exquisite handwork skills of traditional textile artists to produce Indian and fusion clothing that is finding an international market. Some are now branching out into accessories and home decorative products and are using traditional skills to produce table linens, cushion covers, and fashion accessories.

One of the most successful of these designers is Ritu Kumar. In the 1970s, as a young fashion designer, she began experimenting with traditional embroidery. She began slowly, reviving the Mughal art of *zardozi*—embroidery done with silver and gold wire—to create extremely fine evening and bridal outfits. She then began expanding into other types of traditional crafts, such as fine *chikan* embroidery from Lucknow, mirror work from Kutch, elegant Kashmiri embroidery, and handblocked prints. Traditional design concepts were reinterpreted in exquisite silk printing, and everything was incorporated into new versions of traditional Indian outfits. Gradually, she expanded into fusion and Western clothing, as well as accessories and home decoratives. Today, Ritu Kumar has boutiques throughout India as well as in London, and is an international presence. She continues to work with fine master craftspeople, and, more importantly, she has been the inspiration and model for an entire younger generation of designers who now see traditional craft skills as the foundation for a contemporary Indian design aesthetic.

A growing circle of young and extremely talented designers in other fields is also working to revitalize traditional skills within new contexts. One group is working with traditional palm-leaf manuscript painters from the eastern state of Orissa, teaching them carpentry and opening their eyes to the ways in which their paintings can be incorporated into fine furniture. Another is breathing new life into the hackneyed "tourist" designs of the Agra marble inlay workers, and has them producing contemporary dinnerware in stunning designs. The number of such efforts is still small in comparison with the number of crafts producers, but they are the vanguard in what has the potential to be a major trend.

One must of course analyze the distribution of benefits from these efforts. Many of the designers involved with crafts producers see the artisan as a partner, regard their work with some idealism, and accept responsibility for equitable sharing of profits and other returns. Others, of course, do not. The most committed try to work with artisans in their traditional settings. Most find, however, after some time, that the difficulties make commercial success impossible. Those who manage to survive and at the same time to maintain a level of commitment to the artisans generally eventually arrive at a compromise solution, working with artisans in their own villages to some extent, but also bringing some artisans to their workshops in Delhi. Two highly respected and successful commercial firms of long standing (the Delhi-based FabIndia and the Jaipur-based Anokhi) maintain active health, education, and other social programs in their artisan communities. As with the successful nonprofit initiatives, the crucial element seems to be a personal commitment on the part of those involved.

Although any analysis of actual benefits would require substantial study, it is safe to say that the involvement of contemporary Indian designers with crafts has, in general, been responsible for creating a new awareness and a new desirability, which, in the long run, can only benefit the artisan. And although the most famous designers target elite Indian and international markets, growing numbers of young designers are involved with production for a broader domestic market.

Some creative interventions in totally different areas, such as tourism, have also been extremely successful in reclaiming sustainability for traditional craft skills. The southern Indian state of Kerala, for instance, named by *National Geographic Traveler* as one of the 50 paradises of the world, is crisscrossed with an intricate network of inland waterways. These backwaters spawned a unique lifestyle and material culture. One of the products of this lifestyle was the *kettuvallom*, a type of houseboat made from wood, rope, and jackfruit resin. Originally used for cargo transport, they had become obsolete in the modern world, and the craftsmen who knew how to make them found themselves without an occupation. Sensitive development of the concept of "backwaters tourism" has saved the *kettuvallom* and its makers. Now used as private floating hotels, they have become fashionable with high-end international tourists. This is an extremely good model of a way in which a cultural resource can remain alive within a new context.

The problems affecting India's traditional crafts and the artisans who produce them are in some aspects unique to India, and in some ways similar to those facing possessors of traditional skills and knowledge in general. On a global basis, as traditional lifestyles disappear, so does much of the traditional craft heritage that was intertwined with them. New markets, however, are developing for handcrafted goods. These new markets require adaptation, yet they do offer the means to preserve and sustain much of the traditional skills, knowledge, and lifestyles of crafts producers.

In India, the problems affecting crafts producers are immense. The strength of the traditions, however, is also immense, as is the creativity with which many of the problems are being addressed. In one recent project, for instance, several prominent fashion designers were involved in developing an exhibition of garments made from *khadi* or handloomed cloth made from handspun yarn. *Khadi* was the symbolic focus of much of Mahatma Gandhi's vision of India, and in the years since then, massive amounts of government funds have gone into artificially supporting *khadi* as a cheap fabric for mass consumption. The visionary creator of this exhibition, Martand Singh, understood that the future, if any, for this unique cloth lies in customers developing an appreciation for its unusual qualities. Efforts such as these, which show crafts producers the means in which to reposition their skills, are ultimately perhaps most effective way to protect their traditions, their knowledge, and their sense of self-worth. It is also the way in which our contemporary world can provide the rest of us with alternative experiences to McDonalds and Starbucks, linking us to a more textured past, in which creativity and the touch of a human hand enriched the daily experience of life.

APPENDIX: CASE STUDY

Price Spread: Export Markets

The exact ratio between the amount a crafts producer is paid for an item at source and the final retail selling price of that item is extremely difficult to determine. These are matters of extreme secrecy for dealers, traders, and exporters, and crafts producers themselves are reluctant to divulge this information.

The city of Jodhpur in western Rajasthan has become a handicrafts center in the past decade. Intensive interviews conducted there with thirteen crafts producers elicited the information that they are often paid by the day, and that the crafts producer thus has no idea what he is actually being paid per piece. In dealers' workshops, the artisans work 10-hour days, with just a 30-minute break for lunch, and the constantly vigilant eye of the owner or manager ensures productivity. A young craftsman like Shakeel, age 19, with just a few months of experience in wood and metal work, might receive a monthly salary of Rs. 2,400 (US$53). A young painter like Hitish Goel, age 20, receives Rs. 100 (US$2.25) for a 10-hour day, although he is aware that the dealer can sell his day's production for at least five or six times that amount. When he graduates to more senior status, he will be paid at the rate of Rs. 4.50 (US10¢) per square inch and hopes to make more income. Crafts producers who work independently at home and then sell to dealers report a profit margin of only 10 percent over their materials cost, and at most 15 to 17 percent.

Source: Reprinted from "Handmade in India" report, p. 62.

Those extremely skilled crafts producers who can sell by the piece are usually not aware of the final price of their products at the wholesale or retail level. Shyam Lal Soni, an engraver and die-maker whose family formerly worked exclusively for the Jodhpur royal family, says that items he gives to dealers sell in the local bazaar for at least two or three times his selling price. Beyond that, he has no idea what happens to the products.

In March 2000, the Director of the Museum Shop at the Smithsonian's Freer-Sackler Gallery, Martin Bernstein, visited Jodhpur. At the showroom of Lal-ji, one of Jodhpur's most successful dealers, he saw shelves full of decorative brass globes on stands, finished to resemble antique pieces. The local wholesale price was quoted at Rs. 200 (US$4.50), and probably could have been brought down to US$3.50 with hard bargaining for quantity purchases. One assumes that these pieces are made in Lal-ji's workshop and that the crafts producers are paid by the day. If Lal-ji is wholesaling these pieces for US$3.50, the craftsman's payment per piece could not work out to more than US$1.00, and probably to much less.

Mr. Bernstein was very interested in these pieces, since he had seen them on display at the showroom of a New York-based distributor (whom, we later learned, is one of Lal-ji's clients). This distributor was offering the pieces in New York at 25 to 30 U.S. dollars. Mr. Bernstein said that if he had bought them from the New York distributor at that price, he would have placed them on sale in the museum shop for about $70.

This single piece would then have had a crafts producer/retail price ratio of 1:70. Handicraft export is certainly a profitable business, but little of the profit reaches the hands of the creator.

Endnotes

1. This remark is based on the personal experience of Maureen Liebl, who has found on several occasions that when she invited artists to a meeting or dinner at a hotel, they were barred from entering by zealous hotel staff.

2. Information in this section is largely drawn from the "Handmade in India" report.

3. For more information on these organizations, see the "Handmade in India" report, pp. 94–99.

4. Achille Forler, founder member of Asia Europe Copyright Forum, quoted in report on the "Workshop on Rights of Traditional and Tribal Artists," November 24, 1999, India International Centre, New Delhi. (Published by Social Action Forum for Manav Adhikar.)

5. Conversation with *thewa* artist, Girish Raj Soni, Jodhpur, India, April 2001.

References

Gopinath Reddy, S. 2002. "AP Weavers' Misery Spins Out of Control." *Indian Express,* April 29, 2002, p. 4.

Indian Express. 2002. "Digital Knowledge Library to be Launched Today," March 26, 2002.

International Trade Centre, United Nations Conference on Trade and Development/World Trade Organization. 1999. "ITC's Strategy for the Promotion of Trade in Artisanal Products from Developing Countries and Economies in Transition." Geneva.

Jain, Jyotindra. 1989. *National Handicrafts and Handlooms Museum.* Ahmedabad, India. p. 18.

UNESCO (United Nations Educational, Scientific, and Cultural Organization). 1999. "General Conclusions of the Symposium of Experts on 'Culture: A Form of Merchandise Like No Other?' Culture, the Market, and Globalization." June 14–15, 1999. Available at www.unesco.org/culture/industries/html_eng/reunion3.shtml.

Wolfensohn, James D. 1998. "Foreword." In Ismail Sergeldin, ed., *Culture and Development at the Millennium: The Challenge and the Response.* Washington, D.C.: The World Bank, p. 7.

3

ENHANCING INTELLECTUAL PROPERTY EXPORTS THROUGH FAIR TRADE

Ron Layton

The New Partnership for Africa's Development, initiated in July 2001 by the African Union, identifies as one of four main development issues "the creativity of African people, which in many important ways remains under exploited and underdeveloped" (OAU 2001). Actually establishing how to develop and exploit creativity in Africa for development purposes is an important challenge.

Focus on Intellectual Property Exports

Expressions of creativity lie in intellectual property (IP) products, including music, writings, designs, and other copyrightable material, as well as in inventions and brand names. Markets for IP products in developing countries are undeveloped, and domestic revenue is limited by lack of enforcement of IP rights. However, industrial country markets are large and open to IP products from developing countries, and are much more open than to agricultural and manufactured products. This chapter considers how developing countries might receive greater revenue from IP exports to developed markets to assist poverty alleviation and development through a fair trade intervention.

Fair trade in physical goods refers to the process of building direct relationships between importers in developed markets and the poorest and most marginalized

The author invites comments, criticisms, and advice by email to rlayton@lightyearsIP.net, or visit the lightyearsIP.net website and leave thoughts.

producers, thus sharing the benefits of market opportunities and making this shortened supply chain endure so that poverty alleviation benefits are gained. Fair trade (or alternative trade) advocates seek to change the actions of conventional companies to allow more income to reach the producers at the bottom of the supply chain. While seeking to learn from the results of 50 years of fair trade in physical goods, I also draw on personal experience of exporting IP products to industrial country markets.

I use the expression "IP exports" to include the international licensing of the outputs of creativity in content industry products, such as software, music, and literature and in patentable designs and traditional medicines. I also include ethnobotanical assets and consider, as a separate but related issue, brand names, trademarks, and all other IP rights that are related to physical products.

While I believe that changes need to be made to international IP laws to better reflect the interests of developing countries, I primarily assume existing IP laws and explore approaches that reflect business experience of operating within these laws.

The chapter covers

- how fair trade works to share benefits from industrial country markets for physical goods from developing countries;
- evaluations of fair trade and review of recent decisions made to expand and contract fair trade operations;
- IP aspects of the existing fair trade in physical goods and how IP issues might alter the results of fair trade efforts;
- trading and selling issues raised uniquely by IP exports;
- the potential for applying a fair trade approach to IP products;
- how fair trade in IP could alter the behavior of conventional IP business;
- how to secure value from traditional knowledge and how to ensure that decisionmaking on exploitation remains in the hands of the traditional owners.

IP Exports Are Different, Allowing New Opportunities

IP exports differ from exports of physical products in many ways, including the following:

- IP products generally do not require large investments in energy and transport infrastructure.
- Developed markets are open, with few tariff or nontariff barriers on IP exports from developing countries.

- Relative prices can vary radically, even for similar IP products with apparently identical factors of production.
- Distribution chains are not generally as limited by capacity constraints, being more expandable in volume.

Given the expandability of distribution capability, an important opportunity exists to change the behavior of conventional companies currently acquiring developing country IP. Most small-scale sellers of physical goods in developing countries cannot secure business partners who are prepared to share the returns from market opportunities because there are not enough fair trade companies with capacity to handle the volume of physical trade. In contrast, a single substantial IP company operating on principles of greater sharing of developed market opportunities can act as an agent for IP products for a large number of developing country clients.

A small number of "fair trade IP" companies could then become *perceived to be available* to all or most IP owners in developing countries, creating a continuing competitive alternative to existing IP acquirers. Such availability will create pressure on conventional IP importers to adjust their acquisition policies toward more fair terms.

This potential result alone is a worthwhile motivation to consider fair trade in IP products.

Fair Trade in Physical Goods

Fair trade evolved from recognition that trade was not alleviating poverty for the poorest and least empowered producers because of their weak negotiating positions. The new fair trade importers (known as alternative trading organizations, particularly "Northern ATOs") recognized that controlling sales outlets in developed markets meant controlling the allocation of rents from the differential between market prices in rich and poor countries. Northern ATOs were formed to provide disempowered producers with direct sales outlets into developed markets (frequently referred to in fair trade literature as "market access" but not to be confused with the presence or absence of trade barriers).

The Northern ATOs have been focused on fairer supply chain solutions for 50 years. These companies were intended to operate at sufficient profit levels to sustain their presence while sharing the rents with poor producers. Ten Thousand Villages (U.S.) and SERRV International (U.S.) began in the 1940s and remain viable, demonstrating remarkable business sustainability.

The key element of fair trade is the development of respectful long-term relationships with marginalized producers, incorporating:

- contracts for annual supply;
- fair prices;
- advances against future production;
- training for producer skill development;
- provision of market information to producers.

Direct relationships between importers and producer organizations are valued and developed over long periods of time. Paul Myers, chief executive officer of Ten Thousand Villages, believes that sustained purchasing from poor producers is a larger factor in poverty reduction than the higher prices paid by Northern ATOs.[1]

Northern ATOs partner with Southern ATOs, which are generally organizations of growers or artisans (referred to as "producers"). Developing country businesses can be accepted as partners to Northern ATOs if they meet certain criteria, including

- transparency in financial operations;
- efficient management for reasonable profits;
- fair returns for individual producers (for example, coffee and cocoa);
- fair working conditions for plantation workers (tea) and factory workers.

Fair trade volume is likely to grow rapidly, because supermarket chains in Europe and the United States have recently begun handling fair trade products. The Fair Trade Federation estimates that worldwide fair trade in 2001 was valued at US$0.5 billion, half of which was in coffee (Fair Trade Federation 2002).

Groups working for fairer trade are of varying types:

- Importing companies, including Equal Exchange (coffee), Ten Thousand Villages (handicrafts), and SERRV (handicrafts)
- Advocacy nongovernmental organizations (NGOs), including Transfair (U.S.) and Oxfam (U.K.), which seek to influence the purchasing patterns of conventional businesses
- Networking agencies, including Aid to Artisans and the Crafts Center, which provide sales links and technical assistance to producers
- Labeling and certification organizations, including the Fairtrade Labelling Organizations International (FLO), Transfair, the Fair Trade Foundation (U.K.), and Rugmark (certifying hand-knotted rugs that are made without involving child labor)
- Watch groups, including Sweatshop Watch and Corpwatch

The focus of advocacy groups has shifted from importing to retailing because of the vertical integration of conventional supply chains. Hans Bolcher of FLO considers the key task of the fair trade advocates now to be to influence the purchasing decisions of vertically integrated supermarket corporations that control both retail space and supply chains.[2]

Evaluating Fair Trade in Physical Goods

Southern ATOs have developed an effective, well-proven model for distributing income from trade. Northern ATOs regularly check closely on payment of revenues by Southern ATOs to producers and will terminate trading relationships if payments are not made. Terminations are, however, rare because Northern ATOs are satisfied that most revenues are reaching the producers.

The European Fair Trade Association (EFTA) compiles recent impact evaluations of fair trade. Conclusions drawn by EFTA and others from the evaluations include the following (EFTA 2002):

- Prices paid to producers are generally but not always above local market rates.
- The return on labor is above opportunity cost, and the income received is additional.
- "Fair" prices are naturally subjective, but producers generally regard their partners as acting fairly.
- Cash advances against future production and promptness of payment are superior under fair trade.
- Poor producers secure superior supply chains to industrial country markets.
- Long-term relationships are highly valued by producers and allow wider social impacts, such as the ability to budget in order to send children to school for longer periods.
- Empowerment of the poor is improved.
- Dependency on the fair trade importer can develop (dependency varies from 2 percent of sales to 70 percent).

Evaluation Methodology

To consider appropriate criteria for evaluation requires clarification of goals. Many members of the fair trade movement believe fair trade should become the minimum standard of all conventional business. An interesting approach is to regard fair trade as effectively a composite alternative to a minimum wage (composite minimum wage [CMW]) for poor country producers, consisting of long-term relationships, assistance with capacity building, and fair prices. In the absence of international agreement on a world minimum wage or livable wage, fair traders and others committing to this composite set an important standard for conventional business.

Evaluation methodologies used have not included systematic collection of evidence on the impact of long-term trading relationships on poverty. As an example, relying mostly on a single static criterion of local wage opportunity cost of producer labor, an evaluation of Oxfam fair trade in 2000 shows an unweighted average income per hour of 1.28 times the opportunity cost of labor for members of 14 producer groups studied in seven countries (Hopkins 2000). This calculation supports the EFTA conclusions but understates benefits because of widespread underemployment and variability of employment opportunities and does not address the increased ability of producers to improve their lives over time.

To justify enforcing a CMW standard on mainstream conventional business through consumer pressure does require evidence that the composite alleviates poverty. The completed studies provide supporting evidence, and further study of long-term effects might show even greater impact on poverty.

Through their federations, Northern ATOs are challenged to create uniform standards and reach agreement on their purpose. Most want to increase the scale of fair trade, but value is also seen in "proving a point in practice not theory."[3] I discuss in more detail the demonstration value of fair trade later in the chapter.

Intellectual Property Aspects of the Impact of Fair Trade

Expanding the volume of business handled by ATOs is limited by difficulties in competing on price and production capacity. In handicrafts trade, it is common for fair trade importers to be unable to manage successful products by preventing copying of their successful designs. Most fair trade companies have not yet acquired the ability to utilize IP elements such as brand development and brand expansion, design and style recognition, and patenting of designs to limit unlicensed copying and secure higher sales.[4]

It might be considered that the absence of IP capabilities means long-term depreciation of the producers' IP assets, such as designs and styles, that are exposed to markets and hence to unlicensed exploitation by competitors. Given rapid copying and competitive exploitation, the opportunity for producers to address the market happens only once, when the product is first exposed.

Some IP protection can be applied on selected products to protect the market share for the original producers and increase fair trade volume. Our group, Light Years IP, has arranged for a group of IP lawyers to provide pro bono services to fair trade producers and their Northern ATO partners to protect designs and increase brand and trademark protection. A sustainable solution will involve such services being paid from additional revenue generated.

A Recent Decision to Stop Trading

In spite of receiving a positive evaluation of the impact of its fair trade business on poverty, Oxfam (U.K.) decided in 2000 to reduce direct fair trade operations because of the opportunity cost of the resources being applied in the United Kingdom.[5] The Oxfam business had never reached breakeven, and was absorbing more in volunteer and other resources than it produced in direct revenue to producers. In contrast, Ten Thousand Villages[6] and Traidcraft plc (U.K.) are profitable at levels of turnover similar to Oxfam (Traidcraft 2001). Equal Exchange (U.S.) reported being profitable in 9 of the past 10 financial years (Equal Exchange 2001).

Oxfam decided to reassign its U.K. resources toward influencing the behavior of conventional business through advocacy. Oxfam is an effective advocacy NGO, so this decision may be valid but not applicable to all fair trade NGOs. Alternatives to the loss-making situation include improving business management and innovations to overcome the natural business weakness caused by capacity constraints and the cost of sustaining long-term relationships. A few ex-Oxfam producers have formed trading relationships with other Northern ATOs, but most producers have not found a replacement fair trade partner.

Impact beyond Volume

Fair trade companies demonstrate valuable principles by being in existence:

- By staying in business, they challenge the view that intense global competition must drive importers to exploit producers.
- By developing, testing, and sustaining effective supply chains/delivery systems that do alleviate poverty, they provide support for the argument that tariff and nontariff barriers to developing country exports should be lowered to assist development and reduce poverty.

Fair trade companies and advocates have also reached beyond their sectors of trading to change behavior in other conventional business. In the United Kingdom, Traidcraft plc was the first company to publish social accounts in 1990, an initiative that has led to a number of conventional companies adding social elements to their reporting. Fair trade advocates contributed to the current European

Union (EU) debate on corporate social responsibility that led to a green paper on the subject.

Socially responsible stock fund investing is also increasing public awareness. Although it may not be possible to calculate the full effect of any one element of these linked initiatives on the larger goal of fairer and more responsible international business, the overall effort would be much weakened without the continuing business activity of the fair trade companies.

The Coffee Crisis

The crisis affecting the welfare of about 25 million poor coffee producers illustrates the importance of fair trade values and concepts. Since 1999, several factors combined to cause a large oversupply of coffee beans, leading to a collapse in bulk prices and prices paid to producers in producing countries, from US$1.02 per pound in 1999 free on board (FOB) for regular washing arabica to 60 cents per pound in 2001. The most influential factors were large increases in production in Brazil and Vietnam and the ending of supply collaboration among producing countries (Sorby 2002)

A functioning market with competitive conditions should have led to corresponding decreases in retail prices of coffee by the pound to consumers and a responding increase in consumption. However, retail prices have not fallen because of oligopolistic conditions in coffee wholesaling (45 percent of arabica beans are imported by three companies).

The market failure is having a dramatic impact on the welfare of coffee producers. In contrast, fair trade coffee buyers have sustained a minimum purchase price of US$1.26 per pound. It is not possible to know if this price would be a market-clearing price. The question of free market equilibrium price is further confused by the recent imposition of nontariff barriers on soluble coffee now being produced in the EU and the United States.

In a graphic example of the impact of the fair trade alternative on conventional supply chains, FLO reports that in Sierra Leone, a small fair trade company began offering fair terms to coffee growers. Although the fair trade company could take less than 1 percent of the available supply, the dominant buyer, owned by "Mama Toktok," was induced to increase prices paid to producers by 100 percent.[7] FLO also reports that competitors regularly drop local prices offered to producers if they believe that fair trade buyers have reached their financial limits.

In 2000, Transfair succeeded in persuading the Starbucks coffee shop chain to purchase some fair trade coffee at US$1.26 per pound. Starbucks is a small-volume buyer of coffee beans and is purchasing only 1 percent fair trade coffee. To expand this program requires further commitments by the company and some quality improvements by producers. The chain has a high profile with consumers, so public awareness has been raised.

In April 2002, Transfair announced that Seattle's Best Coffee signed an agreement with Safeway Inc., to sell the entire Seattle's Best Coffee line of organic and fair trade coffee in about 1,400 stores across the country. The agreement will result in the largest distribution of fair trade certified organically grown coffee products in North American grocery stores to date (Transfair 2002).

In July 2002, U.S. Representative Pete Stark introduced a House Resolution expressing the sense of Congress that all branches of the federal government should limit purchases of coffee to that which is fair trade certified (Transfair 2002).

In spite of these efforts, regrettably, the vast majority of the world's coffee producers are unable to access fair trade buyers. Expanding fair trade direct capacity and extending fair trade policies to more conventional trade are central to current fair trade efforts.

The Value of Fair Trade

The collaboration of ATOs to create fair trade has reduced poverty, probably with greater impact than has been measured. This collaboration has been sustained over long periods of time, expanding the impact on poverty, the extent of which is still to be measured.

The need to address IP aspects is now being recognized by leading ATOs. Initiated by the author, worldwide discussions are being held within several organizations, including the Fair Trade Federation, the International Federation for Alternative Trade, the Artisan Enterprise Network, and the Artisan Advocacy Network. A workshop was held in October 2002 to mobilize resources for IP work in fair trade.

Influencing conventional business involves both direct consumer pressure and the demonstration effect of ATOs setting minimum standards.

In the huge coffee market, small ATOs have found a few opportunities to influence local market behavior but not world prices. Markets for IP products are, however, unique, and there are special opportunities to influence markets.

Intellectual Property Exports

This section considers two types of IP issues: international trade in IP products and the IP elements of trade in physical products.

As noted by Layton (2001) and discussed further below, markets for IP products are difficult to sell into, and often developing country owners of IP receive no revenue or recognition at all for their product. Penna and Visser (2002) refer to the "iron triangle" as a graphic description for the monopsonistic grip that music buyers exert over the products of musical creativity in West Africa. The Development Economics Group of the World Bank has acknowledged these market failures as a rationale for intervention.[8]

It is valuable to examine what is needed to sell IP from developing countries into industrial country markets and see how a fair trade intervention would work.

Examples of Markets for IP Products from Developing Countries

Three recent productions from the Walt Disney Company, *The Lion King, MuLan,* and *Aida,* reflect interest from the content industry in using developing country themes for major productions. It is probable that the company will extend "exotic" themes in further productions, generating billions of dollars of content industry business, with integrated marketing of live shows, filmed entertainment music, publishing, and merchandising. The integrated exploitation of a single successful title can generate US$3 billion or more in all forms of revenue.[9]

All three Disney products were derived from public domain material, but the relatively small proportionate cost to the studio of paying for underlying rights to copyrighted material would not have prevented the studio from using a copyrighted story, provided that ownership is undisputed. Of course, it would take an agent's persuasive skills to secure placement of a copyrighted story and receipt of license fees.

African music underlies many forms of popular music. The music industry is undergoing major changes because of digital copying of most already recorded music. As these changes prompt new devices that are secure from copying, newly recorded music will be the only music not already copied. This may lead to new opportunities for African music that is substantially unrecorded.

In a completely different sector, Ethiopia is fortunate to have many varieties of pulses and grains, having not specialized production as narrowly as in the United States. This amounts to a national asset base of considerable value to the United States in the event that U.S. varieties become unusable at some time. To derive a rent from making this resource available to U.S. producers would involve the exploitation of an Ethiopian IP asset.

The potential for large revenue from the pharmaceutical exploitation of an ethnobotanical asset or traditional medicine has attracted the attention of a number of developing countries. However, a tiny percentage of such assets can contribute significantly to commercial drugs, and most companies now prefer to develop new compounds rather than acquire them from original natural sources. Very few communities will see substantial revenue from such assets.

Irwin Ziment (Rotblatt and Ziment 2001) argues that belief systems are fundamental to the effectiveness of all forms of medicine, explaining why traditional medicines that are successful in their region of origin often fail in clinical trials. A market for traditional medicines exists within alternative healing processes such as homeopathy, where a new belief system is created around the products.

Everyone Owns Some IP

In theory, every person in each developing country owns a share in some IP, such as its botanical assets, traditional medicines, designs, and artistic material owned by a tribe, regional, or subnational group or country. Poverty can be reduced if exploitation of that IP can provide some basic income to each family.

Earning initial income from a share in collective IP assets requires no labor, so that if initial income is available from IP, a family is free to choose where to apply available labor, whether to cash cropping, other nonfarm income that requires some cash input, or to other purposes. Securing income from IP may be one of the few ways to provide the greater choices that Amartya Sen (1999) shows to be a key factor in poverty alleviation.

To capture revenue from jointly owned IP or to develop income from creativity in African and other developing countries requires effective selling as well as local institutional development for ownership of IP. As the drafters of the New Partnership for Africa's Development envisaged, creativity will be further stimulated in African countries by finding channels for fair exploitation, distribution, and revenue. Increasing awareness of income potential from IP and a greater application of creativity will happen naturally once revenues start to flow.

Exporting as an IP Priority

Domestic markets for IP products in developing countries may be accessed for development and poverty alleviation. However, it is doubtful that the costs of immediate adoption and tight enforcement of IP laws will be justified at this stage in poor countries. Keith Maskus, in his seminal book on IP and development economics (2000), considers this question in depth and concludes that the evidence is not clear.

In my opinion, industry groups in the West supporting the early enforcement of IP laws in developing countries have failed to make their case that the costs of a full system of IP laws and enforcement to a developing country will be justified by the stimulation of valuable IP through innovation for the country's domestic market. Zorina Khan (2002) demonstrates that, historically, most industrial countries, including the United States, adopted policies of far more infringement and for much longer time periods than the Agreement on Trade-Related Aspects of Intellectual Property Rights (TRIPS) allows for countries in similar stages of development.

A further concern arises from the view of Hernando de Soto (2001) that domestic legal priority in developing countries should be placed on the formalization of extralegal real property ownership systems to empower the entrepreneurship of the poor. Enforcing IP laws aggressively at this time in countries with large informal business sectors will decrease the incentive to move a business from the informal sector to the formal by adding the cost of royalties to the high cost of formal business registration cited by de Soto. Surely, a better sequence would have real property title recognition, legalizing informal business and improving contract enforcement, come before enforcing IP laws.

The following paragraphs include comments on alternative IP institutional approaches that serve the developing countries better at this time than copying the IP structures of industrial countries.

From my personal experience with 12 years of IP exporting, any company producing and marketing IP products will be concerned mostly about enforcement conditions in the top 10 to 15 industrial country markets, where almost all worldwide revenue will be gained. IP enforcement is available in these industrial countries, subject to some shortages of experienced IP judges. The IP regime and enforcement within a developing country are low priorities to an IP exporter aiming at world markets.

IP exports represent new opportunities for developing countries, given more open industrial country markets and a better outlook for future profit margins than for manufacturing and agricultural exports. It is our responsibility to uncover the ways in which developing countries can secure critical export revenue from IP products.

Selling IP

I believe that the key factors in successfully selling IP internationally include

- clear and risk-free rights to ownership;
- development of IP products in commercial form and consolidation related IP to enhance salability;
- personal contacts between sellers and buyers;
- market negotiating power;
- marketing to build value in brands and trademarks.

Small ventures in developing countries trying to earn international revenue from IP face the following difficulties:

- lack of knowledge about how trading systems operate for IP;
- lack of access to a distribution chain and to the means to package IP;
- unpredictable prices and demand for their IP;
- weakness in negotiations.

The international market will not function to reward ownership and creation of IP without fair distribution chains for IP products, which are currently lacking. Often, the market fails completely for small-scale developing country designers or owners of IP, who receive no revenue at all for IP that is exploited without recognition or royalty payments.

An Example of Distribution Weakness

The Korean animation industry offers an example of distribution weakness in IP markets. Over the past 30 years, Korean animation companies built up high-quality production capability and excellent design skills through international subcontract production of animation for foreign companies. Korean animation production companies came to be regarded as among the best and most reliable in the world.

In the past 10 years, a number of these successful Korean subcontractors began creating new productions for international markets, aiming to capture the rents available from ownership of successful animated shows. The quality and creativity in these speculative productions were high, but none of the productions were acquired by major worldwide animation buyers, such as Warner Brothers, Canal Plus, and the Cartoon Network. I believe that this lack of success reflected weak inside knowledge of purchasing patterns and poor quality of access to market buyers. The Korean animation industry remained a "manufacturer" of content industry inputs and is now subject to fierce price competition from new manufacturers in China and India.[10]

Applying Fair Trade to IP Exports

Fair Trade Business in IP Products

To work against the negotiating imbalance for developing country IP owners, any new IP Northern ATO would need to have market connections, provide an option to IP exporters, and ensure credibility for the enforcement of rights in industrial country markets. It would need the ability to assist developing country designers in arranging large-scale manufacturing of their design products. If successful, it would deliver critical revenue for poverty alleviation and development.

These functions could be delivered by conventional IP agencies, if they can be persuaded to operate on fair trade terms.

The greatest impact would occur if an ATO could change the behavior of the importing industry by being available and known as an option for IP exporters.

Another approach under discussion is the joint negotiation by regional groups to represent all collectively owned IP in several countries. An agency owned by a group of countries could have the negotiating strength to gain better terms from IP importers. This initiative would also need to focus on establishing legal entities to represent collective ownership of IP.

Some existing Southern ATOs currently producing physical goods will have opportunities for IP exports and could serve as models to stimulate the creation of the new organizations needed in developing countries.

Possible fair trade interventions in IP might include:

- Establishing Northern ATOs to act as agents for IP in industrial country markets.
- Taking action to ensure a fair distribution chain through negotiated agreements with existing IP agents.
- Offering technical and marketing assistance to IP exporters.
- Undertaking capacity building in developing countries, replicating the best elements of the Southern ATO model.

Two Sectors of IP Trade for Poverty Alleviation

As mentioned above, two categories of IP opportunity can be assisted with a fair trade intervention.

1. **IP products trade** in all forms of existing IP, including music, stories, patterns, and ethnobotancial assets, and in all forms of new IP, including inventions and designs, produced by poor people. Publicity and promotion of the availability of fair distribution for developing country IP might be the key to changing the market behavior of IP importers. Publicity of actual revenue flows would be a greater factor in stimulating creative work.
2. **IP elements of existing trade in physical goods.** As noted above, fair trade in physical products is often affected by latecomer competitors undercutting the price of successful items, such as handmade giftware, which reduces the impact of a well-functioning system of poverty reduction. Within some limits, greater brand protection and some design registration can assist. Such a fair trade IP

intervention could also be applied to products that are handled outside the fair trade movement but are similarly linked directly to effective means of poverty alleviation.

The VW "Bug" Project: Extending Fair Trade to Assist Designers

In February 2002, Ten Thousand Villages was approached by representatives of Volkswagen (VW) America in relation to handmade model/gift VW bugs being sold in the United States. Ten Thousand Villages had been importing and retailing a small quantity of gift items in three designs: a wooden model from Traveller's Choice in Tanzania, a ceramic one from Peru, and a wire model from a Congolese group. Ten Thousand Villages was instructed to stop marketing the last product because it was not authorized by VW. VW claimed certain rights in the design of the model gift bugs because they were derived from the design of the actual car, probably relying on "trade dress" or trademark. VW America would not allow the sale in the United States of a VW gift car without its approval and license.

Ten Thousand Villages negotiated a limited license that allowed it to sell out its inventory in return for payment of a small license fee.

In the same sense, each designer or design group that created its own interpretation of the actual car as a model/gift item also has rights in its interpretation. Copies of a designer's interpretation cannot be sold in the United States without license from the designer. Legal enforcement in the United States is equally available to the designer as to VW, if the designer has a U.S.-based IP representative.

Our group, LightYears IP, helped Ten Thousand Villages by obtaining advice from a branding specialist, Seth Seigel, to uncover the potential for a large order from VW for a design from the Congolese group. If the order is secured, the Congolese group will not be able to produce the quantity required from its own resources. As designers, they will need technical assistance to arrange part of the production to be handled by third parties, so that the contract can be secured and managed. This would open an opportunity for the Congolese group to become recognized and compensated as designers of the chosen interpretation and to build market awareness of their design style.

An IP intervention should mean that the skills to find these opportunities and arrange licensing become more available to African designers.

Other Examples

Asian carpets include some valuable regional brands associated with traditional quality of design and weave, but ownership of the brands is not enforced. Recognition of geographical indications for carpets would benefit the owners of such brands, particularly for city/regional brands from the Islamic Republic of Iran.

An herbal tea with some healing properties, Yerba Mate, is marketed under the brand name, Guayaki, which is related to a Uruguayan tribe in the area of the product's origin. The producers have entered into a license agreement to use this name with the tribe that works on the sustainable agriculture plantation. As the market for Yerba Mate grows, Guayaki is at risk of being copied by others. Technical assistance in registering and protecting ownership of the product name will be an important factor in future expansion of sales volume and, hence, impact on poverty.

Protecting Traditional Knowledge from Unwanted Commercialization

Many communities are distressed at the thought of commercialization of their traditions and wish to restrict such use of dance, songs, and other elements. Much has been written on the difficulty of protecting traditional knowledge from exploitation, particularly that which is old enough to be in the public domain.

However, it might be effective to adopt a bold approach of registering copyrights to a whole package of cultural elements, including new and old components, in the name of an incorporated body acting for the traditional group. Exclusive rights to the package would then be licensed to an NGO based in the industrial markets that agrees to hold the rights under instruction from the traditional group.

If the NGO vigorously asserted exclusive rights to the overall package of cultural items, it would make a potential exploiter think twice about liability. In my experience, the boldness of the approach generally turns the exploiter away to look for easier alternatives. Any such assistance provided would need to be grant-funded because no revenue would result.

Capacity Building for IP Exports

Maskus (2000) considers it doubtful that the costs of full IP enforcement in poor countries will be justified by any benefits of innovation for domestic markets. At this time, it is preferable to develop alternative IP institutions that are primarily aimed at IP exporting, and to consider domestic markets only within this context.

In Cuba, exploitation of the work of artists is managed by domestic and export organizations. The artists' association in Cuba, the Asociacion Cubana de Artesanos Artistas (ACAA), offers its 6,000 registered artists the ability to register individual works.

Once a work is registered, an export agency handles the international sale of art and of commercialized products deriving from the art and is responsible for enforcement of rights in developed markets. The ACAA reported that, after the unauthorized use in a U.S. television commercial of a registered Cuban artist's portrait of Che Guevara, the export agency conducted a successful legal action in a U.S. court to stop the infringement.[11]

The ACAA also ensures that the artist is consulted about commercialization of artwork for giftware, handicrafts, and T-shirts, and that commercialization is managed by a specialized entity, AFA. Unlicensed exploitation in the domestic market is limited by AFA to the extent that some domestic enforcement exists. As a command economy, Cuba may be able to exert greater domestic enforcement than other developing countries.

Equivalent Cuban organizations operate to register and manage the IP products of graphic and industrial designers. A design export agency, DISA, handles international exploitation of Cuban design capabilities, both in securing contract work and in exploiting creations in international markets.

These structures suggest relevant alternative options for developing countries oriented toward IP exports. I believe that such structures should be directed to international markets as a first priority, leaving domestic enforcement as a second priority.

Conclusions

Increasing export revenue for poor countries is essential for development and poverty alleviation (United Nations 2002). IP exports are attractive because of open markets and better profit margins than for most agricultural or manufacturing options. The development community needs to embrace the new challenge of uncovering the most effective ways in which to develop IP exports for maximum impact on poverty alleviation.

The products exist and can be stimulated. The markets exist. The IP laws, although somewhat disadvantageous to developing countries, are available for enforcement in the developed markets. Fair trade interventions offer the needed model for market access and delivery systems that ensure that revenues from IP exports do alleviate poverty.

- Fair trade works to share benefits from the opportunities in industrial country markets for physical goods from developing countries, thereby reducing poverty.
- Experience of fair trade suggests that the greatest poverty reduction comes from sustaining long-term trading relationships.

- Applying IP protection in developed markets can increase the scale of existing fair trade in physical goods and stop giving away ownership of designs.
- Fair trade in IP products could make new export revenue available to developing countries.
- Fair trade in IP could alter the behavior of conventional IP business.
- The existence of a Northern ATO working in IP could help reduce the unwanted exploitation of traditional culture.

Notes

1. Paul Myers, Ten Thousand Villages, personal communication, June 2002.
2. Hans Bolcher, Fairtrade Labelling Organizations, address to World Bank Workshop on Grassroots Entrepreneurship, July 2002.
3. Pauline Tiffen, address to International Federation for Alternative Trade, 6th Biennial Conference at Arusha, Tanzania, June 2001.
4. Personal communication with Fair Trade Federation members, 2002.
5. Peter Williams, Oxfam, Personal Communication, October 2001.
6. Personal communication, Ten Thousand Villages, April 2002.
7. Hans Bolcher, Fair Trade Labeling Organization, address to World Bank Workshop on Grassroots Entrepreneurship, July 2002.
8. Keith Maskus, lead economist, Development Economics Group, World Bank, letter dated January 16, 2002.
9. Private content industry sources, 1995–2000.
10. Personal communications, Seoul, Los Angeles, 1999–2001.
11. Personal communication, Havana, May 2002.

References

The word *processed* describes informally reproduced works that may not be commonly available through libraries.

de Soto, Hernando. 2001. *The Mystery of Capital.* London: Black Swan Press.

EFTA (European Fair Trade Association). 2002. "Completed Research on the Impact of Fair Trade." Maastricht. Processed.

Equal Exchange, Inc. 2001. "Annual Report, 2001." Chicago.

Fair Trade Federation. 2002. "Report of the General Manager." Presented at the Fair Trade Federation Conference, Washington, D.C., March 2002.

Hopkins, Raul. 2000. "Impact Assessment Study on Oxfam Fair Trade, Oxfam Fair Trade Programme." Final Report. Oxfam, Oxford.

Khan, Zorina B. 2002. "Intellectual Property and Economic Development: Lessons from American and European History." Commission on Intellectual Property Rights, London.

Layton, Ron. 2001. "Inventions, Designs, Artistic Creations and Fair Trade." *Trade Post.* December.

Maskus, Keith. 2000. *Intellectual Property in the World Economy.* Washington, D.C.: Institute for International Economics.

OAU (Organization for African Unity). 2001. "A New African Initiative: Merger of the Millennium Partnership for the African Recovery Programme and Omega Plan." Approved by the OAU Summit, Lusaka, Zambia, July 11, 2001.

Penna, Frank J., and Coenraad J. Visser. 2002. "Cultural Industries and Intellectual Property Rights." In B. Hoekman, A. Mattoo, and P. English, eds., *Development, Trade and the WTO: A Handbook.* Washington, D.C.: World Bank.

Rotblatt, Michael, and Irwin Ziment. 2001. *Evidence-Based Herbal Medicine.*1st ed. New York: Lippincott Williams & Wilkins.

Sen, Amartya. 1999. *Development as Freedom.* London: Alfred A. Knopf, Inc.

Sorby, Kristina. 2002. "Coffee Market Trends." Background paper for World Bank Agricultural Technology Note 30, "Toward More Sustainable Coffee." World Bank, Washington, D.C.

Traidcraft plc. 2001. "Annual Review/Annual Reports and Accounts." Gateshead, United Kingdom.

Transfair website, April 2002. http://www.transfairusa.org.

United Nations. 2002. "Escaping the Poverty Trap, The Least Developed Countries Report 2002." United Nations Conference on Trade and Development, Geneva.

4

THE AFRICA MUSIC PROJECT

Frank J. Penna, Monique Thormann,
and J. Michael Finger

M usic is a pervasive part of African life. "When you are born, there is music, when you die there is music, and when you are happy there is music," a member of the Senegalese band Rafrache told us.

African music has significant business potential. It currently makes up about half of the fast-growing "world music" segment of recorded music. At the initiation of the work reported in this chapter, Paul Collier, director of the World Bank's Development Research Group, pointed to an important psychological element in the development of the music industry in Africa. To maintain its own resolve to push forward and to prevent its more dynamic young people from going off to Europe or America, Africa has to see itself as succeeding in activities that have some glamour. The music industry has the potential to be an important symbol as well as a substantive element in bringing a poor society forward (Collier 2001).

This chapter is about an ongoing effort by World Bank staff to help Africans to advance the business and cultural potential of their music. The initiative, informally known as the Africa Music Project,[1] began from an odd intersection of interests. Michael Finger, then in the trade group of the World Bank's Economics Department, had concluded from his work with Philip Schuler that the World Trade Organization (WTO) agreement on intellectual property rights (IPRs) did not address the problems faced by knowledge-based industries in developing countries (Finger and Schuler 1999). What would be learned by addressing a "real development problem" in such an industry would suggest ways the WTO rules might more effectively support development.

At the time, Frank Penna of the Policy Sciences Center, Inc. (PSC), a nonprofit, nongovernmental organization (NGO), was managing a project related to indigenous culture in poor countries.[2] The chapters in this book about Indian crafts and about Yekuana folklore are based on work undertaken as parts of Penna's project.

Kreszentia Duer, manager of the Bank's culture program, was Penna's contact at the World Bank. The Bank's culture program had attracted criticism, in large part erroneous, that it did not advance the Bank's poverty reduction and economic development objective. Critics presumed the program to be about the elite going to the opera or museums, rather than about improved marketing of Indian crafts or of ethnobotanical knowledge of the Dhekuana Indians. This joint effort of the Bank's economics and culture programs could help the Bank's culture program to explain what it was really about—*income earning rather than income using* aspects of culture was a helpful catch phrase.

The work thus has three complementary objectives:

- To increase the earnings of African musicians.
- To support African culture and to demonstrate that such support would be a boost to the economy rather than a drain on it.
- To find ways to make the WTO agreement on intellectual property more supportive of development.

This chapter reports on the initial stages of the Africa Music Project and draws lessons from this work. It advances two interrelated themes:

- Culture and commerce often complement each other—advancing what is ingrained in the local economy can generate economic as well as social benefits.
- There would have been no success without active leadership from African musicians. "Local ownership" has been more than a buzzword; it has been a productive reality.

Much of what we report in this chapter we learned from the African musicians and government officials with whom we have worked.

The Dream

Duer, Finger, and Penna knew little about the music business. To begin to learn, Penna organized a workshop held at the Bank in June 2000 that brought together African musicologists and people with experience in the music business in Africa.[3]

The vision for the Africa Music Project that came out of the workshop is an African musician playing a song in an African studio. Computerized equipment records the song, creates the records for his or her copyright, and mounts the song into a dot.com facility that listeners around the world can address. As a listener downloads or plays the song, his or her bank or credit card account is automatically debited, and the musician's account is automatically credited.[4]

Another part of the vision is Nashville, Tennessee. Sixty years ago Nashville was an undistinguished part of Appalachia, the poorest region in the United States. Today it is the seat of U.S. country music, a US$3 billion a year agglomeration of musicians, composers, recording studios, managers, and so forth. At present, virtually all African music that enjoys an international market is produced in Paris or London—the agglomeration of jobs that successful African music generates is not in Africa. The dream for improving the African music industry is that African countries would create their own Nashvilles. The Nashvilles of six or seven African countries would also be connected with a central electronic hub, also in Africa, that would be the seat of the dot.com vendor.

By numbers, African musicians who enjoy international sales are a small fraction of the number of musicians in Africa. In Senegal, for example, they constitute perhaps a dozen of the country's estimated 30,000 musicians. Their story is about Africans in the world music business, not about the African music business.

Part of the dream of the music project is that more African artists make it big in international markets. However, reality here is not to pick such potential winners and promote them along the path successful artists have followed—that path lying mostly outside of Africa. The idea is to build an industry for the 30,000 low-income musicians, recognizing that the measure of success would be a modest increase of earnings for each of them. One would hope that in this more supportive artistic and business environment a few more of the 30,000 will make it big time. The bottom line, however, is that music is an integral part of African life, society, and communications,[5] and the development objective is to enrich African life.

The Dream Confronts Reality: The Structure of the African Music Business

To better understand what possibilities existed in Africa, a team from the Bank and the PSC visited Dakar, on December 4–9, 2000, to discuss with the government and other stakeholders the development of a strategy to support the music industry in Senegal and other African countries.[6]

The reaction from the government was universally positive. Mokhtar Dioup, minister of finance, voiced his approval and stated that the Musicians' Association should be the team's counterpart in Senegal. Other ministers also voiced support, including Kouraïchi Thiam, minister of commerce, who stated that he was "200 percent" behind the idea.

The team also met with the Ministry of Culture's Bureau Senegalais du Droits d'Auteur (BSDA), which is the agency responsible for collecting royalties for artists in Senegal.

Town Hall Meetings

During its visit, the Bank–PSC team spent two full days with local musicians in town hall meetings or meetings with an open agenda. The team asked the musicians to identify their problems, what they viewed as possible solutions, and how outsiders might help. In total, the team heard from about 80 musicians and musicians' agents. Several of Senegal's world-famous musicians—Youssou N'Dour, Baaba Maal, and Thione Seck—participated, but the real significance of the meetings was that less well-known musicians and music producers who earn little income took advantage of the opportunity to express their views and to explain their difficulties.

The following is a sampling of the views expressed and recommendations brought forward:

Problems
- Eighty percent of musicians in Senegal are unemployed or underemployed.
- Most of the radio stations in Senegal do not pay royalties.
- Pirates have more means at their disposal than those responsible for policing them.
- Though the BSDA is vigorous in its pursuit of pirate producers, these pirates are often let off the hook through the intervention of powerful leaders.
- Because the BSDA cannot obtain accurate information on sales from music distributors, BSDA is unable to collect revenues for musicians and composers.
- The BSDA levies too high a level of tax for the services it provides.
- The BSDA should be more accountable to the musicians.
- Financial institutions in Africa will not lend to the music industry—finance until now has had to come from musicians' own earnings.
- The government tax on musical instruments is a major problem.
- Maintenance of instruments and equipment is a major problem.
- The pressing need for short-term income often leads musicians to give up their rights rather than licensing or some other sort of business/legal arrangement that would provide longer-term income.
- There is concern about the extent to which multinational companies impose their views.
- There is little infrastructure—few managers or administrators are in the music field.

- Recording studios are too expensive for ordinary Senegalese musicians to use.
- Because of piracy, musicians are forced to depend on revenue from outside the country.
- Rappers do not have funds for cassette reproduction.

Possible Solutions

- It is important to invest in the low-income musicians.
- Income security for grassroots artists is crucial.
- Informing artists of their rights is critical.
- Traditions can and should be used for cultural exchange.
- Training of backup staff—producers, managers, agents, distributors—is crucial. These roles are not clearly understood in Africa.
- Business development should be a significant part of the program.
- Health and mutual insurance for musicians is important; the model of SIAE in Italy might be an example to follow.
- The legal environment should not be imposed from outside.
- There should be more emphasis on developing the West African market.
- Justice, democracy, honesty, fairness, and equity are essential for the development of Senegal's music industry.

The Musicians' Dream

The mission concluded with a day-long meeting among the team, the president of the Musicians' Association, Aziz Dieng, and several other musicians. The constituents agreed that the PSC would send experts to Senegal to work with the association to help them prepare proposals, in consultation with relevant stakeholders, on a list of topics. The structure followed closely the association's plan that Dieng had presented at the town hall meeting. It included the following elements:

1. IPRs:
    - Education of musicians as to their existing rights and methods of securing these rights, for example, through standard contracts, to include better communication among musicians such as through an association newspaper and a forum bringing together musicians from all parts of the country to hear their views and inform them of the project.
    - Reforms in regulations, institutions, and procedures for policing rights, including assistance to present these changes to the government. BSDA needs to have the means to sue on behalf of musicians.

2. Social Security for Musicians:
   - Contact with musicians' associations from other countries for their experience with social security to research a potential model for Senegal.
3. Training:
   - Artistic training, including rehabilitating the existing music conservatory and possibly establishing a jazz school.
   - Support for music education in public schools, including instruments and training for teachers.
   - A training center for agents, managers, and technicians.
4. Tax Reform:
   - Liberalizing import restrictions on musical instruments and equipment.
   - Making domestic taxes more equitable, less arbitrary, and more oriented toward promoting development.
5. Conservation of Senegal's Musical Patrimony:
   - Archiving, both to maintain music from generation to generation and to reinforce the IPR system.
6. Decentralization:
   - Making areas other than Dakar more attractive locations for music production and performance; build up the role of musicians and communities in the regions in all the activities on this list.
7. Investments in Facilities for Recording and Performance:
   - Creating more widely dispersed recording studios, in Dakar as well as in other regions.
   - Investing in for-hire facilities such as public address systems.
8. Development of the E-Commerce System:
   - E-commerce will contribute to many issues, such as controlling piracy; the Internet is a key way to attract the attention of youth, the next generation of musicians and audiences.

The team later met with officials of several private sector organizations. Among them was Mansour Cama, chairman, National Confederation of Senegal Employers, who suggested that the project should include creating room for local private sector initiatives and should aim to clarify the role of risk taking and competition. He reminded the team again that the legal, regulatory, and fiscal framework needs attention. He noted that the cultural industry is a key part of the country's strategy to develop all the industries in Senegal. Music is a good place to start; it is synergistic with other cultural industries such as crafts and tourism.

From these and follow-up meetings with several of the people who had spoken at the town hall meetings, the team created the following picture of the music industry in Senegal.

The Reality of the African Music Industry

Many African musicians have been successful in international markets, but their recording is done almost exclusively outside of Africa. The agglomeration of studios, agents, technicians, and other music managers, which is an important part of the music business in Nashville, has not emerged in Africa.

Piracy, or the unauthorized copying and selling of recordings, is a pervasive problem. Almost no country in Africa has a piracy level of less than 25 percent; some estimates for West Africa suggest that the piracy level is as much as 85 to 90 percent. The situation in Senegal is typical. Piracy also scares away potential investors.

Collection societies are the organizations that track the use of music and ensure that artists are paid their royalties. In industrial countries, these are key institutions; unfortunately, in Africa, they are ineffective.

Rampant piracy combined with weak collection societies makes the collection of royalties problematic; hence, African artists and composers often sell their songs to a publisher or recording company for an upfront payment. By contrast, in industrial countries artists and composers usually contract for an initial advance plus royalties on subsequent record sales. Thus, in industrial countries there is an incentive for artist and record company to work together to promote the record. In Africa, there is no such incentive to promote sales. The incentive for an artist who receives a one-off payment is to immediately record another album; the new album often undercuts sales of the previous one. Because recording companies know that the artist-composer will immediately record another album, they factor the undercutting into what they offer the artist-composer.

The weak legal environment tempts both recording companies and artists into duplicity. Royalties promised are rarely paid. Artists who promise to limit the number of albums they record often jump immediately to record with another company. This creates a cycle of increased output from artist-composers at declining prices. The quality of the music, and of the recording companies' marketing of it, likewise declines.

In addition to royalties on disks sold, musicians also make their money from royalties on airplay, synchronization (TV), and live performance. However, in Senegal, and likely in many other developing countries, radio stations do not provide the collection society a list or log of songs played. This means that even if the Senegalese radio stations pay their obligatory annual fee to the collection society, the collection society has no basis on which to apportion royalties among musicians. Distribution, when it takes place, is a political process rather than an objective one.

One private radio station in Dakar, Seven Music Radio FM, claimed that it also faces its own problems just to stay in business. The station manager complained that the government infrequently pays the operating stipend for radio stations. "They tend to pay only during election time," he added. Furthermore, he said, the government limits access by private stations to the market for advertising. Although the station has made efforts to increase its revenues, it continues to struggle not only to meet the annual payment to the collection society, but also to provide staff salaries. The station manager suggested that it would be easier to pay rights to the artists if the government lowered taxes and gave private stations a share of the publicity market, and if the stations could obtain credit from a bank.

Because artists earn little from record sales or royalties on radio play, they make most of their money from public appearances. Musicians described a list of problems they face when they schedule public appearances or concerts. Many complained of dishonest producers and corrupt or incompetent managers of appearances and tours. Import restrictions on musical instruments and sound equipment limit their availability and allow those who own equipment to charge high prices. Artists who have a gig, say, in a nightclub, often have to kick back part of their pay to the owner as rent for equipment and instruments.[7] There is also the tax bite. Although tax rates might be no higher than those on other economic activity, the government can more effectively collect taxes on concerts. Concerts are centralized events that must be advertised. Admission is paid in cash, whereas a large part of exchange in poor economies is barter or takes place undetected in the informal economy.

In the region of Thies, Senegal, for instance, the popular *mbalax* music Rafrache band reported that to perform a concert they must pay for performance space, usually a café or disco, and rental of equipment. For a recent concert to an audience of about 100, the café owner collected 30 percent of the entrance fee; the remaining 70 percent paid for the band's costs for transport and rent of equipment. The café owner also kept 100 percent of all drink sales. There was, the band members complained, only a nominal amount of money left over as income for the band members. The low income of the potential audience limits what a band can charge for admission. Otherwise, band members report, young people in the area could not afford to attend. On average, a ticket to a performance by Rafrache costs about US$2.50. The most urgent need, says the band, is for a free space for performances.

"It is like the country is at a crossroads of history. It is important to have music, but only a few people live off the money made from music. Now, this Musicians' Association came right in time," said a member of Rafrache, who recently joined the Musicians' Association. "We [musicians] can do it if we think we are working for the next generation because things are not able to change so quickly."

Big Fish Eat Little Fish

Because the production and vending of music generate no assets that can be effectively secured in law, financial institutions in Africa will not lend to the music industry. Finance has to come from its own earnings. This creates a strong "first mover advantage," which Africans describe with the phrase "big fish eat little fish." Penna and Visser (2002) label this situation the "iron triangle."

Elite musicians or otherwise capitalized individuals who have their own recording studios pay local composers and performers on a work-for-hire basis. The little fish are paid for their time or by the piece; when the workday is done the output belongs to the hirer, as with working in a factory or contributing a chapter to this book.[8] Because the collection societies that are supposed to collect royalties for performers and composers rarely do so, the little fish hardly have an alternative. The big fish, the first mover, then sells the songs on the international market either through its own record labels or through foreign multinational record companies.

Take the case of "Dou Dou" Sow, a well-known musician in Senegal who started his career singing in hotels in the 1970s. He lives in one room that serves as his sleeping, dining, and living quarters on the outskirts of Dakar. He dismisses the recent amputation of his leg, which doctors removed because of gangrene. What he mourns is his inability to perform music on a regular basis.

"There are less live performances today than in the old days because there isn't enough money [to perform]," Sow said. "Before, it was easy to make money from live recordings. Now, one needs sophisticated material [technology] and it is too expensive."

Before, Sow had informal managers, such as friends or family who did not require a lot, if any, money. Now, he does not have a manager, he says, because he does not have the necessary money.

Thirty-eight-year-old Dread Africa, or Jean Louis Thiam, knows this all too well. Thiam can afford from time to time to record in a makeshift studio located in the home of a friend. These home studios multiplied in Dakar in the 1990s. They do provide musicians a way to avoid the big fish, but they provide no help with marketing and distribution and no resources to resist piracy. Thiam complained that producers often refuse to provide a written contract and pay very little—often only US$5 for a track—even though his music is popular enough that his brother found one of his cassette recordings in a shop in New York City. Dread Africa remains a popular but poor musician.

Other musicians belonging to the Musicians' Association confirm that without financial means, they are often unable to record with the technology that makes a "sellable" recording, hire a promoter of their music, or obtain basic contracts.

"There is not a standard way of working. Sometimes you have to sign a bad contract because you have to eat," said one member of the executive committee of the association. "If there is a possibility to have other employment, then you can wait to resolve such a problem."

Many musicians interviewed said they would do other kinds of work to survive; however, finding a job in Senegal is difficult. The Africa Music Project experts estimate that US$600 is the average annual income for a musician in Senegal.

According to John McIntire, World Bank country director in Senegal, many musicians in Dakar are illegal immigrants from other African countries and, hence, are reluctant to complain to authorities about piracy of their work.

Moving Reality Toward the Dream

Dreaming goes more quickly than building. The dream in the Africa Music Project is still ahead of both the government's pace to put through the reforms that its leadership actively favors and the Bank's pace to bring to implementation projects whose preparation the government has approved.

Still, since the inception of the concept of the Africa Music Project—such as the Bank–PSC field trips; IPR expert missions to advise the government and law enforcement personnel, and the development of the capacity of the Musicians' Association—there have been significant achievements, some "soft," others more concrete. These achievements are described below.

Impact in Senegal

Reform of the BSDA

Work is under way to make the BSDA more effective in serving the interests of the poorer musicians. The possibility of privatization is receiving serious consideration. The work, which has been funded by the Bank-Netherlands Partnership Program, has provided the expertise of Attorney Sybille Schlatter of the Max Planck Institute in Germany to assist the musicians in preparing their inputs into the reform process.

Implementation of an Antipiracy Tracking System

In December 2001 the BSDA installed a copyright tracking system to help combat piracy. The BSDA has begun to provide difficult-to-counterfeit hologram stickers to protect copyright compositions. A sticker on a cassette or compact disc (CD) verifies that the distributor has paid royalties. The holograms can now be seen affixed to many music cassettes and CDs selling in the main Dakar market and in the airport shops. When this method was used in Ghana, it reduced piracy from 80 percent to 20 percent.

The BSDA also conducted a public relations campaign on TV and radio and via flyers to inform the public of the importance—and legal obligation—of buying "hologram" music. Although pirated products are still on the market, the system has had a notable effect. Local newspapers report that the BSDA, with law enforcement assistance, has conducted raids to close the market stalls of vendors who sell music without holograms.

Payment of Dues

Following a letter of warning from the BSDA that those that did not comply would be closed, radio stations have begun to pay annual dues to the BSDA. This was accomplished by Schlatter speaking with the head of the collection society and recommending that legal action should be initiated to close down nonpaying stations. Within two weeks the head of the collection society secured an order from a magistrate to close down one station. Subsequently, all the others began to pay.

Inclusion of Musicians on the BSDA Board

One of the criticisms of the BSDA by local musicians is that there has been a lack of transparency, leading to suspicions about the allocation of revenues collected by the BSDA. In 2000, the president of Senegal appointed the president of the Musicians' Association to serve as president of the board of the BSDA. The president of the Musicians' Association has had an active role in the increased efforts of the BSDA to advance the interests of poorer musicians. A particular subject of internal reform has been the distribution of royalties among musicians.

Changing Legislation

The government is moving on a program to revise the copyright law to define the rights of composers, lyricists, and performers; ensure harmonization with relevant international law; and improve the structure of the collection society. The Musicians' Association has had a strong voice in these revisions, and the Africa Music Project and the competence of Dieng, president of the Musicians' Association, have helped enhance its prestige with musicians and government alike. The proposed changes are currently awaiting approval by respective government ministries before being passed to Parliament.

During her mission trips to Senegal in 2000, 2001, and 2002, Schlatter analyzed local legislation and discussed IPR issues with judges, special government advisors, the executive committee of the Musicians' Association, and the BSDA, as well as Senegal's Royal Bank executives and the Writer's Union. Topics included standardization of contracts, promotion of interministerial efforts to combat piracy, and the need to sensitize consumers, musicians, and TV and radio stations about copyright legislation *before* the law changes. In May 2002, she extensively counseled the president of the Musicians' Association in preparation for an IPR seminar for musicians, and she also met with the chair of the BSDA to discuss legislative cooperation.

This kind of intensive sharing of technical knowledge has assisted in further developing the capacity of the Musicians' Association and the BSDA.

The initiative of the Musicians' Association also led Dakar-based business lawyer Mbaye Dieng to promote copyright legal reform on a pro bono basis. Although not a copyright specialist by training, he already has successfully prosecuted one case for a Senegalese writer who needed copyright protection for a book being produced in South Africa.

In spring 2002, Mbaye Dieng agreed to assist the Musicians' Association by reviewing the draft government copyright legislation and providing recommendations. Mbaye Dieng also advises the president of the Musicians' Association on how Parliament works with respect to changes in legislation.

Empowerment: Increased Influence of the Musicians' Association

The recent dynamism of the Musicians' Association has generated enthusiasm among musicians that it will be an effective instrument to defend musicians' rights.

"Since 1974, musicians have been trying to create an association but it never succeeded because there was no serious leader, no uncorrupt person, and little management capacity. Before, people didn't know the objectives of their meetings," said Sow of the three-year-old Musicians' Association. "Today, musicians understand how they are losing money. Before the World Bank interest and start of the Association, musicians in Senegal did not see the connection between the law and their situation. They thought it depended on the quality—capabilities—of their managers. They knew they were being cheated out of royalties, but did not know how to face a system that deprived them. . . . Now, with the Association, people can be more courageous. This [Africa Music] effort is for all, not just for some privileged people."

"I don't think the government can calculate the power of the musicians. Now we are a force that is born, young, but one that is here," said Aziz Dieng, president of the Musicians' Association, in August 2002.

Other musicians agree. Between 2000 and 2002, membership in the Musicians' Association more than doubled, from 1,500 to about 3,000. The increasing number of musicians willing to join the association indicates growing unity.

During this period, the president of the Musicians' Association traveled to most of the 10 regions of Senegal to explain to local musicians about IPR, the importance of forming an association for and by musicians, and potential opportunities to develop the music industry. This is a form of consciousness raising, giving a sense to the musicians that they must take the reins to change their situation; it is a "soft" side of development.

"Musicians are now more aware of their responsibilities for development," said one member of the Musicians' Association in a meeting in Dakar. "And now people know it [the potential for the music industry and economy] is fundamental."

The organization has also shown the public its social awareness. One executive committee member now represents the association on the National Committee against AIDS, which came about upon invitation by the committee. The Ministry of Education is also involved in helping the association to use musicians to develop effective information and communication campaigns for AIDS awareness.

In spring 2002, the association organized a concert to raise money for flood victims in the north of the country and offset damages to livestock and vegetation. The concert raised about 35,000,000 CFA Francs (approximately US$60,000), which the musicians donated to the victims and their families. This represented one of the first-ever occasions for musicians to conduct such an effort together, according to Aziz Dieng.

"The biggest success is moral. International institutions are now interested in music and culture—that is a big psychological success," points out Dieng. He adds that the Music Project has helped him learn how the *functionnaires* operate; before he did not know the importance of administration. According to Duer, this Africa music effort is "to work with poor producers of music and collective groups bargaining for their rights. It is not an individual effort."

The efforts of the musicians have captured the interest of other groups. In September 2002, the Writer's Union also expressed interest to the government in receiving royalties, in copyright legislation reform, and in joining the Musicians' Association in its efforts.

Musicians believe they are present on the government's agenda for the first time. "The main role of the Musicians' Association is to change the minds of the authorities; now they realize that music is more economically important," said a member of Rafrache band from the Thies region.

To help to carry its message to the government, the association published in 2002 a "Declaration of the Association of Senegalese Musicians":

> Future representatives, here you are canvassing the votes of the electorate once again. As usual, music plays a most important role in this campaign. So you acknowledge its value, its utility. But have you ever thought about observing the law that protects the rights of the authors? Have you ever considered to remunerate the authors? How can you ask people to obey the law if you don't do this yourselves? How to teach respect for intellectual property under such circumstances? By giving realistic answers to these questions, by visiting the Office for the Protection of Property

Rights in Senegal to make sure that you meet your obligations toward musicians, you will show your respect for artists and your ambition to promote the works produced in our country. . . .

Mainstreaming of Culture at the World Bank

According to Duer, what started as simply the Africa Music Project has also helped to embed "culture" into the Bank's private sector development (PSD) efforts. Inside the Bank, many now recognize that cultural activities can be income generating. Duer assisted in the insertion of a "cultural industry" clause into Mali's five-year Country Assistance Strategy (CAS) during a mission to Mali in June 2002, representing the first time culture has been recorded into a CAS. Senegal followed, and Ghana has also incorporated cultural industries into its strategy agreement with the Bank.

The intended Bank loan to Senegal may reflect this increased awareness of culture as a tool for development. The idea is that development of the music industry will be integrated under the PSD themes, such as investment climate, telecommunications, and tourism. Importantly, this approach places the emphasis for success on the capabilities and initiatives of the Musicians' Association and other stakeholders. Initially, the PSD loan aims to support the following:

- **Music tourism.** Since the link between culture and music, or a "living culture" is already present in numerous African countries, including Senegal, this is a niche that can be further used to advance income-earning opportunities. This effort could help to add several thousand formal sector jobs to Senegal's existing estimates of 200,000 employed in the formal economy, thereby making a significant contribution to and impact on the economy.
- **Legal reform.** The revision of IPR legislation is necessary to help ensure distribution of royalties. Efforts will also be made to address issues such as pricing of royalties and the distribution percentage for stakeholders.
- **Training.** Training of the Musicians' Association, particularly in microenterprise techniques for the disadvantaged, such as illiterates, will be part of a regular training plan for other groups in Senegal. The Bank is also considering extending its matching grant management system to the Musicians' Association. This would mean that the Bank would provide 50 percent of funds for microenterprise projects as long as the association contributed 50 percent of its own funds toward the effort. Such an approach helps to give market discipline, and, of course, emphasizes informed participation of the beneficiaries themselves in defining their own economic futures.

- **Private-public partnerships.** These include e-commerce, with assistance from telecommunication experts to promote systems for profitable Internet music distribution, and the creation of public dialogue with involvement from the Board of Investment Promotion to manage the technical aspects of organizing public debates.

Looking Toward the Future

The situation of African music now and U.S. music in the first half of the 20th century has three notable similarities. In the United States, the business structure favored established composers and performers and established music publishers. The business strategy of the existing collection agency was to charge users high rates on the output of established musicians. This left aspiring artists to their own devices in dealing with unauthorized use. The realistic alternative for them was to sell their creations immediately to already established artists and entrepreneurs. As in Africa today, big fish ate little fish.

A second similarity is that technology is creating new challenges and increased opportunities for business relationships. In the United States, the spread of sound recording devices in the 1920s created new opportunities for linking musician to listener. In the decades that followed, radio broadcast of music grew in importance, first of live performances, then of recorded music. We are now entering into the age of digital technology and Internet transmission. The commercial possibilities here are likely to be even more novel than those of analog sound recordings and radio broadcast. They may provide opportunities for Africa that are even more dramatic than those observed 50 to 75 years ago in the United States.

The third element is entrepreneurship. In the United States in decades past, as music distribution increasingly came from radio broadcast of recorded music, an effective collection agency became more important. While an individual musician had some ability to collect on live performances and even on the number of copies of a recording that a record company might print, it was impossible for an individual musician to find out which radio stations were broadcasting what recorded music, and how often. Individuals who saw the challenges and opportunities came forward with a new and entrepreneurial collection agency. It provided a technology for monitoring, that is, "logging" radio broadcasts; it extended its membership to anyone who wanted to join; and it used this broad base to undercut the rates the established collection agency charged.

There is no lack of entrepreneurship among Africans; the initial Bank–PSC mission to Senegal resulted in a number of investment proposals. The challenge is to create an environment in Africa in which it pays Africans to apply this entrepreneurship.

Legal and Business Training

As musicians and other artists increase their control of the collection society in Senegal, enforcement of copyright legislation, old or new, must be a priority. As the pro bono Senegalese lawyer Mbaye Dieng notes, it will be up to the musician to bring a piracy case to the courts. How musicians will finance such actions remains a question.

Furthermore, convincing producers to change will be difficult; their negotiating power over royalties and contract terms is stronger than that of individual musicians. Logging, to get radio stations to provide lists of the music they play, is still not complete. In general, determining how to monitor who receives royalties from live performances, airplay, and synchronization is still a challenge.

To start this process, legal training, development of standardized contracts, legal assistance, and basic business training are needed first steps. Audits of the collection society and the Musicians' Association are also suggested. The Musicians' Association has agreed to an audit and has challenged the collection society to do likewise.

The Bank intends to support legal training efforts and capacity building of the Musicians' Association as first steps in helping to develop a sustainable music industry. There continues, however, to be delay in establishing the Musicians' Association as a legal entity, likely a nonprofit corporation. This delay prevents the association from receiving grant funds from donors such as the Bank. Thus, the obvious instrument for such work remains at a disadvantage.

Enabling Communication

The Musicians' Association in Senegal identified support for a communication system to access other areas of the country as a priority. If musicians are to unite, this is a key step toward that goal. The high cost of traveling to other regions, especially remote areas, has weakened the capacity of the association; regular contact with association members in other areas will be vital for sustainable organization. In the meantime, the association is planning to start a newspaper as one means of communication. When considering replication in other countries, access to communication facilities should be on a checklist of priorities.

Administrative Capacity Building of the Musicians' Association and the BSDA

With no tradition of "civil society" in Senegal, there is a need to develop administration and accountability skills, as confirmed by the president of the Musicians' Association. There lurks a danger that if the administration of the Musicians'

Association is weak, then expansion and efforts by the association will lose credibility among musicians.

How the association in Senegal will support itself is another issue, including salaries for the secretariat and for representatives in the regions. There is an expectation of payment for time rendered with the association, in particular since jobs are hard to come by in Senegal. This also poses the question of how the World Bank is viewed in this regard: as another "government" or as a "benefactor"? With the president of the association working a regular day job in order to eat, the effectiveness of the association in the long term begs the question of how the association will retain its effectiveness and key members. Delegation of tasks and support for the infrastructure of the association are therefore essential.

The Potential of E-Commerce

Electronic commerce has considerable potential to contribute to African music— to provide a mechanism for poor musicians to advertise and to sell their music to the world market. In Senegal, the project has already begun instructing musicians in several outlying regions how to use MP3.com as a way of selling unencrypted music over the Internet.

The dream (described above) of an electronic system to record and sell encrypted music may be closer to reality than someone from the preelectronics generation would suppose. For encrypted sales, the commissioner of patents in South Africa has given consent to establish a hub for hardware and software in South Africa. Then each participating country could have a small digital studio— or even a mobile digital studio—from which they would send a music recording to the hub in South Africa for advertising, production, distribution (including export), and payment.

The World Bank approved in summer 2003 a US$46 million credit for private investment promotion. One component will finance music industry ventures; another component will finance rewriting the copyright law. Rewriting the copyright law began in January 2003, financed by an advance on that credit. The attention the project has brought to what the music industry contributes, to its potential to contribute more, plus the attention it has focused on possibly corrupt practices has stimulated action on further legal and regulatory reform. More immediately, it has sparked action by the existing collection society to reduce piracy of recorded music and to collect royalties from radio stations for payout to musicians.

In sum, the major success of the Africa Music Project to date has been to assist musicians in Senegal in recognizing that they can help themselves. The project has involved and activated local musicians and empowered them to identify their own interests, to deal with the government, and to deal with the market. The musicians themselves now have a clearer idea of how they will proceed, and a stronger feeling that they will be successful.

"We want to share something with each other. Most of the time it is not TV or cinema. It is not the kind of life we want. What we want is to show each other I am here, I am living. When you play *mbalax* or reggae, everyone is together," said home studio owner Lamine Faye, 41, in Dakar. "There has been a lot of development money into Senegal but not for music. Now is the time to organize ourselves because I am sure it is something that will last for the next generation and will truly help the development of the country."

Endnotes

1. In the strict sense of World Bank usage, a "project" is a specific lending operation. In this sense the activity described here is not a "project."

2. Penna's project was funded by the World Bank's Development Grant Facility, a facility that funds projects that complement Bank work but might be more effectively undertaken by an outside agent such as an NGO than by the Bank itself.

3. Among the participants were musicologists Dr. Lucy Duran, University of London, on Francophone countries, and Dr. John Collins, University of Ghana, on Anglophone countries. Among the business experts who participated was a senior executive of the leading international recorder-publisher of African music, Gerald Seligman, senior director for EMI Hemisphere and Special Projects, EMI Classics.

4. Experts who participated in the workshop indicated that the technology was about to come forward to allow secure electronic marketing of music over the Internet.

5. When we visited the "On Air" room at the Seven Music Radio FM station in Dakar, the rap group Keene Bougoul was chanting antidrug and antiprostitution lyrics, as well as complaints about the inaction of the government. Separately, a Senegalese government minister told us that he often buys rap tapes. "They help me to keep up with what is going on in the country," he said.

6. The decision to begin in Senegal was influenced by two elements: (1) musicologists and people in the music business suggested considerable commercial potential and (2) the government of Senegal was interested and supportive. Hence, the World Bank's country director for Senegal, John McIntire, was supportive of including development of the music industry in the Bank's Senegal portfolio.

7. Rap musicians bragged that the cost of musical instruments is not a problem for them. They do not use instruments, only a computer-generated background drumbeat.

8. Usually a contributor to a scholarly book receives an honorarium upon delivery of his or her contribution, while the copyright for the book rests with the publisher.

References

Collier, Paul. 2001. "The Rationale." In World Bank, Policy Sciences Center, Inc. Workshop on the Development of the Music Industry in Africa web page at http://www.worldbank.org/research/trade/africa_music2.htm.

Finger, J. M., and P. Schuler. 1999. "Implementation of Uruguay Round Commitments: The Development Challenge." World Bank Policy Research Working Paper 2215. Available at www.worldbank.org/trade.

Penna, Frank J., and Coenraad J. Visser. 2002. "Cultural Industries and Intellectual Property Rights." In Bernard M. Hoekman, Philip English, and Aaditya Mattoo, eds., *Development, Trade, and the WTO: A Handbook*. Washington, D.C.: The World Bank.

5

PREVENTING COUNTERFEIT CRAFT DESIGNS

Betsy J. Fowler

Artisan crafts production is a major economic force in many nations.[1] The benefits of effective protection of artisan creations go beyond concrete economic benefits, although those are certainly important, to include preservation of a culture's history and way of life. Through preserving and protecting indigenous art, intangible benefits accrue to the whole society, and the preservation of livelihood is ensured.

Global competition to provide products at the lowest possible price point has proliferated to counterfeiting of original handmade crafts. An example of this is conveyed through the sale of Native American arts and crafts that are actually imported copies from Asia. "Some are of sufficient quality to be virtually indistinguishable from the originals by all but the most practiced eye. But they *are* almost always distinguishable by one factor: price. Southwestern Indian-type basketry is now made in Pakistan, and Romania has begun manufacturing and selling knockoffs of Taiwanese knockoffs of Indian jewelry. In almost every case, the prices of such items are less than what would be charged for authentic material. Since the unwary often buy up "bargains" that are imitations, this trade shrinks the market for, and lowers the price of, the legitimate work of the tribes of the Southwest, thus diminishing and even eliminating the livelihood of thousands of people (Page 1998, p. xix).

Although standard legal mechanisms are in place to protect artisans in general, in most countries this protection is not sufficient to prevent counterfeiting of artisan crafts. Artisans, organizations, and governments have developed measures to further protect their crafts and fill the gaps. The following case studies will examine legal and extralegal measures and their effectiveness.

Background

Originating in cultural traditions, the production of crafts is an avenue for economic growth and cultural preservation. Artisan handicrafts represent an estimated US$30 billion world market. In addition, handicraft production and sales represent a substantial percentage of gross domestic product (GDP) for some countries: Burkina Faso, 70 percent; Morocco, 10 percent; and Peru, 50 percent (Ramsay 1999). Handicrafts production can be an effective approach to poverty alleviation because it is generally the rural poor who are creating the handmade items. In Colombia, 80 percent of handcrafted production comes from indigenous and rural areas (Duque Duque 1996). In Latin America alone, about 25 million individuals are engaged in crafts production (Ramsay 1999).

Increasing incidence of design theft has brought artisans and the protection of their intellectual property (IP) to the forefront of international discourse. While the framework of legal protection for artisans has been in place in the global market for decades, the issues of protection of ancient designs, symbols, and traditional knowledge utilized in artisan crafts are not well established.

After a brief review of the standard international tools of IP protection, this chapter discusses the varying approaches some artisans, organizations, and countries have taken to extend legal protection to artisans—reinforcing the fact that more can be done to protect artisans' original crafts.

Overview of IP Tools as They Apply to Crafts

The World Intellectual Property Organization (WIPO) divides forms of protection into two main categories: copyright and industrial property. Within these two categories are the tools most commonly used to protect artisan crafts throughout the countries of the world, and each country has its own preferences and interpretations of applicability. The most common tools of protection are copyright and trademark.

Copyright

The standard form of protection for artistic works has traditionally been a copyright. "Copyright protects the *form* of expression and not the idea itself" (Gasaway 1999). This is a key aspect of the difficulty in protecting indigenous art wherein a culture's significant traditions and symbols are reflected in their material art.

The Western cultural values of propertization do not coincide with many indigenous collective mores. With the use of copyright to protect an artist's creations, if one registers a design, it becomes the legal property of the individual. This approach does not merge with traditional approaches to community property and culture. "We, as native peoples, do not understand this concept of 'ownership.'"[2]

Copyright registration applies only to the nation in which it is registered (WIPO 2002). In other words, if your craft has a copyright in Peru, that protection is not automatically transferable to any other nation. One must apply in each country in which protection is sought. In one case, European designers toured Andean crafts communities and subsequently used traditional designs in their jewelry collections. The designers then registered the designs and the appellation they "stole" from the original Peruvian communities, thereby preventing the indigenous artisans from marketing their own creations in certain countries. The artisans were "unable to fulfill contracts with importers for a number of years, and the abuses went as far as the confiscation of the craftsperson's jewelry at trade fairs" (WIPO-ITC 2001).

This brings to light an additional consideration in the protection of artisan crafts both nationally and internationally: copyright enforcement responsibility lies with the artisan. If counterfeit products are being marketed within the country, the artisan with the copyright must bring this to the attention of the proper authorities. This level of market awareness and monitoring is overwhelming and expensive, in some cases outweighing the value of acquiring a copyright to begin with.[3]

Trademark

"A trademark is either a word, phrase, symbol or design—or combination of words, phrases, symbols or designs—which identifies and distinguishes the source of goods of one party from those of others" (Joseph 2000). Trademark duration after registration is a much shorter time period than copyright, but unlike copyright, can be renewed in perpetuity. Trademarks can be further broken down into two categories that hold promise for the protection of indigenous crafts. These are known as collective and certification marks.

"Collective marks are owned by an association whose members use them to identify themselves with a level of quality and other requirements set by the association" (WIPO 2002). These marks are most often used for associations of professionals within a field—perhaps all members have to pass a professional exam or earn a degree that identifies them as having a level of knowledge. Panama actively utilizes the collective mark for registered elements of traditional knowledge that may be owned or shared by communities.

Certification trademarks are used to establish that a product meets a certain established standard, but there is no membership requirement. Certification trademarks are now used by a variety of indigenous groups as a tool for identifying products created by their tribe or community.

Examining the History of Protection

The following case studies, both in industrial and in developing country scenarios, reveal the trend toward the demand for protection of our universal culture as well as individual rights. The cases reveal that problems in defending poor peoples' knowledge exist in rich countries, despite their stronger IP rights laws, and not just in developing countries. Each story shows the differing responses to instances of IP rights offenses. Some countries have successfully defended artisans' rights through existing legal tools, some have developed new laws, and some artisan groups have paved their own way.

The reader will find that nongovernmental organizations (NGOs) have proved instrumental in combating counterfeiting in both rich and poor countries. Given the differences across countries in the quality of general legal institutions, it is perhaps not surprising that organizations in rich countries have enjoyed more success in using the courts to defend artisans' claims. In all countries, however, networks of artisans work tirelessly to raise awareness about problems of counterfeiting—among both producers and consumers, as well as in government.

Case Study 1: Protection of Crafts in Australia

Overview

The market for indigenous Australian arts and crafts was estimated at US$200 million in 1999, with half of those sales from the tourist market, yet only about 25 percent is received by the indigenous artists, the balance going mainly to traders. No accurate statistics have been compiled to estimate the value of counterfeit crafts, but it is a serious problem, not only economically but also culturally. "As indigenous culture attracts increasing commercial interest, Indigenous people are concerned that they do not have the necessary rights to ensure appropriate recognition, protection and financial compensation for the contributions" (Frankel and Janke 1998, chapter 2, p. 1).

Analysis of IP Protection

Presently, there are no separate laws for the protection of traditional knowledge, and the Australian aboriginal crafts are protected through standard IP mechanisms, although in some cases the court shows respect for indigenous customary law.

Aboriginal custom provides for collective ownership of culture, but individuals or groups can be custodians of specific aspects or items of heritage. The custodians are responsible to the best interests of the community (Frankel and Janke 1998, chapter 1, p. 8).

In the case of *Milpurrurru v. Indofurn*, also known as the "Carpets" case, in 1994 an Australian importer was charged with copyright infringement. The company imported carpets from Vietnam that were reproduced from designs of aboriginal artisans that were contained in a portfolio that had been produced by the Australian National Gallery without getting permission from the artisans.

The importing company claimed that copyright infringement did not apply because there was no "original owner" and the designs were drawn from preexisting traditional design. The court did not agree, and even though some of the designs were altered in the copies, the Copyright Act states infringement has occurred with "substantial reproduction."

The court ordered US$188,000 in damages paid and all unsold carpets turned over. The most interesting aspect of the award was the court's inclusion of financial compensation for "cultural and personal interests." This was the court's recognition of the harm caused by the culturally inappropriate way in which the carpets were reproduced. As mentioned above, the artists, as cultural custodians, were responsible for the infringement even though they had no way to prevent it, and it is a punishable offense within the community. "The Court made a collective award to the artists rather than individual awards so the artists could distribute it according to their cultural practices. In this way, the Court indirectly recognised the communal ownership of Indigenous arts and cultural expression" (Frankel and Janke 1998, chapter 5, p. 11).

The issue of traditional communal ownership is highlighted in the case of *Bulun Bulun and Another v. R&T Textiles* in 1997. In this case, the artisan, Mr. Bulun Bulun sued Mr. Milpurrurru et al. for copyright infringement for importing clothing that had been printed with a design from a painting of Mr. Bulun Bulun's. Both parties were from the same indigenous group, the Ganalbingu of the Northern Territory, and Milpurrurru claimed communal property ownership of the traditional waterhole design from the painting. Mr. Bulun Bulun claimed that his ancestors had been given the responsibility "to maintain and preserve all of the Mayardin (corpus of ritual knowledge) associated with Ganalbingu land, and it was his responsibility to create paintings in accordance with the laws and rituals of the Ganalbingu" (WIPO 1999, p. 6).

The court decided in favor of Mr. Bulun Bulun for copyright infringement. On the issue of equitable, communal ownership of copyright, the court determined that because there was no precedent whereby artists' creations were held in "trust" by the community, the responsibility of Mr. Bulun Bulun was fiduciary, or simply to "act in the best interest of the community," which he had fulfilled by pursuing enforcement of his copyright. The community had no equitable interest in the copyright (WIPO 1999, p. 7).

Trademarks

There are many instances of misrepresentation of aboriginal crafts in the Australian market. "Aboriginal-style" products by nonaboriginal artists confuse the purchaser tourist into thinking it is original art. "A large amount of 'ripoff' material is mass-produced overseas in countries where labour is cheap and there are no copyright laws. These goods are imported into Australia and sold in tourist shops alongside authentically produced Indigenous products" (Frankel and Janke 1998, chapter 3, p. 6).

In the manufacture of some items, aboriginal people contribute some of the steps, and the products are then sold as "aboriginal-made." An answer to this confusion about origin could be the use of a certification mark for aboriginal communities. "According to the AIPO (Australian Intellectual Property Organization), the certification provisions are well suited for protecting and authenticating Indigenous people's products. This option is also favoured by many Indigenous groups" (Frankel and Janke 1998, chapter 5, p. 17).

Effectiveness of Australian Model

Aboriginal Australians have a strong NGO lobbying for their rights. This organization, the Australian Institute of Aboriginal and Torres Strait Islander Commission (ATSIC), is active in the search for the best protection of aboriginal traditional knowledge and culture through in-country presence as well as at international forums. Its activism in the promulgation of aboriginal rights is an essential element of the establishment of indigenous rights.

In addition to active indigenous organizations and effective legal enforcement, Australian indigenous groups are pursuing the use of a certification trademark that verifies the source of the crafts.

Case Study 2: The Native American Experience in the United States

Overview

The Native American experience in the protection of arts and culture yields an interesting case. As an indigenous population geographically located within one of the world's most industrial countries, Native Americans have faced a substantial threat to their livelihood from counterfeit copies of their art. Their battle provides insight into the difficulties of awareness and enforcement even with an extensive legal infrastructure and economic resources available within the country.

The Native American community has been quite proactive in the establishment of legislation, both federal and state, to protect Indian arts and crafts. The following two acts provide the legal framework from which to prosecute those who seek to exploit Native American crafts for profit.

The Omnibus Trade and Competitiveness Act   The Omnibus Trade and Competitiveness Act of 1988 requires that Indian-style imported products be indelibly marked with the country of origin. This provides the buyer clear evidence of where a product is made to allow informed decisionmaking in reference to authenticity.

Indian Arts and Crafts Act   The Indian Arts and Crafts Act of 1990 (effective 1996), Public Law 101-644, is federal legislation prohibiting the illegal marketing of non-Indian goods as Indian made (Indian Arts and Crafts Association [IACA] 2000). Armed with severe penalties for the first time, the courts can impose fines of up to US$250,000 and up to 5 years in prison for fraud.

Present-Day Status

Even with an extensive legal infrastructure, enforcement of protection for artists is difficult. "Although estimates vary, foreign fakes are now believed to account for as much as half of the market in Indian arts and crafts, worth US$1 billion a year" (Brooke 1997).

Andy Abeita, artist and president of the Council for Indigenous Arts and Culture (CIAC), has devoted his career to the protection of American Indian artists. CIAC literature states:

> The federal government and the State of New Mexico both have Indian arts and crafts protection laws that are quite ample in their protection. The biggest problem has been a lack of education on their behalf. CIAC research has found that government agencies needed to learn how to apply the Indian arts and crafts protection laws. The Indian artists are not aware of the laws that protect their art, and when confronted with unscrupulous tactics by importers intent upon circumventing existing laws, the Indian community is negatively affected. Since 1995, the Indian Arts and Crafts Association (IACA)[4] and the CIAC has [sic] been providing that information with some progress finally on its way.[5]

With an estimated 90 percent of families depending on crafts as a primary or secondary source of income (Bureau of Indian Affairs 2000), Abeita says the fraud inflates the marketplace with false prices and devalues the authentic products.

In addition, he claims that it is demeaning to the value and the essence of what the true cultural art is.

In 1998, New Mexico's Director of Indian Tourism said that the counterfeiting had driven profits down 40 percent for most Native American artists (Shiffman 1998). A Zuni[6] jeweler claimed that over the course of five years to 1998, his income dropped by one-third, and that a lot of families dependent on traditional arts and crafts for their livelihood are suffering. "A lot of families have had their vehicles taken and their lights shut off" (Smith 1998).

A variety of devious tactics are used to deceive the purchaser. Imported goods arrive with country-of-origin stickers instead of indelible markings, and disreputable retailers and wholesalers simply peel the stickers off or cover them with their own, and then sell the goods as being made by Native Americans. In another example, Andy Abeita tells the story of how both a corporation and a town named "Zuni" were formed in the Philippines. Goods were manufactured and brought into the United States with "Made in Zuni" stamps, flooding the market with fakes. Through his work with the United Nations, Abeita was able to get the Philippine government to rescind the incorporated name. Abeita says that, in his experience, he has yet to find a Filipino, Indonesian, or Korean company making the copied goods on their own. "They are all Americans taking the design overseas, reproducing them cheaply, and smuggling them back into this country to be sold as originals."[7]

In some cases, Indians are "used" by dealers to string beads or assemble foreign, mass-produced parts, and then the goods are sold as Indian made. "The imitators often use nickel instead of sterling silver. They use dust and colored plastic instead of turquoise. Synthetic fibers become 'all-natural' rugs" (Shiffman 1998). With awareness of the depth at which fakes have permeated the market, the public is becoming wary of making any purchase.

Both Native American artisans and retailers advise consumers desiring authentic goods to purchase only from reputable dealers that provide "certificates of authenticity" with each Native American piece. This certificate forces the dealer or retailer to commit to paper the guarantee of authenticity and provides the purchaser proof that the item was marketed to them as authentic.

Traditional Knowledge and Tribal Trademark Legislation

Presently, CIAC is working on moving tribal trademark legislation through the tribal administrations. The legislation, which would allow the establishment of a tribal trademark for each federally registered tribe, must first be approved by the tribes and then by the tribal legal departments; then it will be written into policy.

The trademark would provide an authenticating mark to be used on each design and product produced by the tribe. The tribe must first authenticate the goods of every member of the tribe and register them. This process would be time-consuming, and a community education program would help the tribal administrations, communities, and artisans understand the benefits and importance of the trademark usage.[8]

The U.S. Patent and Trademark Office (USPTO) advised the tribes to draw up a list of their tribal symbols, and stated that the office would provide protection against outside use or registration incorporating the symbols. The USPTO advised that a tribal resolution would be used as sufficient authorization for a tribe to claim a symbol. "Once the list of symbols is established, in theory a tribe or another party— say a coalition supporting Native American rights—could push for the cancellation of existing trademarks incorporating Native American symbols" (Patton 2000).

According to Abeita, Zuni was the first tribe to complete the internal review of its tribal trademark resolution, and the next step was a formal tribal vote in June 2002. The measure was approved into law, although it had yet to be implemented as of October 2003 because of funding constraints. The tribe must apply for grant monies to support the implementation process; therefore, the new regulatory structure is on hold.[9]

Key Elements of Effectiveness of the Native American Model

As Native Americans continue to seek a solution to the problem of exploitation of their culture through counterfeit articles, the public is simultaneously being educated about the importance of preserving traditional culture. The successful elements of progress center around a proactive nonprofit sector and an effective consumer marketing campaign.

The CIAC and IACA, both headed by Native Americans, have worked hard to raise the issue of counterfeit art in the public consciousness. The intensive lobbying efforts at the state level in New Mexico have garnered the attention of lawmakers and brought new legislation to protect Native American arts.

In addition, Native Americans have effectively used "certificates of authenticity" and are actively pursuing the use of certification trademarks.

Case Study 3: Indigenous Artisans and Crafts Protection in Canada

Overview

Indigenous art and its protection is a prominent topic in Canada's economic discourse. A 1996 Canadian census showed that there was tremendous growth in aboriginal self-employment in the last two decades of the 20th century in a variety of businesses, many of which are crafts-related.

Analysis of IP Protection

Aboriginal Canadians have been quite proactive in investigating present-day IP protection to the fullest extent of its ability to protect indigenous culture. Within their culture, aboriginals see themselves as "custodians," not owners, of their traditional knowledge. This approach goes against standard Western IP law that focuses on individual ownership of a design or symbol.

Consequently, the best approach for legally maintaining what is culturally "theirs" has evolved from a combination of existing IP tools, traditional knowledge systems within the community, and other mechanisms such as collectives.

"Because of costs, most IP holders file in countries which are important markets, such as the United States, United Kingdom, Japan and France, or in countries that are likely to produce infringing products for sale in export markets" (INAC 1999, p. 14).

Artisans have chosen to address the overwhelming task of enforcement through the use of collectives. Copyright owners join a collective that handles the collection of fees and tariffs, as well as copyright infringement suits.

In addition, trademarks, particularly the certification trademark, are widely used by aboriginal groups and organizations.

Present-Day Status

In 1999 the Pauktuutit, the Inuit Women's Association of Canada, was looking into the protection benefits of a collective trademark because of repeated experiences of traditional knowledge exploitation from both Canadian and international companies. The Pauktuutit believe that their designs and patterns have been exploited by the fashion industry, and they want to find the legal protection they need to protect the history of their 1,000-year-old culture. One example cites a visit by a representative of the fashion house Donna Karan, who purchased US$10,000 to US$15,000 in designs from the Inuit women, then used them as "inspiration" for a collection being designed (Mofina 1999).

In a recent effort in 2001, the Pauktuutit sought to copyright the traditional *amauti* or parka worn by women that has a hood that is designed for holding babies. The Inuit women "want to make sure the *amauti* doesn't go the way of the kayak, copied and mass-marketed by southern companies without giving credit— or profit—to the Inuit who designed it" (*Canku Ota* 2001).

Even with the efforts to copyright the garment, the Inuit Women's Association Executive Director Tracy O'Hearn says that the laws are not comprehensive enough to protect the traditional, collective nature of ownership in the Inuit culture, as well as being time-limited. The organization is lobbying for a change in the IP laws to include traditional knowledge protection (*Canku Ota* 2001).

This protection would prevent anyone from legally using the Inuit's designs—a kind of "cultural protectionism."

Key Elements in the Effectiveness of the Canadian Model

Canadian collectives, associations, networks, and organizations have paved the way for recognition of the need for IP protection for indigenous traditional crafts. Networks of aboriginal communities have joined to form groups with lobbying power, both within and outside Canada.

The Inuit Circumpolar Conference (ICC) includes representatives from Canada, the Russian Federation, the United States, and Greenland, and is an active lobbying organization with 150,000 members. The ICC was a participant in the WIPO Roundtable on Intellectual Property and Traditional Knowledge in 1999— one of the first international efforts at establishing a forum for the discussion of traditional knowledge and cultural protection.

Many other, smaller organizations are active within their regions and have pursued the use of certification trademarks and other tools to protect their designs. Although the costs of monitoring and enforcing IP protection lie with the artisan, the Canadian court system is effective in enforcement of existing standards and is working toward accommodating and respecting the indigenous customary law within the system.

Case Study 4: Latin American Experiences

Overview

The Latin American countries of Panama, Peru, Bolivia, and Colombia have established extensive organizations and systems within their countries for the protection of indigenous crafts. These approaches include official, legal protections and extralegal measures.

Status of IP Protection

A diverse collection of crafts protection tools is represented within the Latin American region. From sui generis traditional knowledge protection laws[10] in the case of Panama, to the use of craft certificates of origin, as in Bolivia, countries have established mechanisms to protect their heritage.

Panama

Panama established the first comprehensive system of protection of traditional knowledge ever adopted in the world in June 2000 through the use of copyright. The Department of Collective Rights and Forms of Folkloric Expression grants copyrights for the collective rights of indigenous peoples over their creations and other aspects of traditional knowledge. A special system was developed to "register, promote and market their rights, in order to highlight the socio-cultural values of indigenous cultures and render social justice unto them" (*Cultural Survival Quarterly* 2001). No form of traditional culture can be registered for IP protection by a third party—thereby preventing any copying by anyone outside of the community. The copyrights granted never expire.

The National Crafts Department of the Ministry of Commerce and Industry uses a certification stamp to guarantee authenticity of the products, and people are prohibited from importing any products resembling indigenous crafts or other aspects of culture unless permitted by the associated indigenous community.

The legislation is the culmination of efforts by the Kuna[11] people to stop the flow of cheap copies of *molas,* the traditional dress scooped up by tourists. The tourist industry in the Kuna Yala, or Kuna lands, is tremendous because of cruise ship traffic, and the sales of poor quality, mass-produced, nontraditional *molas* were offensive to the strict adherence of cultural mores practiced in the region (Snow 2001).

Peru

The trademark is the tool that is most frequently used in Peru for effective indigenous craft protection. The trademark is valid for 10 years and is renewable in perpetuity. "It can be said that a significant number of craft businesses have set in motion the process for the registration of trademarks in order to secure a position on the market and an identity for their products; this idea is being promoted by the majority of development projects or by certain NGOs that support the marketing of craft products" (Rosario 2001b, p. 3). Many craft guilds, organizations, and cooperatives in Peru are utilizing the strength of their associations for economic development, informational resources, and training. The groups can work for the artisan in promoting IP protection through the use of certification trademarks.

Peru does not have a system to protect traditional knowledge, but has developed a sui generis draft law that has been published. In the meantime, efforts are focused on using the standard IP legal provisions to the best advantage for indigenous craftspeople and their communities. The problem lies with the lack of publicity about the best way to utilize the tools already available. "Work therefore has to be done on publicizing and teaching its use and applying the intellectual property protection system. The purpose of the publicity exercise has to be to make the (legal and extralegal) means available to the craft sector with which to protect craft creations, and to do so in clear and simple language" (Rosario 2001b, p. 3).

Extralegal Mechanisms

Certifications and organizations are actively used in Latin American countries to protect artisans and promote authentic indigenous crafts. Handmade certifications and certificates of origin are required for export to many countries because of the application of tariffs—handmade goods are generally free of tariff.

These certifications are provided through government agencies or state-owned ventures. Artesanias de Colombia (Artisans of Colombia) worked in conjunction with the Colombian Foreign Trade Institute to establish a procedure for certifying the origin of products that will now allow the export of about 7,000 craft products internationally. Presently, a handmade certification is also being developed in Colombia (Castro 2000, p. 33).

Bolivia has a national registry of artisans producing crafts that includes all of the details about the artists and the types of crafts they make.

Peru has an organization that operates as a union, the Central Interregional de Artesanos del Peru (CIAP), which promotes mores of behavior based on honesty, transparency, responsibility, and a will to excel. Members agree to abide by Incan principles of *Ama Sua* (not to rob), *Ama Llulla* (not to lie), and *Ama Quella* (not to be lazy). If these principles are not followed, membership is not retained. Bylaws specifically state that designs may not be copied or sold to third parties (Castro 2000, p. 35). The organization works to prevent counterfeiting through example, and pools together artisans who have the same values and work ethic. The CIAP model has been used by other organizations.

Venezuela has a Law on the Development and Protection of Craft Development through which the National Directorate of Handicraft was established and the National Registry of Artisans and State Councils of Artisans were created (Boza 2001).

Key Elements in the Effectiveness of IP Protection in Latin American Countries

Organizations are a key element in the progress of Latin American IP protection. Through the use of trademarks, certifications, registries, and other measures, these groups can develop and use a combination of tools to protect artisans' creations. With the majority of indigenous peoples of the world residing in Latin America,[12] it is important for communities to prevent the "disassociation of the craft works from the traditions in which they originated with the attendant loss of the cultural identity that gave rise to them" (Rosario 2001a, p. 4).

The first sui generis IP protection law for traditional knowledge was enacted in Panama, and Peru is well on its way to development of the same broad coverage.

These laws must be effectively implemented and enforced to provide a substantive example of the effects such coverage has on the welfare of indigenous craftspeople.

Case Study 5: Ghana

Overview

Ghana has no specific IP laws relating to the protection of traditional knowledge.

According to the chief state attorney, Betty Mould-Iddrissu, the importance of IP rights enforcement has only recently become highlighted within the economy, both for the protection of foreign rights within Ghana (as a means for attracting foreign investment) as well as for the protection of Ghanaian rights from (mainly) copyright infringement. Even though a modernized Copyright Law was enacted in 1985, it was not enforced, and piracy reached alarming rates. "I want to underscore the fact that mere passage of legislation is no guarantee that a law is being enforced, and if there is no enforcement, the passage of legislation is useless. This has been most apparent with regard to copyright legislation in Africa" (Mould-Iddrissu 1999).

What happens to an artisan's unique creations when the legal infrastructure fails to protect his/her designs? In the following case, the artisan relies on the quality of his/her creations to distinguish them from copies.

Status of IP Protection

An example of the limiting aspect of standard IP mechanisms in protecting indigenous art is *Kente* cloth, a traditional Ghanaian form of weaving through which meaningful designs are created designating various significant life events.

Although a law was passed in the 1960s specifically for the registration of textile designs,[13] some well-known designs such as *Kente* were purposefully excluded because of their communal nature.

Africancrafts, a nonprofit organization founded by an American, Louise Meyer, has worked to help preserve the tradition of *Kente* cloth weaving through the support of a Ghanaian artist, Gilbert "Bobbo" Ahiagble. Although Bobbo's traditional weaving has been featured at the Smithsonian and his creations are sold through various channels, there is no legal protection for the traditional design cloths he creates. Theoretically, if he registered a copyright for each design, only he would be able to reproduce them. This approach is not realistic, as the designs are used to mark events in tribal life. Bobbo would have a cultural monopoly, something he feels unable to do.

There was no legal recourse for Bobbo when J.C. Penney reproduced his designs on bedsheets and marketed them to the American public. This is offensive to the artisan's community because each design is specific to events in tribal life. According to Louise Meyer, Bobbo's attitude toward copies has gone through a metamorphosis. "Twenty years ago he was very worried about copying, but then he realized that his skills are traditional, and the weavings are of much higher quality than the copies. He has recognized that the publicity gained through his creations helps promote his school, support 16 teachers, and promote learning about his culture. Bobbo is very quality conscious. He still buys all the threads for the school himself to guarantee the dyes won't run, and anyone who shortcuts on quality is not allowed to stay at his school."[14]

These days, Bobbo is using labels to distinguish his products—his version of a certificate of authenticity. In addition, all his weavings have to be specially ordered from his school, thereby ensuring original work.

Key Elements of the Ghanaian Model

The Ghanaian experience highlights the importance of enforcement of IP rights.

"The piracy of copyrighted works in Africa, and in Ghana in particular, over the years contributed to (the) retardation of the cultural creativity of our local communities, which, for a developing country whose national identity and cultural roots are inextricably linked with its national economic development, may have far-reaching consequences," reported Ghanaian Roundtable representative Betty Mould-Iddrissu at the 1999 WIPO Roundtable on Intellectual Property and Traditional Knowledge (WIPO 1999).

Summation

The most prevalent sentiment within the artisans' reactions to protecting their indigenous art was the implementation of Western values in non-Western cultures: the phenomenon of individual versus collective ownership. This one cultural element distinctly sets indigenous cultures apart, and creates a loophole in the legal system when it comes to the materialization and commercialization of traditional art.

The need for public communications and awareness training on IP, its tools, and uses is also a common thread throughout the analysis. Lack of knowledge about avenues of protection for their art sometimes prevents artisans from seeking formal protection. This was the case in every country examined. While some countries have networks and organizations that provide a source for answers, much more can be done to educate the public—not only the artisans but also the consumers.

NGOs and associations helping with lobbying and enforcement efforts have had a successful impact on the awareness level of the general population, as well as within governments. While some individuals have really made a difference, it is the combined efforts of networks of indigenous populations that have brought the counterfeiting problem to the forefront. One might have expected that individuals in industrial countries, given their better access to legal information, would rely less on organizations and associations than artisans in developing countries. The cases reviewed show that networks in both rich and poor countries have played a critical role in raising awareness about legal options available to artisans.

Yet, even when the information about standard legal mechanisms is available, the cost of registering copyrights and pursuing legal redress in home and foreign countries may be too overwhelming. Consider the impact of a US$35 copyright registration fee on an individual artisan whose annual income is about US$600. It is out of reach.

Although many individual attorneys and associations come to the aid of individuals or members who are fighting for their IP rights, this service should be available to all who need it. There are a few successful examples of such organizations, including American Crafts Project, a nonprofit organization providing legal services to small artisans whose original creations have been copied and marketed by others without recognition or permission of the original artist. How can a small, developing country artisan pursue a large American company that is copying and remarketing his/her ideas? How would he/she have the resources? Even if he/she had a registered copyright (or other IP mechanism), how could he/she afford to legally pursue such infringement? These difficult situations can seriously limit an artisan's livelihood, both through decreased sales and through costs of enforcement.

Until such time as all countries have implemented traditional knowledge protection, the use of networks and associations is an effective tool for pooling resources for lobbying, information and awareness training, and enforcement. Networks have been quite useful in all countries, and have provided the strength of numbers needed to gain the attention of governments and outside interests. Within these organizations, the use of certificates of origin, handmade certifications, and certificates of authenticity have developed into effective marketing tools by guaranteeing quality and authenticity.

Many artisans provide a certificate of authenticity with their artistic creations, thereby ensuring the originality of the piece. Although fraudulent certificates have been found in some cases in the United States with Native American jewelry, this approach has been successful for those purchasers concerned with obtaining the original artisans' work.

Globalization is touching every corner of the earth, reaching the most remote places. While this fact seems inescapable, the process itself can be influenced to provide an avenue for the most needy to benefit while preserving the cultural uniqueness of each global community.

Protection of IP for indigenous cultures around the world is a challenging but essential part of this process. Although there are legal instruments to protect artisan creations, these tools do not entirely cover the needs of indigenous cultures in protecting their heritage. As individuals, organizations, and governments devote their energies to researching potential solutions to effective protection, learning occurs, and integration of approaches will hopefully yield a framework that can apply regionally or even globally.

Notes

1. A comprehensive definition of handicrafts is provided by the Crafts Center, a recognized international resource for crafts information and networking, as the following: Crafts are defined as objects which are predominantly hand made, with the aid of tools or power-driven equipment, as long as the direct manual contribution of the artisan remains the most substantial component of the finished product; they should reflect, in their form or technique, the identity of specific communities, groups or geographical regions, or should reflect the creativity of the individual artisan. They should generally be made of national raw materials compatible with sustainable development. They can be utilitarian, aesthetic, artistic, creative, decorative, functional, traditional, religiously and socially symbolic.

2. Interview, Andy Abeita, president, Council for Indigenous Arts and Culture, March 24, 2000.

3. As noted by the Indian and Northern Affairs Canada (INAC 1999) in its discussion on certain Canadian indigenous communities' use of common law copyright rather than formal copyright protection.

4. The IACA is a not-for-profit trade organization that works to promote and protect authentic Indian handmade arts and crafts in the United States and worldwide.

5. Interview, Andy Abeita, March 24, 2000.

6. Zuni is a Native American pueblo tribe of New Mexico.

7. Interview, Andy Abeita, March 24, 2000.

8. Interview, Andy Abeita, March 24, 2000.

9. Telephone interview, Andy Abeita, October 22, 2003.

10. Specific legislative framework to protect indigenous cultural and IP rights and traditional knowledge.

11. The Kuna are an indigenous, politically independent people residing on the northeastern coast of Panama.

12. "Guatemala, Bolivia, Peru and Ecuador currently account for 80% of the world's indigenous populations" (INAC 2001).

13. Textile Designs (Registration) Regulations, L.I. 512, June 1966.

14. Phone interview, Louise Meyer, March 18, 2002.

Bibliography

Aageson, Thomas H. 1999. "Indigenous Artisans and Sustainable Development in Latin America and the Caribbean." Aid to Artisans Keynote Address to the World Bank Working Meeting on Cultural Heritage Partnerships. February 16, 1999. Available at http://www.aid2artisans.org/docs/EVENTS/Speech/toma.htm. Accessed March 2002.

Adad, Mohammed. 1997. Speech at World Crafts Council Meeting, Kyoto, Japan.

Allal, M., and E. Chuta. 1992. *Cottage Industries and Handicrafts: Some Guidelines for Employment Promotion.* Geneva: International Labour Office.

Beck, Rochelle. 1999. "The Challenge of Successfully Marketing Handmade Products from Peru: Lessons from 19 Years in the Field." World Bank Learning Program, Washington, D.C.

Becker, Ellie. 1998. "Foreign-Made 'Indian' Crafts Are Difficult to Detect, Stop." *Albuquerque Journal,* April 13, 1998.

Boza, Dolores Isabel. 2001. "Artisanal Works and Copyright." WIPO/ITC Workshop on Legal Protection of Original Craft Items, Havana, Cuba, February 2001 (WIPO-ITC/DA/HAV/01/6).

Brenner, Malcolm. 1997. "IACA Director Declares War on Fake Indian Jewelry." *The Indian Trader,* June 1997.

Brooke, James. 1997. "Sales of Indian Crafts Boom and So Do Fakes." Editorial, *The New York Times,* August 2, 1997.

Bureau of Indian Affairs. 2000. Available at http://www.doi.gov/bia.

Canku Ota (Many Paths): An Online Newsletter Celebrating Native America. 2001. "Inuit Women Seek Parka Copyright." Issue 37, June 2, 2001. Available at http://www.turtletrack.org.

Castro, Juan David. 2000. "Legal and Other Measures to Protect Crafts, Bolivia, Colombia and Peru." International Trade Centre, Geneva, Switzerland.

Cernea, Michael M. 1993. "Culture and Organization: The Social Sustainability of Induced Development." *Sustainable Development* 1(2):18–29.

"Crafts Classification and World Trade." 1999. *Crafts News,* Washington, D.C.

Cultural Survival Quarterly. 2001. "Intellectual Property Rights, Culture as Commodity." Issue 24.4. Cambridge, Mass.

Dell, Jerri, ed. 1999. *Investing in Culture: The Artisan as Entrepreneur.* Washington, D.C.: World Bank Institute Learning Program.

Duque Duque, Cecilia. 1996. "Handicrafts: A Path Toward Peace." *Grassroots Development* 20(2).

Durham, Debbie. 2000. Executive Director, One World Market. Interview, April 2000.

Elkin, Vicki. 1992. "Fairer Trade." *World Watch* 5(4):5.

Engender. 1998. "Export Competition and Women's Labor." Prepared for United Nations Development Fund for Women. Available at http://www.unifem.undp.org/trade/sa7.htm.

Fair Trade Federation. 1999. Available at http://fairtradefederation.org.

Federal Trade Commission. 2000. "American Indian Arts and Crafts 'Surf Day'." Available at http://www.ftc.gov/opa/2000/10/indianart.htm.

Frankel, Michael, and Terri Janke. 1998. "Our Culture—Our Future." Report on Australian Indigenous Cultural and Intellectual Property Rights. Updated November 25, 1999. Available at Http:icip.lawnet.com.au. Accessed March 2002.

Gasaway, Laura N. 1999. "Intellectual Property Overview." UNC-CH Professor of Law's Course Overview Fall 1999. Available at http://www.unc.edu. Accessed March 2000.

Goulet, Denis. 1971. "An Ethical Model for the Study of Values." *Harvard Educational Review* 41(2):205–27.

Grubel, Herbert G. 1998. "Economic Freedom and Human Welfare: Some Empirical Findings." *Cato Journal* 18(2):287–304.

IACA (Indian Arts and Crafts Association). 2000. Organizational literature. Albuquerque, New Mexico. Available at http://www.iaca.com.

INAC (Indian and Northern Affairs Canada.) 1999. "Intellectual Property and Aboriginal People: A Working Paper." Research and Analysis Directorate. Available at http://www.ainc-inac.gc.ca. Accessed February 2002.

_____. 2001. "Indigenous Women of the Americas." Last updated April 30 2001. Available at http:www.ainc-inac.gc.ca/ch/dec/wmn_e.html. Accessed January 2002.

International Trade Centre, United Nations Conference on Trade and Development/World Trade Organization. 1999/2000. Available at http://www.intracen.org.

Joekes, Susan, and Ann Weston. 1994. *Women and the New Trade Agenda.* United Nations Development Fund for Women, pp. 43–50.

Joseph, Joel D. 2000. "Protect Your Name and Your Work." *The Crafts Report,* March 2000, p. 34.

Kathuria, Sanjay. 1988. "Indian Craft Exports for the Global Market." *Artisan Industries in Asia: Four Case Studies.* Ottawa, Canada: International Development Research Centre.

Mofina, Rick. 1999. "Culture 'Confiscated' for High Fashion: Inuit Women Want to Trademark Tradition to Fend Off Fashion Industry's 'Exploitation.'" *Ottawa Citizen*, Can West Interactive, November 16, 1999.

Mould-Iddrissu, Betty. 1999. "Introduction to Intellectual Property Rights: A Developing Country's Perspective." U.S. Department of State website. Available at http://usinfo.state.gov. Accessed March 2002.

Page, Susanne and Jake. 1998. *Field Guide to Southwest Indian Arts and Crafts*. New York: Random House, p. xix.

Patton, Phil. 2000. "Trademark Battle over Pueblo Sign." *New York Times*, Section F, January 13, 2000.

Pye, Elwood. 1988. *Artisans in Economic Development*. Ottawa, Canada: International Development Centre.

Ramsay, Caroline. 1999. "Characteristics of World Trade in Crafts." The Crafts Center, Washington, D.C.

Rosario, Victor Manuel Loyola. 2001a. "Problems Arising from the Inadequate Protection of Craft Creations." WIPO/ITC Workshop on Legal Protection of Original Craft Items, Havana, Cuba, February 2001 (WIPO-ITC/DA/HAV/01/1).

_____. 2001b. "Towards a More Effective System of Protection: In the National Environment." WIPO/ITC Workshop on Legal Protection of Original Craft Items, Havana, Cuba, February 2001 (WIPO-ITC/DA/HAV/01/3).

Sala, Maria-Mercedes. 2001. "Codification of Artisanal Products in Trade and Customs Nomenclatures." WIPO/ITC Workshop on Legal Protection of Original Craft Items, Havana, Cuba, January 30–February 1, 2001.

Shiffman, John. 1998. "$1 Billion Industry Reeling as Faux Crafts Flood Market." *USA Today*, April 8, 1998.

Smith, Scott S. 1998. "The Scandal of Fake Indian Crafts." *Cowboys and Indians*, September 1998.

Snow, Stephen. 2001. "Kuna Yala of Panama." *Cultural Survival Quarterly*, Issue 24.4, Cambridge, Mass.

Trade and Development Centre, a Joint Venture of the World Trade Organization and the World Bank. 2000. Available at http://www.itd.org.

Turham, David. 1994. "What Can We Learn from Past Efforts to Encourage Employment-Intensive Development?" Background paper for the 1995 World Development Report, Organisation for Economic Co-operation and Development.

UNIFEM (United Nations Development Fund for Women). 1999. "Strengthening Women's Economic Capacity." Available at http://www.unifem.undp.org.

WIPO (World Intellectual Property Organization). 1999. "Roundtable on Intellectual Property and Traditional Knowledge." Geneva. (WIPO/IPTK/RT/99/3). Available at http://wipo.org. Accessed 2002.

_____. 2002. "About Intellectual Property." Available at http://www.wipo.int. Accessed March 2002.

WIPO-ITC (World Intellectual Property Organization–International Trade Centre). 2001. "WIPO-ITC Workshop on Legal Protection of Original Craft Items." Havana, Cuba, January 30–February 1, 2001 (WIPO/ITC/DA/HAV/01/1).

World Bank. 2000. "Culture in Sustainable Development." Social Development Network. Available at http://www.worldbank.org.

World Bank Institute. 1999. "Investing in Culture: The Artisan as Entrepreneur." World Bank conference, November 9, 1999. Washington, D.C.

WTO (World Trade Organization) website. 2000. Available at http://www.wto.org.

6

BIOPROSPECTING AGREEMENTS AND BENEFIT SHARING WITH LOCAL COMMUNITIES

Kerry ten Kate and Sarah A. Laird

In the closing decades of the last century, the conservation, development, and human rights agendas began to merge. Equity was increasingly acknowledged as the central plank in law and policy on access to genetic resources and traditional knowledge, as can be seen from the Convention on Biological Diversity (CBD), national law to implement it, and the recent International Treaty (IT) on Plant Genetic Resources for Food and Agriculture. These encapsulate the principles of prior informed consent, mutually agreed terms, and benefit sharing. "Facilitated" access is encouraged by these regimes, but not at the expense of rights. Over the same period, researchers and indigenous peoples' groups were exploring the parameters of what constitutes equitable research relationships and were beginning to articulate appropriate terms for collaboration. A range of indigenous peoples' statements and declarations, researchers' codes of ethics, and institutional policies have been developed in response.

This change in the policy and ethical environment has been matched by some equally dramatic scientific and technological developments, which shape market demand for access to genetic resources and associated traditional knowledge. Scientific developments in the fields of biochemistry, molecular biology, cell biology, immunology, and information technology continue to transform the process of product discovery and development. For example, advances in molecular biology and genomics have produced a previously inaccessible range of disease targets for the development of new drugs. New technologies—such as combinatorial chemistry, high-throughput screens, and laboratories-on-a-chip—have provided unprecedented numbers of compounds to test in high-throughput screens. They have also given us better ways to turn the new knowledge into molecules, whether conventional ones or those produced by biotechnology, for screening. In this environment, natural products are often viewed as too slow, costly, and problematic. In healthcare, research dollars are flowing into synthetic chemistry for rational drug design, combinatorial approaches, and genetics that focuses largely on human material, with natural products currently left behind.

However, genetic resources and associated traditional knowledge continue to provide leads in the discovery, development, and manufacture of products. Annual global markets for products in the healthcare, agriculture, horticulture, and biotechnology sectors derived from genetic resources lie between US$500 billion and US$800 billion (ten Kate and Laird 1999). In the case of healthcare, there are still sales of between US$75 billion and US$150 billion of pharmaceuticals and between US$20 million and US$40 billion worth of botanical medicines derived from genetic resources each year. Direct links can still be made between many products on the market and knowledge systems dating back millennia. For example, of the approximately 120 pharmaceutical products derived from plants in 1985, 75 percent were discovered through the study of their traditional medical use (Farnsworth and others 1985). Grifo and others (1996) demonstrated that for the base compound in most of the top 150 plant-derived prescription drugs, commercial use correlates with traditional medical use. As we discuss, companies continue to access ethnobotanical knowledge as part of discovery programs, although the manner in which different sectors make use of it varies greatly, so that benefit-sharing arrangements are comparatively rare.

This is a broad and wide-ranging subject, and in this chapter we can touch on only a few areas. We look at how the new legal and ethical frameworks and trends in science and industry can create conditions for local communities and indigenous peoples to control access to and the use of their knowledge, and to benefit from this use. We also discuss the nature of agreements designed to share benefits with local groups.

Establishing Equity and Rights to Control the Use of Traditional Knowledge

A number of significant changes in the legal and policy framework over the past decade have set the scene for better recognition of the rights of indigenous and local communities in transactions involving genetic resources and traditional knowledge. These changes include intergovernmental agreements, national measures, and codes, statements, and policies adopted by communities, researchers, and companies.

Intergovernmental Agreements

In recent years, states have agreed on a range of intergovernmental agreements that include provisions supporting indigenous peoples' right to control and benefit from the use of their traditional knowledge systems. Some of these agreements—such as the 1993 Convention on Biological Diversity, the 1994 Convention on Desertification and Drought, and the 1989 International Labour Organization Convention 169 Concerning Indigenous Peoples—are legally binding. Others—such as the 1994 United Nations Draft Declaration on the Rights of Indigenous Peoples and Agenda 21 and the Rio Declaration of 1992—are not legally binding, but place a moral obligation to conform with their provisions on countries adhering to them. (Helpful analyses of the full range of these measures can be found in Posey [1996] and Dutfield [2000].)

We focus on the CBD and the IT as particular focal points for dialogue on traditional knowledge associated with genetic resources and bioprospecting. Biodiversity prospecting (often contracted to "bioprospecting") was first defined as "the exploration of biodiversity for commercially valuable genetic resources and biochemicals" (Reid and others 1993).The CBD sets out provisions according to which states should regulate access to genetic resources and associated traditional knowledge. It balances sovereignty and the authority of national governments to regulate access to their genetic resources with the obligation for them to facilitate access for environmentally sound purposes. Access to genetic resources is to be subject to governments' prior informed consent, on terms mutually agreed by the provider and recipient that promote the fair and equitable sharing of benefits. Similarly, subject to national law, access to the knowledge, innovations, and practices of indigenous and local communities requires the prior approval of the holders of that knowledge, and the resulting benefits should be shared fairly and equitably with the communities concerned.

The 183 parties to the CBD are developing guidelines to spell out these provisions and translate them into action. When the parties to the CBD met in The Hague in April 2002, they adopted the voluntary Bonn Guidelines on Access and Benefit-Sharing (see www.biodiv.org). These guidelines provide operational guidance for "users and providers" of genetic resources and serve as information for governments that are drafting national laws and for governments, communities, companies, researchers, and others that are involved in access and benefit-sharing agreements. The scope of the guidelines is "all genetic resources and associated traditional knowledge, innovations and practices covered by the CBD and benefits arising from the commercial and other utilisation of such resources," with the exclusion of human genetic resources. The guidelines describe steps in the access and benefit-sharing process, with sections on prior informed consent and mutually agreed terms; possible measures that countries and organizations should consider in response to their roles and responsibilities as providers and users of genetic resources and traditional knowledge; recommendations for the participation of stakeholders; and incentive measures, accountability, national monitoring and reporting, verification, dispute settlement, and remedies. One appendix sets out suggested elements for material transfer agreements and another, monetary and nonmonetary benefits that may be shared. The guidelines state that access and benefit-sharing systems should be based on an overall access and benefit-sharing strategy, at the country or regional level. Given the complexity and uncertainty involved in access and benefit-sharing arrangements, such strategies can help communities and other groups involved to derive optimum benefits (ten Kate and Wells 2001).

In a related field, the CBD has developed a program of work on Article 8j (which concerns the knowledge, innovations, and practices of indigenous and local communities). A number of the 18 tasks outlined by the Working Group on 8j relate to access and benefit sharing, including the following:

- Guidelines on participation of indigenous and local communities in decision-making, policy planning and development, and project implementation and strategic, environmental, and social impact assessments on lands or waters occupied or used by indigenous and local communities
- Guidelines to help states establish legal frameworks, including sui generis systems that recognize, safeguard, and fully guarantee the protection of the cultural heritage, customary laws, innovations, and traditional knowledge. Others relate to how to respect, preserve, and maintain these legal frameworks; apply them more widely; and obtain an equitable share of the resulting benefits, including national incentive schemes
- Models for codes of ethical conduct for research, access to, use, exchange, and control of information concerning traditional knowledge, innovations, and practices on reporting and prevention of illicit appropriation of traditional knowledge

Another recent development is the IT, which has provisions on prior informed consent, benefit sharing, and farmers' rights. One of the important elements of the IT, which was finalized in Rome in November 2001, is a multilateral system for access, for food and agriculture, to 35 crop genera and 29 forage species and associated benefit sharing. Its conditions for facilitated access to in situ plant genetic resources for food and agriculture will be according to national law (to allow for protection of property and other rights of communities). While most benefits will be shared on a multilateral basis (rather than with the specific provider of genetic resources), benefits such as the exchange of information, access to and transfer of technology, capacity building, and even a commercial benefit-sharing package should be available to communities through the system. The article on farmers' rights encourages countries to take steps to "to protect and promote Farmers' Rights," including protection of their traditional knowledge and the right to participate in benefit sharing and in national decisionmaking. Communities may also benefit through involvement in conservation and sustainable use activities. (See ftp://ext-ftp.fao.org/waicent/pub/cgrfa8/iu/ITPGRe.pdf or http://www.fao. org/ag/cgrfa/News.htm.)

Intellectual Property Rights

The potential use of existing or innovative models of intellectual property rights (IPRs) to protect traditional knowledge is also under examination. At the regional and national levels, there are various initiatives to apply and develop intellectual property law consistent with prior informed consent for access to genetic resources, prior approval for the use of traditional knowledge, and benefit sharing (for sources of information, see, for example, U.K. Commission on Intellectual Property Rights http://www.iprcommission.org/). For example, in Decision 486 "Common Regime on Industrial Property," adopted in September 2000, the five countries of the Andean Community have attempted to harmonize the World Trade Organization's (WTO) Trade-Related Aspects of Intellectual Property Rights (TRIPS) with the CBD. Among other aspects, the decision provides that certain life forms shall not be considered inventions, patent applications based on the region's genetic resources require a copy of the access contract, and applications for a patent on an invention obtained or developed from tradi-tional knowledge shall include a copy of the license from the community. (See http://www.comunidadandina.org/ingles/treaties/dec/D486e.htm.)

At the international level, there are discussions on the review and implementa-tion of TRIPS (see, for example, the Doha WTO Ministerial Declaration, November 20, 2001, at http://www.wto.org/english/thewto_e/minist_e/min01_e/mindecl_e. htm, paragraphs 17–19; and TRIPS Council http://www.wto.org/english/tratop_e/ trips_e/trips_e.htm). The World Intellectual Property Organization (WIPO) Intergovernmental Committee on Intellectual Property and Genetic Resources, Traditional Knowledge and Folklore is considering intellectual property issues that arise in the context of access to genetic resources and benefit sharing, the pro-tection of traditional knowledge, innovations and creativity, and the protection of expressions of folklore. For example, it is reviewing clauses related to IPRs in access and benefit-sharing agreements (see http://www.wipo.org/globalissues/igc/index.html). WIPO is working to devise a format for an electronic database of contract clauses and practices concerning access to genetic resources and benefit sharing. It is also considering elements of a sui generis system for the protection of traditional knowledge, and the Intergovernmental Committee has been considering ways to improve access to traditional knowledge for patent examiners so that patents are not improperly granted.[1]

A range of proposals has emerged concerning patents, from the meaning of "prior art," the scope of patents, and the test of "inventive step," to procedural requirements such as disclosure of country of origin and even proof of prior informed consent in patent applications. Indigenous peoples' groups have engaged with the patent system to challenge the granting of patents. For example, the Coordinating Body of Indigenous Organizations of the Amazon Basin (COICA), an umbrella group that represents more than 400 indigenous tribes in the region, joined with the Center for International Environmental Law (CIEL) to file a request before the U.S. Patent and Trademark Office asking it to reexamine a patent it had issued on a purported variety of *Banisteriopsis caapi*, or Ayahuasca, a plant that has a long traditional use in religious and healing ceremonies. The patent was annulled shortly thereafter (Ruiz Muller 2000; Wiser 2002), but has subsequently been reinstated. Work in this area continues.

Other forms of IPRs are also being investigated as a potential source of protection against expropriation of traditional knowledge. Geographical indications and trademarks have looked particularly promising (see Commission on Intellectual Property Rights 2002; Downes and Laird 1999; Dutfield 2000; Moran 1993).

National Laws on Access to Genetic Resources and Traditional Knowledge

The CBD leaves parties a great deal of discretion to decide how to regulate access, and, in practice, the number of countries developing national laws and policies on this subject has grown fast. About 100 countries have already introduced, or are developing, laws and other policy measures to regulate access to genetic resources and benefit sharing.[2] Two (the Philippines and Peru) have also introduced laws that regulate access to traditional knowledge, independent of whether this is obtained in conjunction with genetic resources. The CBD states that the right to determine access to genetic resources rests with government, but several national laws on access to genetic resources make such governmental consent contingent on prior informed consent and benefit-sharing agreements with affected communities. Laws on access to genetic resources define terms such as "knowledge," "traditional knowledge," "intangible component," and various categories of peoples such as "local communities" and "indigenous cultural communities." The exact circumstances in which the "prior approval" of local and indigenous communities are needed—and for what—vary from country to country and are sometimes unclear. Some access laws require prior informed consent from local and indigenous people for access to genetic resources on their lands but do not address access to their traditional knowledge concerning those resources, while others explicitly require prior approval from local and indigenous peoples for access to their traditional knowledge, but not to genetic resources.

The Philippines and the five countries of the Andean Community were in the vanguard with such legislation. The Philippines' Executive Order 247 on Access to Genetic Resources requires the prior informed consent of indigenous cultural communities, in accordance with customary laws, for prospecting of biological and genetic resources within their ancestral lands and domains. The Philippines' 1997 Indigenous Peoples Rights Act (IPRA) recognizes a wide range of rights held by the country's numerous indigenous groups, including land rights and a considerable measure of self-government within ancestral domains, including rights to "preserve and protect their culture, traditions and institutions." In guaranteeing and upholding these rights, the state must consider them in the formulation of all national plans and policies (Barber, Glowka, and LaVina 2002).

The Andean Community's Decision 391 establishes a Common Regime on Access in Bolivia, Colombia, Ecuador, Peru, and República Bolivariana de Venezuela. Decision 391 states that an applicant wishing to access genetic resources or derivatives with an "intangible component" (any knowledge, innovation, or individual or collective practice of actual or potential value associated with the genetic resource, its derivatives, or the biological resource containing them, whether or not it is protected by intellectual property systems) must identify the supplier of the intangible component and negotiate a benefit-sharing agreement with them. Since other contracts are needed with the owner, holder, or administrator of the biological resource containing the genetic resource, or of the property on which the biological resource containing the genetic resource is found, the community's consent should be sought prior to accessing their knowledge. To complement the Andean Community's Common Regime on Access to genetic resources, Peru is developing a law on the collective IPRs of indigenous peoples related to biodiversity (box 6.1).

More recent examples of access legislation can be found in India (in draft form) and Brazil. The Biological Diversity Bill (No. 93 of 2000) in India stipulates that no foreigner may obtain any biological resource occurring in India or knowledge associated thereto "for research or for commercial utilisation or for bio-survey and bio-utilisation" without prior approval of the National Biodiversity Authority, nor apply for any intellectual property right for any invention based on a biological resource obtained from India without the Authority's approval. A National Biodiversity Fund will channel benefits received from foreign bioprospectors to

BOX 6.1 The Peruvian Proposal on the Protection of Traditional Knowledge

In 1996, the Peruvian government established five groups to explore options for the protection and regulation of traditional knowledge and access to genetic resources. A range of governmental and nongovernmental organizations as well as indigenous groups were involved. The proposal was based on the following elements:

- To access a community's traditional knowledge for research, prior informed consent is required and is sufficient.
- To access a community's traditional knowledge for "exploitation," a license agreement as well as prior informed consent is required. Although such knowledge may be common to more than one community, an agreement with one community is sufficient. The terms of the license will address benefit sharing, for example, through royalties. Two payments with communities are envisaged. One payment is made when the license agreement is signed. This is obligatory and can be monetary or nonmonetary, such as building schools, medical posts, and communication centers. The second payment is when some benefits have arisen following exploitation of the traditional knowledge. The minimum payment envisaged is 0.5 percent of the gross sales.
- The proposed protection regime intends to prohibit the patenting of an invention based on indigenous traditional knowledge without demonstration of authorization for use of the knowledge.
- Traditional knowledge in the public domain (that is, that anyone not belonging to the community has acquired) does not require prior informed consent or a licensed agreement for its exploitation, but a contribution must be made by the user to a fund.
- A confidential register is proposed to protect traditional knowledge that is not in the public domain.

Source: Dr. iur. Ana María Pacón, presentation to United Nations Conference on Trade and Development (UNCTAD) Expert Meeting on Systems and National Experiences for Protecting Traditional Knowledge, Innovations and Practices, Geneva, October 30, 2000.

"benefit-claimers," conservation, and development in the area from which the genetic resource or knowledge comes. Indian citizens and corporations must also give "prior intimation" to State Biodiversity Boards before obtaining any biological resource for commercial utilization or biosurvey, through which benefits will be shared at the state level (Sections 26–29). Local bodies are to constitute "Biodiversity Management Committees" to promote the conservation, sustainable use, and documentation of biodiversity within the area.

The Brazilian Medida Provisoria (No. 2, 186-16 of August 23, 2001) establishes a management council whose permission will be needed to access components of the national "genetic patrimony" (defined as "information of genetic origin" contained in samples and living or dead extracts of all life forms) and associated traditional knowledge (defined as individual or collective knowledge or practice of indigenous or local communities or real or potential value associated with genetic patrimony). National public or private institutions with research and development activities in biological areas will be authorized to access genetic patrimony and associated knowledge in exchange for a sharing of benefits with the contracting parties.

Indigenous Peoples' Declarations, Codes of Conduct, Institutional Policies, Research Agreements, and Corporate Policies

Complementing developments on the national and international policy front, a range of documents developed by indigenous peoples, researchers, professional associations, and companies has marked a significant shift in the ethical context for bioprospecting partnerships. Although implementation often remains a challenge, these documents have helped to make equitable relationships between local communities and indigenous peoples, and various outside groups, more likely (Alexiades and Laird 2002; Laird 2002). These documents include codes of ethics, research agreements, indigenous peoples' statements and declarations, and corporate and institutional policies. These documents have influenced the language incorporated into national and international law and contractual agreements. Because they have been developed by groups with focused concerns and interests, they have brought some helpful specificity and detail to national and international dialogue.

Over the past 20 years, indigenous peoples' organizations have issued a range of declarations and statements with clear demands in terms of bioprospecting. These demands include ownership and inalienable rights over their knowledge and resources; requirements for their prior informed consent; right of veto over research and/or access to their land, knowledge, or resources; and benefit sharing. In some cases, these demands have included calls for a moratorium on bioprospecting until the legal framework is established to allow for equitable partnerships (Dutfield 2002; for copies of statements see www.biodiv.org and http://users.ox.ac.uk/~wgtrr/decin.htm).

Researchers have developed a number of codes of ethics and research guidelines through professional societies such as the International Society of Ethnobiology, the American Society of Pharmacognosy, and the Society of Economic Botany. These lay out general principles for research partnerships, obligations of the partners, and sometimes include recommended guidelines for researcher behavior in the field (Laird and Posey 2002).

A number of research organizations have developed institutional policies that establish general principles for their employees and associates. An example is the set of Principles for Participating Institutions, in which 28 botanic gardens and herbaria from 21 countries developed common standards on access to genetic resources and benefit sharing (Latorre and others 2001; www.rbgkew.org.uk/con-servation). The Limbe Botanic Garden in Cameroon, and other institutions working with indigenous peoples and local communities, have endorsed these principles, and then developed in more detail their own policies to translate them into action. These policies address practical issues confronted on a daily basis by the institution concerned, including the nature of their relationship with local communities (Laird and Mahop 2001; www.rbgkew.org.uk/peopleplants/manual).

A number of bioscience companies have also developed corporate policies setting out their approach to compliance with the CBD. These policies generally describe the scope of resources covered by the policy; the standard to which the company means to be held accountable (for example, absolute commitments, or commitments to make reasonable or best efforts); how to obtain prior informed consent and ensure that genetic resources and information are obtained legally; and commitments to obtain clear legal title to the materials and information acquired, to share benefits fairly and equitably, and to support conservation through environmentally sustainable sourcing. Some corporate policies describe the process followed to develop them and indicators to gauge success in their implementation (ten Kate and Laird 1999).

In the GlaxoSmithKline Policy Position on the CBD approved in February 2002, the company states that it is increasingly focused on drug discovery by screening synthetic chemical compounds, and thus has limited interest in collecting and screening natural material. Collecting programs have drawn to an end, and screening is no longer conducted in-house, but by partners in countries such as Brazil and Singapore. However, the policy supports the principles enshrined in the CBD when conducting relevant activities. The document does not address prior informed consent from local communities per se, but states that it has always undertaken only to work with organizations and suppliers with the expertise and legal authority to collect samples, and to ensure that the governments in developing countries are informed of and consent to the nature and extent of any collecting program.[3]

Commercial Demand for Traditional Knowledge

The trends in law and policy described above set the context for contractual agreements, which increasingly incorporate terms and conditions to comply with or are inspired by binding and voluntary measures, thus improving the likelihood that biodiversity prospecting partnerships involving local communities will be fair and equitable. However, the very existence of such agreements depends on academic and commercial demand for access to traditional knowledge. This section outlines the nature and scale of commercial demand for traditional knowledge and how it is used by companies.

As we have mentioned, many companies, such as GlaxoSmithKline, are scaling back their research on natural products, but the screening of existing ex situ collections of genetic resources continues, and even a modest range of targeted collecting activities. Compared with the demand for access to genetic resources, demand for access to traditional knowledge is more rare. In 1998–99, we carried out a survey of 300 scientists in companies and research organizations conducting discovery and development on genetic resources. Of the 24 pharmaceutical companies interviewed, all of whom used genetic resources, about half used traditional knowledge. By contrast, all 21 representatives from botanical companies used documented traditional knowledge. Of the companies using traditional knowledge, 80 percent relied solely on literature and databases as their primary source for this information (ten Kate and Laird 1999). Some of the others conducted or commissioned ethnobotanical field collections.

The manner in which companies use traditional knowledge in research and development programs is summarized in table 6.1. In drug discovery efforts, traditional knowledge can be used as a general indicator of nonspecific bioactivity suitable for a panel of broad screens; as an indicator of specific bioactivity suitable for particular high-resolution bioassays; and as an indicator of pharmacological activity for which mechanisms-based bioassays have yet to be developed (Cox 1994). The International Cooperative Biodiversity Groups (ICBGs) have found that the most common use of traditional knowledge in their programs is as a guide for initial plant selection, and for easily diagnosed diseases of relevance to the communities holding the knowledge. Traditional knowledge is less likely to be useful in discovery programs for blockbuster drug disease categories such as cancer, human immunodeficiency virus, and Alzheimer's.[4] Effectively integrating ethnomedical knowledge into large-scale, high-throughput screening systems that seek high levels of specific targeted biological activity is difficult (Rosenthal and others 1999).

Publication of academic research results is the most common route by which traditional knowledge makes its way to the private sector. Because traditional knowledge is predominantly gleaned from public-domain publications, it does not usually trigger benefit-sharing negotiations. However, there are cases in which companies have entered into agreements with local groups or intermediaries for their knowledge and resources. One of the most celebrated cases in recent years is that of the compound P57 derived from the Hoodia plant in southern Africa that

**TABLE 6.1 The Use of Traditional Knowledge by Industry
              Sectors**

Sector	Manner of Use	Source
Pharmaceuticals	TK is not considered a useful tool during the early stages of high-throughput screening, but once an active compound is identified, most companies use TK (when available) to guide subsequent research. A (very) few companies direct their research programs based on TK; some will use TK as the basis for setting up screens to select for competing (or better) compounds with similar bioactivity, that is, as a reference compound to select more active synthetic analogue compounds.	Literature, databases, intermediary brokers. A minority of companies commission field ethnobotanical collection. Ethnobotanical information is often attached to samples as an "add-on," even if collections are primarily chemotaxonomic or ecology driven.
Botanical medicine	TK is used as the basis of identification of potential new product development; in safety and efficacy studies; and formulation. It is widely used in marketing commercial products, sometimes in developing wildcrafting or cultivation strategies for raw materials.	Literature, databases, tradeshows, Internet, and so forth. Middlemen brokers will follow up on leads in literature with local communities and research institutions. In rare cases the literature leads marketing companies to conduct field-based research on species of promise; this is directed, rather than bulk collecting, research.
Personal care and cosmetics	TK is used as the basis of identification of potential new leads and to direct research on a species' commercial potential. It is used in safety and efficacy studies; is widely used in marketing commercial products; and is sometimes used in developing sourcing strategies for raw materials.	Literature, databases, trade shows, Internet, and so forth. Occasionally, middlemen brokers will follow up on leads from the literature with local communities.Companies conducting high-throughput screening will commission the collection of ethnobotanical samples with identified uses. Other companies have entered into direct, field-based partnerships with communities to use their TK in product development.

TABLE 6.1 (Continued)

Sector	Manner of Use	Source
Crop protection	A small proportion of companies use TK to guide the collection and screening of samples. As with pharmaceuticals, once activity is demonstrated, TK is sometimes used to decide on the direction of subsequent research.	Literature, databases.
Biotechnology	Many biotechnology applications, such as brewing and bread-making, are based on TK dating back millennia, but contemporary biotechnology makes little use of TK.	
Seeds	Companies make little use of TK, but they do use germplasm that has been prebred by other organizations to which genes from traditional varieties may have made an important contribution.	
Horticulture	Many popular ornamental varieties and horticultural vegetable crops owe their existence to traditional domestication and selection over long periods of time. However, TK is rarely used in the selection and breeding of new horticultural varieties today.	

TK, traditional knowledge.
Source: Laird and ten Kate 2002.

is under development by Pfizer. In this case there is a direct correlation between traditional use—collected in the 1970s—and the commercial product. However, it was only in 2002 that a memorandum of understanding (MOU) was signed between the San bushmen, from whom the traditional knowledge was collected, and the collectors of traditional knowledge—the South African Council for

BOX 6.2   The CSIR-Phytopharm-Pfizer Commercialization of Hoodia on the Basis of San Traditional Knowledge: Evolution of Agreements

For thousands of years, the San (bushmen) of the Kalahari, numbering about 100,000 across South Africa, Botswana, Namibia, and Angola, have used species of the succulent *Hoodia* genus (of the family Asclepiadaceae) to stave off hunger and thirst on hunting trips. In the 1970s, as part of wider research into traditional uses of local species, the CSIR collected and began investigating Hoodia. The CSIR is one of the largest research organizations in Africa, performing 12 percent of all industrial research and development on the continent; 40 percent of its funding comes from government and 60 percent from clients.

At the time of collections, the CSIR did not sign an agreement with the San. Nor did it do so in 1998 after CSIR patented an appetite-suppressing compound known as P57 from the plant and signed a licensing agreement with Phytopharm plc, a small U.K. research-based pharmaceutical company. Soon after, Phytopharm sold the rights to an exclusive global license for P57 for US$32 million in license fees and milestone payments to Pfizer, a U.S. pharmaceutical company better equipped to take promising leads through the development phase. Phytopharm had just successfully completed the third and final stage of clinical trials. Meanwhile, throughout this process both companies appeared to be ignorant of their legal and ethical obligations under the 1993 CBD and were unaware until 2001 that the San constituted a legitimate stakeholder group. Although benefits had begun to flow back to CSIR in the form of laboratory facilities, and milestone and royalty payments for the CSIR were written into an agreement, no arrangement was in place to benefit local groups for their traditional knowledge.

As a result, in 2001 the San organized demonstrations and hired a lawyer to defend their rights to benefit from the use of their knowledge. Following five months of talks with the CSIR, they have entered into an MOU that acknowledges the need to provide benefits for the use of traditional knowledge should a commercial product be developed, but does not include specific details of this benefit-sharing package. The MOU acted as the basis for negotiation and, most importantly, recognized the San as the originators and custodians of traditional knowledge associated with the use of Hoodia. The MOU was a first step toward reaching a full agreement, which was signed in March 2003. Benefits for the San in this agreement include 6 per-

Scientific and Industrial Research (CSIR). For a number of years it was not deemed necessary to include the San in agreements, and it was only after a series of protests that the MOU was developed. The MOU recognizes the San as the originators of the knowledge used to make the commercial product (box 6.2).

cent of all royalties and 8 percent of all milestone payments received by the CSIR. These benefits will be paid to the San Hoodia Benefit-Sharing Trust set up jointly by the CSIR and the South African San Council.

There is an absence of national legislation to guide such agreements, although a Biodiversity Act and a Indigenous Knowledge Systems Bill are in development. In part as a result of this policy and legislative vacuum, the terms of the agreement met with mixed reactions. They were hailed by Roger Chennells, an attorney representing the South African San Council, as "... notable recognition and acknowledgement of the importance of the traditional knowledge and heritage of the San peoples" (South African San Council and the CSIR 2003). Others expressed concerns about the deal, including the emphasis on benefits linked to uncertain commercial product development and the relatively small size of royalty rates (Wynberg 2003).

Sources: Barnett 2001; Kahn 2002; Madeley 2002; South African San Council and CSIR, 2003; Wynberg 2002, 2003.

Biodiversity Prospecting Agreements

The variable demand for access to genetic resources and traditional knowledge has influenced benefit sharing with local communities and companies. The types of benefits that result from these partnerships, including reciprocal access to other genetic resources, opportunities for in situ and ex situ conservation, access to information and research results, participation in research, technology transfer, and training and capacity building, can all arise within access partnerships. Where partnerships result in commercial products, financial benefits can include fees, milestone payments, and royalties (see ten Kate and Laird 1999 for a more detailed discussion of benefit sharing in the pharmaceutical and other industries). However, few such benefits have yet accrued at the local level.

Different Kinds of Agreements

Different contractual arrangements may contain provisions related to access to genetic resources, traditional knowledge, benefit sharing, and IPRs. These arrangements include:

- Intellectual property licenses
- Material transfer agreements
- Environmental permits

- Real estate leases/land tenure
- Shrinkwrap licenses
- Option agreements
- Letters of intent
- MOUs

Each of these arrangements is outlined in Gollin (2002). The new breed of biodiversity prospecting agreements or access and benefit-sharing agreements that have been developed in response to the CBD tend to follow the basic principles of general commercial contracts, but may also include elements of the different agreements listed above and also address issues such as sovereign rights, prior informed consent, access to land and resources, benefit sharing, conservation, and environmental permitting.

The Structure of Agreements

In most cases involving the commercialization of genetic resources, several actors are involved in a value-adding chain from communities and intermediaries, such as universities and genebanks, to companies that discover, develop, manufacture, and retail products. As described by Gollin (2002), two main approaches have emerged to allow a group of separate entities to collaborate in these activities: "hub-and-spoke" and consortium or "club" structures.

In a consortium or club, numerous collaborators work in a group to develop products derived from genetic resources or traditional knowledge. In such a multilateral arrangement, all the parties typically enter into one contract that sets out all the promises of them all. This approach can help with transparency and in addressing environmental, economic, equitable, and ethical goals, but it is complicated to determine the roles of each party. Negotiations can be challenging because no deal is done until all parties agree and are ready to sign the same document.

A hub-and-spoke arrangement, by contrast, involves more than one contract (the spokes) with one entity common to each of the contracts (the hub). The arrangement is more flexible, since it is easier to alter aspects of each agreement, for example, by substituting a new commercial partner if the original one withdraws. In addition, bilateral agreements are easier to negotiate than a single multilateral one, and offer what some companies see as an important advantage; namely, they can avoid direct negotiations with local communities. The hub institution, however, must carry the principal burden of negotiation and coordination among all the contracts.

Terms and Conditions

Whatever the nature of the agreement, it will typically involve terms and conditions (see Bonn Guidelines at www.biodiv.org and Latorre and others 2001) on:

- **Introductory provisions:** Preambular reference to the CBD, IT, and any other applicable international, regional, or national law; description of the legal status of the provider and user of genetic resources; mandate of the parties and their general objectives in establishing the agreement.
- **Conduct of the collaboration:** The roles, rights, and responsibilities of the different parties in the collaborative research process; confidentiality; duty to minimize environmental impacts of collecting activities.
- **Access and benefit sharing:** Prior informed consent and legal acquisition of the genetic resources and associated traditional knowledge; description and permitted uses of genetic resources and associated traditional knowledge covered by the agreement (research, breeding, commercialization); conditions under which the user may seek IPRs; benefits to be shared and with whom they are to be shared; clauses on whether the recipient of the resources/knowledge may pass them on to third parties, and, if so, on what terms.
- **A range of legal provisions:** Definitions; length of agreement; notice to terminate the agreement; fact that the obligations in certain clauses (benefit sharing) survive the termination of the agreement; independent enforceability of individual clauses in the agreement; events limiting the liability of either party (Act of God, fire, flood); arbitration and alternative dispute settlement arrangements; assignment or transfer of rights; choice of law.

The Negotiating Process

Tobin (2002) identifies some steps for local and indigenous communities in negotiating mutually agreed terms for access to their traditional knowledge or genetic resources on their lands. These steps include identifying the resources and parties that are the basis for negotiation, establishing rules for negotiation, considering the potential role of mediating institutions, and defining who are the "providers" of genetic resources and traditional knowledge. He also poses questions for communities and companies involved in prior informed consent negotiations to consider:

- Can all communities, custodians of relevant knowledge, be identified, and if so, is it feasible that they all be required to give consent for its use?
- What happens when communities live in neighboring countries?
- Is it possible to prevent use of material in the public domain?

- How can equitable sharing of benefits within communities be secured without state paternalism?
- Can equitable sharing among communities be achieved, in particular between communities which do not have a history of cooperation, again without resorting to paternalism?
- In what form can information be held, e.g., in a register, and for what purpose?
- If the value of the knowledge lies in keeping it confidential, how can it be ensured that potential users are aware of which communities must be consulted for use of knowledge?
- How can transaction costs be kept down? If the system is overly expensive, benefits will end up being consumed by its maintenance and will not reach communities.
- With whom should companies negotiate? All communities, custodians of particular knowledge, all community members, or only with shamans, healers, leaders, and the like?
- How can legal certainty be secured, in order to ensure that a company is protected against future claims for benefits brought by other custodians of knowledge following development of an interesting product?
- Should warranties be sought from indigenous peoples regarding their rights to enter into agreements?
- Can indigenous peoples be required to accept confidentiality obligations regarding research and development reports, and if so, will they be in a position to comply?
- To what extent are companies responsible for ensuring equity in distribution of benefits within and among communities?
- Are companies obliged to pay royalties after patents expire?
- What happens when competitors are not paying royalties for information in the public domain? Is it fair that companies that entered into agreements should be prejudiced in their competition with companies that are not paying royalties?

The Sharing of Benefits

The categories of benefits that arise from access to genetic resources and traditional knowledge are now fairly well known (ten Kate and Laird 1999). Several different forms of monetary and nonmonetary benefits are indicated in appendix II of the Bonn Guidelines on Access and Benefit-Sharing as Related to Genetic Resources (see box 6.3 and www.biodiv.org) and are also illustrated in the cases of the ICBGs, San–CSIR, and Kani–Tropical Botanic Garden and Research Institute (TBGRI) partnerships outlined below (see boxes 6.2 and 6.4, respectively). While

BOX 6.3 Appendix II of the Bonn Guidelines on Access and Benefit-Sharing as Related to Genetic Resources. Monetary and Non-monetary Benefits

1. Monetary benefits may include, but not be limited to:

(a) Access fees/fee per sample collected or otherwise acquired;
(b) Up-front payments;
(c) Milestone payments;
(d) Payment of royalties;
(e) License fees in case of commercialization;
(f) Special fees to be paid to trust funds supporting conservation and sustainable use of biodiversity;
(g) Salaries and preferential terms where mutually agreed;
(h) Research funding;
(i) Joint ventures;
(j) Joint ownership of relevant intellectual property rights.

2. Non-monetary benefits may include, but not be limited to:

(a) Sharing of research and development results;
(b) Collaboration, cooperation, and contribution in scientific research and development programmes, particularly biotechnological research activities, where possible in the provider country;
(c) Participation in product development;
(d) Collaboration, cooperation, and contribution in education and training;
(e) Admittance to *ex situ* facilities of genetic resources and to databases;
(f) Transfer to the provider of the genetic resources of knowledge and technology under fair and most favourable terms, including on concessional and preferential terms where agreed, in particular, knowledge and technology that make use of genetic resources, including biotechnology, or that are relevant to the conservation and sustainable utilization of biological diversity;
(g) Strengthening capacities for technology transfer to user developing country Parties and to Parties that are countries with economies in transition and technology development in the country of origin that provides genetic resources. Also to facilitate abilities of indigenous and local communities to conserve and sustainably use their genetic resources;
(h) Institutional capacity-building;
(i) Human and material resources to strengthen the capacities for the administration and enforcement of access regulations;
(j) Training related to genetic resources with the full participation of providing Parties and, where possible, in such Parties;

(k) Access to scientific information relevant to conservation and sustainable use of biological diversity, including biological inventories and taxonomic studies;
(l)   Contributions to the local economy;
(m) Research directed towards priority needs, such as health and food security, taking into account domestic uses of genetic resources in provider countries;
(n) Institutional and professional relationships that can arise from an access and benefit-sharing agreement and subsequent collaborative activities;
(o) Food and livelihood security benefits;
(p) Social recognition;
(q) Joint ownership of relevant intellectual property rights.

the nature and magnitude of benefits and how these are divided among potential beneficiaries varies considerably from case to case, there are often broad commonalities between agreements. For example, the contracts used by the different ICBGs vary in structure and content, but since they were all developed in part to offset inherent bias against societies less technologically advanced in IPR and related regimes, "most include provisions for an inventorship role on patents by traditional people where appropriate, and others have evolved various novel means of recognition and/or control by indigenous organizations (eg know how licenses, grant back provisions, authorship, etc…" (Rosenthal 1999).[5] The policy of the ICBG program is that when traditional ethnomedical knowledge is involved in a patentable invention, if the traditional knowledge provider cannot be recognized as an inventor, the contribution should be treated as valuable "know how," the contribution should be credited in any related publications and in the patent as prior art, and the providers should be compensated for their contributions, as appropriate. Prior art citations formalize the contribution of such knowledge but do not claim any monopoly rights to its use. The absence of important prior art citations may constitute grounds to deny or invalidate a patent (Rosenthal and others 1999, p. 18).

The Latin American ICBG contracts divide the royalties that flow from any sales of products from genetic resources and traditional knowledge sourced under the agreement into a "collectors' share" (5 percent), an "inventors' share" (in which all named inventors will divide the inventors' share of 45 percent), and a "conservation share," which stipulates that a conservation fund will receive 50 percent of royalties (Timmerman and others 1999).

BOX 6.4   Benefit-Sharing Agreement between the Kani and the Tropical Botanic Garden and Research Institute

The Kanis, with a population of 16,181, are a traditionally nomadic tribal community, who now lead a primarily settled life in tribal hamlets, each consisting of 10 to 20 families, in and around the forests of the Western Ghats (southwestern India). A lead provided by the Kanis relating to the antifatigue properties of a wild plant, *Trichopus zeylanicus,* led to the development of the drug Jeevani by the TBGRI, which transferred the manufacturing license to the Aryavaidya Pharmacy, Coimbatore Ltd. for a license fee of Rs 10 lakh (1 million rupees, or approximately US$25,000). The TBGRI agreed to share 50 percent of the license fee and royalty with the tribal community.

Kanis in different areas of Thiruvanathapuram district held differing opinions on the arrangement with TBGRI, which primarily interacted with Kanis from the Kuttichal Gram Panchayat area, and hired as consultants three Kanis from this area who imparted the knowledge of *Aarogyappacha.* This group of Kanis supported and were appreciative of TBGRI's role. However, Kanis in other Panchayat areas felt overlooked and consequently believed that the benefit-sharing arrangement was not sufficiently inclusive or participatory. In September 1995, a group of nine medicine men (called *Plathis*) of the Kani tribe wrote a letter to the Chief Minister of Kerala, objecting to the sale of their knowledge to "private companies." TBGRI acknowledged these problems and wanted to organize a trust fund to overcome them.

In 1997, the Kerala Kani Samudaya Kshema Trust was registered. It is fully managed by Kani tribes and is the first trust established by the tribes. It marks the first time that the different Kani clans have worked together in this way. More than 700 Kani families, which constitute more than 65 percent of the Kani population in Western Ghats, are members. Fifty percent of the license fee of nearly IRs 10 lakh (US$33,000) received by TBGRI, Trivandrum, was transferred to the Kani Trust in February 1999. This amount is kept as fixed deposit by the trust in a bank. The interest accrued is used for the welfare activities of the members of the Kani tribes. In 2000 the interest received (about Rs 50,000) was given to the three Kani consultants who initially provided the knowledge. The Kani Trust is now regularly receiving 50 percent of the royalty through TBGRI. As of the end of 2001, IRs 1,350,000 of royalties had been paid into the trust. The Kani Trust Society has launched various self-employment schemes for unemployed Kani youth and has granted them loans from the interest generated from the fixed deposit and the royalties. Special financial assistance of IRs 25,000 was given for the welfare of two young tribal girls whose mother was killed by a wild elephant.

Sales of Jeevani have grown. There are big orders from different parts of India and from Japan, the United States, and other international markets. Because of limited supply of the raw material, the manufacturing company is unable to meet the growing demand. The Forest Department has now agreed to permit the Kani to cultivate the plant and sell the raw drugs in semiprocessed form to the manufacturer. This cultivation project, coordinated by the Kani Trust, will not only meet the increasing demand for the raw material, but will also provide additional income to a large number of Kani tribespeople.

Sources: Anuradha 1998; personal communication, R. V. Anuradha, March 15, 1999; personal communication, Dr. Pushphangadan, May 16, 2002; ten Kate 1999; and case study submitted to the CBD Secretariat by the government of India, 1998.

The ICBG-Africa project involves more than 20 collaborating institutions, ranging from African universities and protected areas to U.S. universities and research institutes, with benefit sharing to take place in the short and long term:

- **Short-term benefits:** The emphasis for short-term benefits is on capacity building rather than short-term cash payments, to help Nigeria and Cameroon add value to their resources before trading the samples. In addition, small cash payments were made to informants and collectors, and support was provided for community development projects. The medical member(s) of the ethnobotanical team consulted local healers and provided volunteer medical assistance when requested.
- **Long-term benefits:** Twenty percent of any royalties from licenses of products developed under the project are to be distributed among those who contributed intellectually to the invention, taking into account their relative contribution and ensuring that the investors receive not less than 15 percent. Fifty percent goes to the Bioresources Development and Conservation Programmes (one of the project partners) to be used solely for programs and projects to promote sustainable economic development relating to biodiversity conservation in Nigeria and Cameroon, to be distributed through a trust fund—the Global Fund for Health, whose board comprises representatives from the United States, Cameroon, and Nigeria. The remaining 30 percent of royalties are to be donated to the Tropical Disease Drug Development Program at the U.S. Walter Reed Army Institute of Research to further research into understudied developing country diseases.

In the meantime, market and industry forces have taken the case in new directions, outside the control of the San and others in southern Africa. Pfizer recently announced it would return the rights to develop P57 to Phytopharm, following closure of its Natureceuticals groups (www.phytopharm.com), and numerous companies have begun to sell raw forms of Hoodia products on the Internet (for example, www.hoodiashop.com and www.hoodis-dietpills.com). Although products such as Hoodia Diet Tabs™ and Hoodoba™ Hoodia Diet Pills make claims about their products' efficacy by citing the long history of traditional use of Hoodia by the San, no established partnerships for benefit sharing, and no prospects for access and benefit-sharing agreements exist in these cases.

Conclusions

A growing number of national laws and international guidelines require the acquisition of prior informed consent and the sharing of benefits with local communities when researchers wish to access genetic resources on their land or their traditional knowledge about those resources. The range of legal, ethical, and policy developments that have taken place over the past two decades, particularly since the advent of the CBD, have created an environment that is more conducive to equitable partnerships with local communities. The increasing use of access and benefit-sharing agreements—unheard of 10 years ago, but now often a requirement—is one example of this development. Such agreements can generate real benefits through partnerships.

From the perspective of communities, the most enabling policy environment in the future will be a balanced and flexible package of international, national, and institutional measures. Such a package would include participatory national strategies and laws on access and benefit sharing, the International Treaty on Plant Genetic Resources for Food and Agriculture, and the Bonn Guidelines, as well as codes of conduct and model agreements that translate these into clear actions for researchers, companies, and communities themselves to use in the specific context of their work.

Benefit sharing has the potential to help communities in the short term by offering some employment (collaboration in collecting and cultivating samples) and grants for facilities needed by the community (help with clinics, schools, and transport). In the longer term, royalties from the sales of any successful commercial products could be channeled through trust funds for community development and biodiversity conservation.

However, two major limitations inhibit the value of bioprospecting agreements to local communities. The first barrier is the set of constraints in the policy environment, which can be corrected by improving laws and agreements. A number of challenges still remain for the implementation of access legislation and other laws that empower communities. One challenge is to ensure that national authorities have the resources to administer the laws, and to take a suitably flexible approach that enables the negotiation of fair partnerships on a case-by-case basis to meet the needs of all partners in the specific case. Those individuals or organizations that can grant prior informed consent on behalf of indigenous and local communities must also be established, as must the manner in which benefits can most appropriately be shared with them. Another challenge is to ensure that more benefits reach local communities and also that some are dedicated to conservation.

The second constraint on the benefits available to communities from bioprospecting results from the limited demand by industry for access to genetic resources from communities' land or their associated knowledge. Demand for genetic resources in general is limited, and demand for traditional knowledge more so. Traditional knowledge is regularly used in the discovery and development of products, but it is generally already in the public domain and sourced through publications. It is rare for traditional knowledge to be sourced from interviews with local and indigenous communities themselves in such a way as to require prior informed consent and trigger benefit-sharing negotiations.

To optimize the benefits they receive from those wishing to access their genetic resources and knowledge, communities and their representatives should work with policymakers to establish workable mechanisms for ensuring prior informed consent and for channeling benefits. They should also protect their knowledge and agree on a strategy for its disclosure. Provided it is used with care, "defensive publication" may be a helpful tool. This involves positive disclosure of information, generally through publication, so that users cannot claim IPRs on it in the form received. Alternatively, the knowledge can be kept as a trade secret, so that access can be acquired only with permission that can trigger benefit-sharing negotiations.

Notes

1. Personal communication, Graham Dutfield, May 2002.

2. Countries and regional groups already regulating access to genetic resources to ensure prior informed consent and benefit sharing include the Andean Pact (Bolivia, Colombia, Ecuador, Peru, República Bolivariana de Venezuela); Australia (the States of Western Australia and Queensland); Brazil (at the federal level and the States of Acre and Amapa); Cameroon; Costa Rica; the Republic of Korea; Malaysia (the State of Sarawak); Mexico; the Philippines; and the United States (within Yellowstone and other national parks). Those planning to regulate access to genetic resources to ensure prior informed consent and benefit sharing include the member countries of the Association of Southeast Asian Nations (ASEAN); Australia (the Commonwealth); Côte d'Ivoire; Cuba; Eritrea; Ethiopia; Fiji; The Gambia; Guatemala; India; Indonesia; Kenya; Lao PDR; Lesotho; Malawi; Malaysia (at the national level and the State of Sabah); Mozambique; Namibia; Nicaragua; Nigeria; the Organization of African Unity; Pakistan, Papua New Guinea; Republic of Yemen; Samoa; the Seychelles; the Solomon Islands; South Africa; Sri Lanka; Tanzania; Thailand; Uganda; Vanuatu; and Vietnam. Belize, China, El Salvador, Ghana, Guyana, Hungary, Iceland, Panama, the Russian Federation, and Zimbabwe may also be planning to regulate access to genetic resources in the near future. (Personal communication, Lyle Glowka, February 2001.)

3. Personal communication, Tod Hannum, GlaxoSmithKline, February 28, 2002.
4. Personal communication, J. Rosenthal, National Institutes of Health, 2002.
5. Personal communication, J. Rosenthal, National Institutes of Health, 2002.

References

Alexiades, M. N., and S. A. Laird. 2002. "Laying the Foundation: Equitable Biodiversity Research Relationships." In S. A. Laird, ed., *Biodiversity and Traditional Knowledge: Equitable Partnerships in Practice*. London: Earthscan.

Anuradha, R. V. 1998. "Sharing with the Kanis. A Case Study from Kerala, India." Case study submitted to the fourth meeting of the Conference of the Parties to the Convention on Biological Diversity (CBD). Secretariat of the CBD, Montreal.

Barber, C. V., L. Glowka, and A. G. M. LaVina. 2002. "Developing and Implementing National Measures for Genetic Resources Access Regulation and Benefit Sharing." In S. A. Laird, ed., *Biodiversity and Traditional Knowledge: Equitable Partnerships in Practice*. London: Earthscan.

Barnett, Antony. 2001. "In Africa the Hoodia Cactus Keeps Men Alive. Now Its Secret is 'Stolen' to Make Us Thin." *Observer*, June 17, 2001.

Commission on Intellectual Property Rights. 2002. "Final Report: Integrating Intellectual Property Rights and Development Policy." Available at http://www.iprcommission.org/graphic/documents/final_report.htm.

Cox, P. A. 1994. "The Ethnobotanical Approach to Drug Discovery: Strengths and Limitations," In *Ethnobotany and the Search for New Drugs*, Ciba Foundation Symposium 185. New York: Wiley.

Downes, D. R., and S. A. Laird. 1999. "Innovative Mechanisms for Sharing Benefits of Biodiversity and Related Knowledge: Case Studies on Geographical Indications and Trademarks." Prepared for United Nations Conference on Trade and Development Biotrade Initiative, Geneva.

Dutfield, G. 2000. *Intellectual Property Rights, Trade and Biodiversity: Seeds and Plant Varieties*. London: Earthscan.

————. 2002. "Indigenous Peoples' Declarations and Statements on Equitable Research Relationships." In S. A. Laird, ed., *Biodiversity and Traditional Knowledge: Equitable Partnerships in Practice*. London: Earthscan.

Farnsworth, N. R., O. Akerele, A. S. Bingel, D. D. Soejarto, and Z. Guo. 1985. "Medicinal Plants in Therapy." *Bulletin of the World Health Organization* 63:965–81.

Gollin, M. A. 2002. "Elements of Commercial Biodiversity Prospecting Agreements." In S. A. Laird, ed., *Biodiversity and Traditional Knowledge: Equitable Partnerships in Practice*. London: Earthscan.

Grifo, F., D. Newman, A. S. Fairfield, B. Bhattacharya, and J. T. Grupenhoff. 1996. "The Origins of Prescription Drugs." In F. Grifo and J. Rosenthal, eds., *Biodiversity and Human Health*. Washington, D.C.: Island Press.

Kahn, Tamar. 2002. "Prickly Dispute Finally Laid to Rest: San Reach Agreement with CSIR over Use of Appetite-Suppressing Cactus." *Business Day*, Johannesburg, Opinion, March 22, 2002.

ten Kate, K. 1999. "Legal Aspects of Regulating Access to Genetic Resources and Benefit-Sharing: The Convention on Biological Diversity, National and Regional Laws and Material Transfer Agreements." In K. ten Kate and S. A. Laird, *The Commercial Use of Biodiversity: Access to Genetic Resources and Benefit-Sharing*. London: Earthscan.

ten Kate, K., and S. A. Laird. 1999. *The Commercial Use of Biodiversity: Access to Genetic Resources and Benefit-Sharing*. London: Earthscan.

ten Kate, K., and A. Wells. 2001. "Preparing a National Strategy on Access to Genetic Resources and Benefit-Sharing. A Pilot Study." Royal Botanic Gardens, Kew and United Nations Development Programme/United Nations Environment Programme Biodiversity Planning Support Programme.

Laird, S. A., ed. 2002. *Biodiversity and Traditional Knowledge: Equitable Partnerships in Practice*. London: Earthscan.

Laird, S. A., and K. ten Kate. 2002. "Biodiversity Prospecting: The Commercial Use of Genetic Resources and Best Practice in Benefit-Sharing." In S. A. Laird, ed., *Biodiversity and Traditional Knowledge: Equitable Partnerships in Practice.* London: Earthscan.

Laird, S. A., and T. Mahop. 2001. "The Limbe Botanic and Zoological Gardens Policy on Access to Genetic Resources and Benefit-Sharing." Limbe, South West Province, Cameroon.

Laird, S. A., and D. A. Posey. 2002. "Professional Society Standards for Biodiversity Research: Codes of Ethics and Research Guidelines." In S. A. Laird, ed., *Biodiversity and Traditional Knowledge: Equitable Partnerships in Practice.* London: Earthscan.

Latorre García, F., C. Williams, K. ten Kate, and P. Cheyne. 2001. *Results of the Pilot Project for Botanic Gardens: Principles on Access to Genetic Resources and Benefit-Sharing, Common Policy Guidelines to Assist with Their Implementation and Explanatory Text.* Royal Botanic Gardens, Kew. 78 pp.

Madeley, John. 2002. "Body and Mind: Living Off the Fat of the Land: John Madeley on the Bushmen's Battle with Business over a Diet Pill Made from a Kalahari Plant." *Financial Times*, December 1, 2001.

Moran, W. 1993. "Rural Space as Intellectual Property." *Political Geography* 12:263–77.

Posey, D. A. 1996. "Traditional Resource Rights: International Instruments for Protection and Compensation for Indigenous Peoples and Local Communities." IUCN-The World Conservation Union, Gland, Switzerland.

Reid, W. V., S. A. Laird, C. A. Meyer, R. Games, A. Sittenfeld, D. H. Janzen, M. A. Gollin, and C. Juma, eds. 1993. *Biodiversity Prospecting: Using Genetic Resources for Sustainable Development.* Washington, D.C.: World Resources Institute.

Rosenthal, J. P., ed. 1999. *Drug Discovery, Economic Development and Conservation: The International Cooperative Biodiversity Groups.* Special issue of *Pharmaceutical Biology* 37.

Rosenthal, J. P., D. Beck, A. Bhat, J. Biswas, L. Brady, K. Bridbord, S. Collins, G. Cragg, J. Edwards, A. Fairfield, M. Gottlieb, L. A. Gschwind, Y. Hallock, R. Hawks, R. Hegyeli, G. Johnson, G. T. Keusch, E. E. Lyons, R. Miller, J. Rodman, J. Roskoski, and D. Siegel-Causey. 1999. "Combining High Risk Science with Ambitious Social and Economic Goals." In J. P. Rosenthal, ed., *Drug Discovery, Economic Development and Conservation: The International Cooperative Biodiversity Groups.* Special issue of *Pharmaceutical Biology* 37:6–21.

Ruiz Muller, Manuel. 2000. "Regulating Bioprospecting and Protecting Indigenous Peoples' Knowledge in the Andean Community: Decision 391 and Its Overall Impacts in the Region." Paper presented at Expert Meeting on Traditional Knowledge, United Nations Conference on Trade and Development Biotrade Initiative. Geneva, October-November 2000.

South African San Council and the CSIR (Council for Scientific and Industrial Research). 2003. "The San and the CSIR Announce a Benefit-Sharing Agreement for Potential Anti-Obesity Drug." Press release, March 24, 2003, South Africa.

Timmermann, B. N., G. Wachter, S. Valcic, B. Hutchinson, C. Casler, J. Henzel, S. Ram, F. Currim, R. Manak, S. Franzblau, W. Maiese, D. Galinis, E. Suarez, R. Fortunato, E. Saavedra, R. Bye, R. Mata, and G. Montenegro. 1999. "The Latin American ICBG: The First Five Years." In J. P. Rosenthal, ed., *Drug Discovery, Economic Development and Conservation: The International Cooperative Biodiversity Groups.* Special issue of *Pharmaceutical Biology* 37:35–54.

Tobin, Brendan. 2002. "Biodiversity Prospecting Contracts: The Search for Equitable Agreements." In S. A. Laird, ed., *Biodiversity and Traditional Knowledge: Equitable Partnerships in Practice.* London: Earthscan.

Wiser, Glenn. 2002. "The Ayahuasca Patent Case: Indigenous People's Stand against Misappropriation." In S. A. Laird, ed., *Biodiversity and Traditional Knowledge: Equitable Partnerships in Practice.* London: Earthscan.

Wynberg, Rachel. 2002. "Institutional Response to Benefit-Sharing in South Africa." In S. A. Laird, ed., *Biodiversity and Traditional Knowledge: Equitable Partnerships in Practice.* London: Earthscan.

———. 2003. "Sharing the Crumbs with the San." Biowatch South Africa. Available at www.biowatch.org.za.

7

BIOPIRACY AND COMMERCIALIZATION OF ETHNOBOTANICAL KNOWLEDGE

Philip Schuler

This volume explores obstacles and opportunities confronting people in developing countries who want to earn more from their creativity and intellectual property (IP). Many of the cases presented in other chapters underscore the obstacles people face when trying to commercialize traditional knowledge—some flowing from the problem of applying conventional intellectual property right (IPR) laws, others rooted in the basic commercial environment. This chapter takes a slightly different approach. It analyzes where inventors or entrepreneurs succeeded in overcoming these difficulties, but did so in rich countries rather than in developing countries. In all of these cases, researchers or businesses in an industrial country received patents on ethnobotanical knowledge[1] or plants that originated in a developing country, and to varying extents were able to bring a product to market. A popular term applied to these cases is "biopiracy"—a spin on "bioprospecting," conveying the view that the patents were not merely inappropriate but that the patentees were outright thieves.[2]

What do these celebrated cases of biopiracy tell us about the capacity of developing countries to earn more from their knowledge and creativity? Did rich countries succeed where poor countries failed because IPR regimes in the latter provide inadequate protection? Did developing countries fail to benefit because industrial countries grant too much IP protection too easily? Does commercial success depend primarily on business factors unrelated to IP rules? Are there policies that could help developing countries earn more in similar cases? We also want to know how patent awards in rich countries affect prospects for commercialization in poor countries. This chapter will argue that, while property rights regimes are flawed in both rich and poor countries, formal legal structures do not determine who benefits from commercialization of traditional knowledge.

Before getting into the specific cases, one must first address the criticism that commercializing traditional knowledge is difficult because it simply has no commercial value. The literature is replete with examples of the commercial value of ethnobotanical knowledge (amounts are in U.S. dollars):

- "Studies have shown that as many as 74 percent of the plant derived human drugs are used for the same purpose for which native people discovered their use" (Society for Research and Initiatives for Sustainable Technologies and Institutions [SRISTI] n.d.).
- "At least 7,000 medical compounds used in Western medicine are derived from plants. The value of developing-country germplasm to the pharmaceutical industry in the early 1990s was estimated to be at least $32,000 million per year. Yet developing countries were paid only a fraction of this amount for the raw materials and knowledge they contribute" (Rural Advancement Foundation International [RAFI] 1994).
- "For example, 25 percent of US prescription drugs are said to have active ingredients from Indian plants. The sale of these drugs amounted to $4.2 billion in1980 and $15.5 billion in 1990. In the EU, Australia, Canada, and the US, the market value for both prescription and over-the-counter drugs based on Indian plants amounts to $70 billion."[3] (Srinivas 2000)
- "The pharmaceutical TNCs of the North have thus appropriated colossal wealth from collection of tropical biodiversity which is expected to reach an amount of $47 billion by the year 2000" (*The Statesman* 1998).

There is at least prima facie evidence that traditional knowledge and the genetic material identified by traditional knowledge can be commercialized. The question to address is how to accomplish this.[4]

The central criticism in the biopiracy literature is that businesses in industrial countries are getting rich off of poor peoples' knowledge at developing countries' expense. The stylized story is one where researchers learn of a traditional herbal remedy or food crop, perform only a limited amount of laboratory testing or selective breeding to determine how the remedy works or how to produce it in an industrial setting, and then receive a patent on what is little more than the traditional product. It comes as no surprise that research centers and companies in industrial countries seek IPRs over any new product they develop, whether or not it was ultimately derived from publicly available knowledge, but in some cases applicants seek protection over the original knowledge itself. Some of these patents have been challenged successfully on the grounds that the innovations claimed in the patents are not novel because of their widespread prior public use in developing countries.

The cases reviewed below support the critics' complaint that industrial country governments are too quick to grant patents. In place of a complete examination of an applicant's claims, patent offices tend to rely on postaward litigation to resolve issues of patentability. Challenging patents is expensive, particularly for organizations and individuals in developing countries, and there are countless claims voiced about biopiracy that never result in an official challenge.

The available evidence provides far less support for claims that these biopiracy patents make rich people richer at poor peoples' expense. The new commercial products made using these patents did not displace traditional products in developing countries. In only one case was a biopiracy patent used to prevent people in a developing country from turning their traditional knowledge into a commercial product. Furthermore, all cases indicate that commercialization in industrial countries requires more than simply receiving a patent—holding an IPR is neither necessary nor sufficient.

I move now to some specific cases.

Biopesticides from the Neem Tree

Everyone's favorite biopiracy story involves U.S. and European patents on pesticides made from neem seeds. The neem tree (*Azadiracthta indica*, called Margosa in English) is a member of the mahogany family that is indigenous to India, although the tree is grown in arid regions throughout Africa and Asia. It is mentioned in Indian texts written more than 2,000 years ago. Products are made from every part of the tree. Neem products have been used in human and veterinary medicine, toiletries, and cosmetics and as an insect repellent and fungicide in agriculture.

Its use as a fungicide is at the heart of the present controversy. Indian farmers traditionally soaked neem seeds in water and alcohol and then sprayed the emulsion on their plants. Western businessmen were attracted to neem because, unlike most chemical pesticides, it has few damaging side effects.

The Patent Controversy

The present controversy involves two patents held by the specialty chemicals company W.R. Grace: European patent EP0436257 and U.S. patent 5,124,349.[5] Both of these controversial patents were awarded for controlling fungi on plants using a stable extract from neem seeds. Both applications were filed in 1990; the U.S.

patent was awarded in 1992 and the European patent in 1994. Both sets of patent documents acknowledge that pesticides have been made from neem tree products for years. They point out that the drawback of the traditional process is that the fungicide begins to degrade if the emulsion is not used right away; commercial production requires a storage-stable product. The documents go on to enumerate various steps for processing neem seeds using a variety of solvents at a variety of strengths, steps that the inventors claim are novel.

There were public demonstrations against Grace's joint venture in India as early as 1993, and a collection of advocacy groups joined together in 1995 to challenge the European and U.S. patents on the grounds that the product/process was not novel.[6] Indians had been using neem products in the same fashion for centuries, and Grace's extraction process was not radically different from the traditional process, they argued. The company's response was that its procedure extracts azadiracthin in a way that permits longer storage life than traditional procedures, extending it from a few days to at least two years, and that its patent (specifically the U.S. patent 5,124,349) in no way prevented Indian farmers from producing and distributing their own extracts (Burns 1995; *PR Newswire* 1995).[7] The European Patent Office (EPO) revoked patent EP0436257 in May 2000. The EPO's press release states: "The patent was revoked since the claims were not novel in view of public prior use, which had taken place in India" (EPO 2000; *Deccan Chronicle* 2000). The U.S. patent remains valid.

It is important to point out that even though these two patents have received all of the media attention, they are by no means the only neem patents issued in the United States and Europe. As of September 2002, the U.S. Patent and Trademark Office (USPTO) database listed more than 400 U.S. patents involving either neem or, more commonly, azadiracthin (the pesticidal agent in neem). The EPO database contains several hundred patents as well. The oldest U.S. neem patent was granted to Japanese researchers in 1980 for toothpastes containing neem, among many other ingredients. Robert Larson secured the first patent involving azadiracthin in 1985 (which he later sold to W.R. Grace) for a method of extracting azadiracthin from neem seeds without it losing its effectiveness as a pesticide. There are also more than 50 Indian patents on neem products or methods of producing neem-based pesticides.

History of Commercialization

Unlike some of the other cases involving ethnobotanicals, there was already quite a bit of research, development, and commercial production of neem products in the home country before they became popular in industrial countries. There have been efforts to develop neem products commercially in India for more than 70 years.

Early work seems to have been motivated by the goal of import substitution—encouraging the use of traditional, village-level products in place of their imported counterparts (in much the same spirit as Gandhi's *khadi* [homespun fabric] campaigns; Shiva n.d.). In more recent years there has also been study and commercial development of neem in India beyond traditional village-level uses. The first report in the scientific literature of neem's insect-repelling capabilities was published by two Indian scientists in 1928, and the first scientific tests of its antifungal properties were conducted by Indian scientists in 1962 (National Research Council [NRC] 1992). The Indian firm Ajay Bio-Tech has been making a fungicide derived from neem since 1990.[8] In 1993, P.J. Margo Private Ltd. (W.R. Grace's Indian partner) began producing and marketing stabilized neem biopesticides in India (Kocken and van Roozendaal 1997).

Research and development work in industrial countries followed somewhat later. In 1951 Heinrich Schmutter, a German scientist, conducted the first scientific studies of neem outside of India after he observed that neem trees were the only ones surviving a plague of locusts in Sudan. Efforts to commercialize neem products in the West began in the 1970s. A businessman from the United States learned of neem's antifungal properties while on a visit to India in 1971. He then brought back samples, tested them, and began investigating commercial applications.[9] The U.S. Department of Agriculture (USDA) began studying neem as a source for biopesticides in 1975. Robert Larson (of Vikwood Botanicals in Wisconsin) developed the first storage-stable extract of azadiracthin in the United States, which he patented in 1985.[10] The U.S. Environmental Protection Agency (EPA) first approved neem's use as a pesticide (under the trade name of Margosan-O) in 1985 (NRC 1992). At about this point neem's popularity really took off, aided in part by a 1992 NRC study, ambitiously titled *Neem: A Tree for Solving Global Problems*. There are now countless neem products made and sold in industrial countries, ranging from cosmetics to herbal remedies to pesticides. Box 7.1 below shows the timeline of patents, investments, and mergers involved in this case.

Economic Impact

What is the economic impact of the biopiracy patents and commercialization of neem fungicides in industrial countries on efforts to commercialize neem pesticides in India? Since there are quite a few other patents on neem-related products and processes, holding or losing one patent has little effect on neem producers' ability to assert their property rights and sell commercially.[11] Furthermore, by the time the EPO revoked its neem patent in 2000, W.R. Grace had long since exited

BOX 7.1   Chronology of Commercialization of Neem Biopesticide

1985:   Robert Larson receives patent for stable neem extract.

1989:   **W.R. Grace** buys Larson's patents, trademarks, and registrations.

1991:   Grace awards license to sell neem-based products to **Ringer Corp.**, which will focus on home/gardening market.

1992:   **Agridyne** goes public after receiving EPA registrations for Azatech and Azatin.

1992:   Ringer begins selling Neemix and Bioneem to gardeners through mail-order channels.

1993:   Grace announces joint venture with **P.J. Margo Pvt. Ltd**. (Karnataka, India) to build first commercial facility for producing neem biopesticides. **Margo Biocontrols** is the subsidiary dealing with neem and other biopesticides. Demonstrations begin against Grace in India.

1993:   Agridyne announces joint venture with **Tata Oil Mills** (Bombay). It receives a patent on a neem-extract purification procedure (5,229,007) and EPA registration for Align (agricultural market).

1993:   **Hindustan Lever Ltd**. (a subsidiary of Unilever PLC) purchases Tata Oil Mills from the Tata Group. (Hindustan Lever holds a 1991 Indian patent on neem extraction.)

1994:   Agridyne receives its second U.S. patent for neem extraction (5,352,697) and licenses its neem patents to **Rohm & Haas**. (Rohm & Haas presently holds four Indian patents on neem products or processes.) Agridyne announces agreement with **Farnam Companies** to market animal husbandry biopesticides.

1994:   Grace and Agridyne engage in a legal quarrel over patent infringement.

1995:   Grace and Agridyne settle patent dispute. Grace licenses patents 5,001,146 and 5,124,349 to Agridyne.

1995:   **Biosys** buys out Agridyne.

1996:   Grace sells biopesticides division to **Thermo Ecotek**, which folds it into its new subsidiary, **Thermo Trilogy**.

1997:   Biosys declares bankruptcy and sells assets to Thermo Trilogy.

1998:   Ringer changes its name to **Verdant Brands**, which sells products under a variety of brand names.

2000:   Verdant Brands sells its retail products division to **Woodstream**; it continues to market commercial products through the **Consep** subsidiary.

2000:   Thermo Electron announces that Thermo Trilogy is a "non-core" business and seeks buyer.

2001:   **Mitsui** purchases Thermo Trilogy and creates a subsidiary, **Certis**, to produce and sell pesticides.

2001:   Verdant auctions off Consep's assets and ceases operations.

2001:   Grace files for Chapter 11 bankruptcy protection because of asbestos-related claims.

the biopesticides business (as had its erstwhile competitor Agridyne), so the EPO's decision had no effect on Grace's business. One dimension of the question is how the larger collection of neem patents has affected traditional users and producers. Here one must recognize that there is no evidence that Grace, Agridyne, Thermo Trilogy, or any other U.S. companies holding patents on neem products have attempted to block Indians from producing neem-based biopesticides or exporting them to the United States or Europe. Certainly there is no way that they could have legally blocked farmers from mixing their own fungicides using a traditional formula on the strength of their patents, given that the patents purport to cover novel and different processes of extracting the active ingredients.

A second dimension is whether commercialization in the United States prevented Indian firms from developing their own commercial neem fungicides. The answer is no. The Indian firm Ajay Bio-Tech has been making a fungicide derived from neem since 1990 (*Europe Agri* 2000). Could Indian companies have produced for export to industrial countries? In fact, they do. E.I.D. Parry (based in Chennai/Madras) manufactures Neemazol in India for both the domestic and world markets. In 2001 it opened a subsidiary in Sacramento to market Neemazol in the United States, and it plans to manufacture the product in the United States for sale throughout the Americas (*Business Line* 2001a).[12] At least three other Indian companies sell neem-based pesticides to the world market.[13] The Indian start-up firm Fortune Biotech holds a U.S. patent and EPA registration for Fortune Aza, and has plans to export to the U.S. market. There is no evidence that Grace or other companies in the United States have attempted to assert their patent rights to block these Indian products. There *were* accusations of patent infringement, but these were accusations made by U.S. producers against each other: Grace and Agridyne engaged in a patent infringement lawsuit before settling out of court (Grace agreed to license its patents to Agridyne and shortly thereafter it sold its biopesticides business).

There are undoubtedly secondary economic effects. Commercialization in industrial countries generates a demand for neem seeds in India. Revenue from sales of neem extract does not compensate Indians for the knowledge about neem that they had developed over the centuries, of course, but it is revenue that the country might not have otherwise received.

This can have a detrimental effect on traditional users, however. W.R. Grace built a large facility in India to process neem seeds and has bid up the price of seeds out of the reach of former users in India (IFOAM n.d.). Over the past 20 years, the price of neem seeds rose from Rs 300 per ton to more than Rs 8,000 per ton[14] (Shiva n.d.). Of course, one would have observed this impact on prices even if only Indian firms had commercialized the new product.

Lessons of Neem

The neem case clearly shows that it is too easy to win a patent in the United States and Western Europe.

This case also reveals that the patents granted in industrial countries did not prevent commercialization of neem in India. Indian businesses are similarly unlikely to benefit from the cancellation of the European patent.

Is this a failure of IPR regimes? Is there an IPR solution? To some extent this patenting controversy arose because it is too easy to get a patent in the United States and Europe but too hard in India. The EPO ultimately rejected one of W.R. Grace's patents on the grounds that "the claims were not novel in view of public prior use, which had taken place in India" (EPO 2000). As is discussed below, patent regimes in these countries are coming to rely less on examination of patent applications and more on postaward litigation. This applies to all patents, not just those involving ethnobotanical knowledge. An additional failing of industrial country patent regimes is their apparent xenophobia—the examination process tends to discount information from developing countries.

But this case also suggests that, even if too much IPR protection is granted too freely in the industrial countries, this does not prevent people in developing countries from commercializing local knowledge. Indian companies were not deterred from entering the market for producing neem-based biopesticides.

Could Indians have worked out contracts with foreign investors that would have compensated Indians for their original knowledge? This is unlikely in the case of the original patent, given the way the knowledge was transmitted to the West. At one time both Agridyne and Grace were reportedly prospecting for new compounds with the aid of ethnobotanists (*Business Week* 1993). Had they pursued this line of research, there might have been scope for benefit-sharing arrangements, as discussed in the chapter in this volume by ten Kate and Laird.

Medicinal Uses of Turmeric

The root of the turmeric plant (*Curcuma longa*) has long been used in Asian societies in cooking, cosmetics, and medicine. Turmeric's uses as a spice and coloring agent are widely known. While there is perhaps less familiarity with its medicinal uses in industrial countries, in traditional Indian Ayurvedic medicine turmeric is used to treat anemia, asthma, burns, conjunctivitis, dental problems, diabetes, diarrhea, pain, and many other ailments. Turmeric does enjoy popularity among sellers of dietary supplements, where its traditional Ayurvedic uses are touted to lend credence to marketing claims.[15] In recent years, turmeric has attracted the attention of the mainstream medical community as well. There are presently more than 350 scientific or medical studies indexed in the Medline database involving turmeric or curcoma, its active ingredient, although no turmeric-based medical therapies have yet been approved for sale as drugs in the United States.[16]

In 1995 two Indian scientists at an American university received a U.S. patent for a method of using turmeric to treat wounds. In response to a challenge filed by an Indian research organization, the USPTO overturned the patent in 1997. This event is frequently billed as the first case of successfully reversing a biopiracy patent (Indian Council for Scientific and Industrial Research [CSIR] n.d.). What is interesting about this case is the transmission mechanism: instead of researchers or businesspeople scouring the globe in search of new products, Indian researchers brought the ethnobotanical knowledge to the industrial country.

The Patent Controversy

Suma K. Das and Hari Har P. Choly, two scientists working at the University of Mississippi Medical Center, were granted U.S. patent 5,401,504 in March 1995 for the use of turmeric in treating wounds. Their patent records claim a method of healing wounds, specifically skin ulcers, by administering a wound healing agent (orally and topically) that contains an effective amount of turmeric. The patent application details controlled laboratory experiments performed on rats and two clinical case histories documenting how turmeric was used successfully on humans after other therapies had failed. To nonexpert eyes this appears to represent only a modest step beyond confirming what was already well known among medical practitioners in India. The New Delhi–based CSIR challenged this patent, citing Ayurvedic texts as evidence that the invention lacked novelty. The USPTO initiated an examination in 1996 and ruled against the inventors in August of the following year. CSIR reportedly spent Rs 500,000 to overturn the patent (Sharma 2001).[17]

I should point out that this is by no means the only patent award involving turmeric, even if it is the only one to spark such a controversy. There are presently close to 400 U.S. patents involving turmeric, the earliest of which was approved in 1974. Seven of these patents were granted for medical uses of turmeric that— again to nonexpert eyes—might be considered to be similar to their traditional uses. These patents are listed in table 7.1 below.

Furthermore, the USPTO has awarded a number of other patents for using turmeric as a seasoning or coloring agent in ways that do not appear particularly novel or nonobvious, including Spicy Popcorn with Natural Ingredients (6,207,205), awarded to three Indian inventors in 2001, and Oleomargarine with Natural Yellow Food Covering (3,940,504), awarded to two U.S. inventors in 1976. In 1979 the USPTO awarded patent 4,138,212 for the method of washing ground

TABLE 7.1   U.S. Patents on Medical Uses of Turmeric

Patent Number	Description of Invention	Year Issued
5,401,504	Use of turmeric in wound healing	1995
5,494,668	Method of treating musculoskeletal disease and a novel composition therefor	1996
5,897,865	Turmeric for treating skin disorders	1999
6,048,533	Turmeric for treating health ailments	2000
6,200,570	Herbal formulation useful as therapeutic and cosmetic applications for the treatment of general skin disorders	2001
6,224,871	Dietary supplement for nutritionally promoting healthy joint function	2001
6,264,995	Herbal composition for reducing inflammation and methods of using same	2001

Source: USPTO.

turmeric roots in warm soapy water to extract curcoma—a process that does not seem far removed from traditional household processing methods. One thing these patents reveal is that the USPTO makes little effort to verify the prior art, suggesting that efforts to document traditional knowledge in developing countries could be useful in preventing patents.

The various U.S. patents awarded to traditional uses of turmeric tell us something about how traditional knowledge is transmitted from poor to rich countries: in many of the cases above the inventors are Indians, some working in India and others in U.S. research institutions. In fact, one of these patents (6,200,570) is assigned to CSIR—the same organization that successfully challenged another turmeric patent as an act of biopiracy. CSIR's director, Anant Mashelkar, has stated a commitment to making India "an export house for knowledge," one step toward which is pursuing patents on traditional Indian knowledge (*The Sunday Pioneer* 1998). According to newspaper accounts, CSIR challenged the turmeric patent partly for symbolic reasons and partly to acquire expertise in U.S. patent reexamination procedures. It subsequently adopted a policy of opposing only those foreign patents on traditional knowledge that pose economic harm to India (*The Hindu* 1999). One finds in reading the turmeric patent awards that these are not examples of multinational corporations sneaking through villages in the jungle looking for medicinal knowledge to expropriate. Rather, the conduit is expatriate scientists and resident inventors with access to industrial country patent offices.

Lessons

As in the neem case, this case also reveals the need for better examination of patent applications to ensure that they are truly novel and that they take into account the prior art as it exists in other countries. The turmeric case also highlights the reliance on postaward legal challenges to establish the validity of a patent claim. In this case the adversarial process "worked," in the sense that CSIR succeeded in overturning the American patent.

This case is important for the channel through which traditional knowledge was transmitted. Most of the patent recipients are Indian researchers, whether in India or the United States; this is not an example of a multinational corporation actively trolling for traditional knowledge.

Ayahuasca: Patenting without Commercialization

The first two cases deal with patents on products using traditional knowledge. The next several cases involve patents on plants themselves. One celebrated case is the U.S. plant patent granted to a variety of Ayahuasca (*Banisteriopsis caapi*), a South American vine with hallucinogenic properties that is used in traditional Amazonian Indian rituals. An American pharmacologist obtained a U.S. plant patent in 1986 on the basis of his claim that he had bred a new variety of the plant using cuttings he had obtained in South America. This patent was challenged by organizations representing indigenous Amazonian communities a decade later, was revoked in 2000 on the grounds that the plant covered by the patent was similar to specimens already in herbarium collections in the United States, but then was reinstated the following year. More than any other biopiracy case, this example shows that a patent need not have anything to do with commercialization.

The Patent Controversy

Loren Miller obtained samples of Ayahuasca in Ecuador when he was a pharmacology student. Miller is the founder and director of a company called International Plant Medicine Corporation, about which little is known. Its website implies that the firm conducts research into developing commercial drugs (particularly for cancer) from tropical plants. There is no information on any such products, however, other than the plant patent for Ayahuasca (International Plant Medicine website n.d.).

Miller received a U.S. plant patent for the cultivar "DaVine" in 1986. The patent documents describe a number of ways that the new cultivar differs from the original (various physical characteristics, such as flower color, leaf shape, and so forth). There is no evidence that Miller attempted to commercialize his patent. In his own recounting of the patent affair, Miller claims that his research into medicinal properties of Ayahuasca was blocked in 1995 "by political maneuvering," but also that he made no attempt to use his patent on Ayahuasca: "this patent has been gathering dust sitting unused in a drawer" (International Plant Medicine website n.d.).

News of this patent took some time to travel back to South America. Various Amazonian Indian tribes became aware of the patent in 1994, after which they launched a protest against the patent. In March 1999, the Center for International Environmental Law (CIEL), a public interest law firm based in Washington, D.C., filed a request to reexamine the patent on behalf of two Amazonian Indian organizations. One of these two, the Coordinating Body of Indigenous Organizations of the Amazon Basin (COICA), objected to the patent because it gave a U.S. citizen rights to a plant that is sacred to many indigenous peoples of the Amazon, who use the plant in religious and healing ceremonies.

The USPTO rejected the patent in November 1999, making this decision final in April 2000, basing its action on the fact that publications describing *B. caapi* were "known and available" prior to the filing of the patent application. The USPTO ruled that specimen sheets at the Field Museum in Chicago constituted "prior publication," which suggests that other scientific field research publications might be used in other cases. The USPTO skipped over the question of whether the knowledge and use of a product by indigenous people in another country constituted "prior use" under the patent acts (Wiser n.d.). In an unusual turn of events, the USPTO accepted an appeal by Miller in late 2000, and in January 2001 issued a notice terminating the examination and reversing the earlier decision—thereby reinstating the patent. Lawyers at CIEL maintain that the USPTO failed to follow correct legal procedures on evidentiary standards for patentability challenges (Wiser 2001).

Lessons

Two points about the decision itself are worth noting. First, the USPTO did not recognize the claims of indigenous groups that patents should not be granted to sacred plants. This disappointed those who hoped that IPR laws could be used to defend against cultural misappropriation (indigenous groups compared the patent on Ayahuasca with patenting the Eucharist). Second, the USPTO granted the plant patent on the basis of the unique physical attributes of the plant (leaf shape, color of flowers, and so forth) and not for its actual or potential medicinal properties. It therefore provides no IPR protection that would be useful for drug development, nor does it give anyone the means to block traditional uses of the plant. And, in fact, the "inventor" made no attempt to commercialize the patent or use it to prevent others from using the plant.

What this case shows above all else is that simply receiving a patent does not translate into either commercialization or preventing existing uses of a product. It also suggests that existing IPR laws are a poor instrument for blocking cultural degradation.[18]

Basmati Rice in America

Basmati rice is a long-grain rice native to the Indian subcontinent known for its taste and aroma—the word "basmati" means "queen of fragrance"—that has become popular with consumers around the world. It consequently commands a premium price in international markets. It has been cultivated in present-day India and Pakistan for thousands of years. Formal scientific research into and development of improved commercial varieties of basmati rice date back at least to work done in the 1930s at the Rice Research Institute in Pakistan (Jamil 1998). A number of new, semidwarf varieties have been developed since the 1950s as part of the green revolution, bred to produce higher yields than traditional varieties. In 2001 the Indian Agricultural Research Institute released the world's first hybrid basmati rice, Pusa RH-10 (*Business Line* 2001b).[19] Even before the controversy erupted over the basmati rice patent, the governments of India and Pakistan were taking steps to protect the reputation associated with basmati by limiting commercial use of the name to only certain rice varieties that are cultivated in designated areas.

In recent decades rice researchers around the world have bred localized varieties of basmati rice that are able to grow outside of South Asia. Most media attention focuses on RiceTec, a Texas agricultural company that developed, trademarked, and patented new strains of basmati rice, which it sells under the trademarked names "Kasmati" and "Texmati." Others have developed localized basmati rice varieties as well: a California company sells "Calmati," researchers at Louisiana State University distribute "Dellmati," Uruguayan farmers grow "Urumati," Thai farmers grow "Siamati," and basmati is reportedly now grown in Egypt and Australia (*Economic Times* 2000).

After the Indian government lodged a protest, RiceTec and the USPTO significantly narrowed the patent's scope, but the basic claims remain in place, as do other forms of IPR protection. This case, like the others, reveals weaknesses in the patent examination process. While the more hysterical claims that the U.S. patent forces poor Punjabi farmers to pay royalties to Texan agroindustrialists are unfounded, South Asian growers will suffer some competition in the marketplace from American-grown basmati.

The IPR Controversy

Researchers at RiceTec, a company located in Alvin, Texas, bred several new strains of basmati rice in the 1980s and 1990s, which the company protects using a variety of IPR instruments.[20] The company holds U.S. Plant Variety Protection Certificates on seven varieties of rice, including one strain of basmati.[21] It holds trademarks on "Kasmati" and "Texmati," along with other trade names it uses to market its rice. At the center of the controversy, though, is U.S. patent 5,663,484, which RiceTec received in September 1997 for three of its basmati rice varieties.[22] The original patent made claims on 20 characteristics of the plant, its seeds, and its breeding process.[23] The patent asserted rights over the three new basmati strains identified explicitly (and their offspring), as well as rights over any other rice variety grown in the Western Hemisphere that possesses traditional basmati rice characteristics combined with a low content of "chalked grains."[24]

The Indian government challenged this patent, arguing that existing varieties of basmati already possess many of the same attributes claimed in the patent. The Indian government stressed that the patent's overly broad claims posed a threat to future sales of Indian basmati rice. In response, RiceTec dropped some of the claims. In August 2001 the USPTO further limited the scope of the patent, rejecting all but 4 of the original 20 claims. The revised patent essentially grants RiceTec protection over only the three new varieties it had developed.

Media and NGO accounts of the controversy often presume that the patent gives RiceTec the right to stop South Asian farmers from continuing to plant the basmati rice they've always planted. It seems clear, however, that RiceTec could not have blocked South Asian cultivation of basmati rice on the strength of its U.S. patent, since it applies only to basmati grown in the Western Hemisphere (where traditional varieties do not grow). Nor does it block researchers in India and Pakistan from developing new commercial basmati rice varieties—as noted above, Indian researchers recently developed the world's first hybrid basmati rice. When confronted on this issue in a 1998 interview, RiceTec Chief Executive Officer Robin Andrews responded that the patent covered only the unique method of breeding the new variety, and not basmati rice itself (*Rediff Business Interview* 1998). This is not at all how the patent documents read, however, and presumably a clever IP lawyer could block competing varieties grown in the Western Hemisphere, even if only temporarily, as patent infringement.[25]

The Indian government, along with several nonprofit organizations, also challenged the use of the words "basmati" or "jasmine" to market American rice, arguing that these legitimately apply only to certain rice varieties grown in South and Southeast Asia. The U.S. Federal Trade Commission rejected this challenge in 2001 on the grounds that U.S. agricultural regulations treat these terms as examples of aromatic rice, independent of where the rice is grown. It also argued that there was little likelihood of consumer injury resulting from confusion between American and Asian rice varieties.[26] In contrast, the U.K. Food Standards Agency (2002) recently issued labeling guidelines recognizing as "basmati" rice only those varieties that the Indian and Pakistani authorities recognize officially as basmati.[27]

Even if U.S. consumers are not harmed or confused, Asian producers will almost certainly suffer lost or lower sales because of competition from new American varieties, which were bred and are marketed explicitly as substitutes for traditional Asian varieties.[28] How large these losses will grow is uncertain. A 2001 *Bangkok Post* article refers to an estimate that India lost US$200 million after RiceTec trademarked "Jasmati" (another of its rice varieties), though this clearly overstates the impact, given that total U.S. imports of basmati rice from all countries have never amounted to even one-tenth of that amount.[29] Table 7.2 shows U.S. imports of basmati rice over the past decade.

By way of contrast, RiceTec's total sales of seeds and consumer rice sold through supermarkets amounted to US$10 million in 2000 (Ivanovich 2001). This figure cannot be compared directly with the value of imports since it includes seed sales and sales of rice other than its localized basmati varieties, and because consumer rice sales reflect retail markups that import prices do not.

TABLE 7.2   U.S. Rice Imports, 1989–2001

	Value (millions of dollars)		Quantity (thousands of metric tons)	
Year	Total rice	Basmati rice	Total rice	Basmati rice
1989	60.1	4.8	121.9	4.7
1990	71.6	7.4	148.5	7.2
1991	80.3	9.1	162.1	8.5
1992	91.6	10.9	175.4	9.2
1993	106.4	11.2	203.1	11.1
1994	129.8	10.1	246.7	11.4
1995	121.1	7.4	224.4	8.5
1996	156.9	9.2	275.4	10.2
1997	200.5	11.0	312.4	12.1
1998	187.7	18.3	296.3	18.9
1999	187.1	18.4	353.6	19.8
2000	180.4	19.5	304.5	23.2
2001	168.5	17.6	405.8	22.5

Source: U.S. International Trade Commission.

The flip side is that this figure obviously excludes sales of other American-grown basmati rice varieties.

Lessons

- The basmati case reinforces the observation that developing countries have intellectual property worth protecting. Centuries of breeding by South Asian farmers resulted in a high-quality rice variety that commands a premium in international markets.
- While "basmati" may not meet the technical definition of a *geographical* indicator (as the word does not refer to a geographic area of origin), it does carry with it a reputation for quality rice with certain characteristics. Traditional basmati rice growers have the same interest in preventing dilution of this reputation as do producers of Champagne.
- The second observation is that Indian companies developing new commercial basmati rice varieties are harmed not by foreign patents per se, but by competition in the marketplace. This is a commercial problem that requires a commercial response.
- It would help to print location of origin on bags—much as wineries use single-vineyard or Port producers use single-vintage to differentiate their products of high quality from those of low quality.
- The true competitors are high-yield variety producers in South Asia. RiceTec's competition is the Indian Agricultural Research Institute, not a poor Punjabi farmer.

Yellow Beans: Mayacoba from Mexico or Enola from Colorado?

One biopiracy example that involves clear economic harm is the patenting of yellow beans from Mexico. This is a case where a U.S. patent holder sued importers (as well as U.S. growers) of yellow beans on grounds of patent infringement, halting imports while the lawsuit is resolved in the courts.

Mexican farmers have been growing yellow-colored beans at least since the Aztecs. More recently, Mexican agronomists developed a variety of yellow bean that they registered in 1978 as "Mayacoba."[30] The Asociacíon Agricultores de Rio Fuerte Sur, a growers' group with about 1,000 members in Sinaloa, Mexico, subsequently developed an export market in Southern California for yellow beans. The growers' association invested approximately US$420,000 in a new drying and bagging facility to provide beans directly to U.S. supermarket chains such as Price Club-Costco and Safeway. As of early 2000, yellow beans imported from Mexico were selling for 27 cents a pound in Los Angeles (Friedland 2000). Annual sales in the United States are reportedly about US$50 million (Accola 2000).

The Patent Controversy

A Colorado farmer, Larry Proctor, bought a bag of what he found to be unusual yellow beans when he was traveling in Mexico during the early 1990s. He bred the beans to produce a variety with a distinctly yellow color that held true across generations, named it "Enola" (after his wife), and in 1996 applied for a patent and plant variety protection certificate, which he received in 1999.[31] Proctor envisioned a huge market for the yellow bean with Latino immigrants in the United States as well as a potential to export to Mexico and the rest of the Western Hemisphere (Raabe 1999). As of November 2001 his company, Pod-Ners, had licensed Enola bean production to 80 growers and 8 processors (*AgJournal.com* 2001).

An importer in Nogales, Arizona, who grew up eating yellow beans in Mexico, started importing them into the United States in 1994. Within five years her firm, Tutuli Produce, was importing 6 million pounds of Mayacoba beans annually from Mexico. Larry Proctor's lawyers sued her in 1999, notifying her that she needed to license from him (at up to 6 cents a pound) the right to sell yellow beans in the United States, which would result in a total royalty payment of US$360,000 in 1999. Proctor maintains that Enola is not the same as Mayacoba, but that Mexican farmers have likely been raising his Enola beans and selling them as Mayacoba.[32] Mexican exports of yellow beans have slowed to a trickle while the lawsuit and patent dispute are resolved.[33] At the request of Pod-Ners, U.S. Customs officials have been stopping bean shipments from Mexico to search for any beans with the same yellow color as Enola beans (Friedland 2000). The Asociacíon Agricultores de Rio Fuerte Sur filed a countersuit in U.S. District Court in December 1999, with the support of the Mexican government and Tutuli Produce.

Pod-Ners also filed suit against 16 bean processors and growers based in Greeley, Colorado, in November 2001 for illegally growing and selling Enola beans. Proctor stated that there are as many as 50 nonlicensed bean growers and processors working with the Enola variety. The suit seeks damages and an injunction against further property right infringement (*AgJournal.com* 2001; *Denver Business Journal* 2001). Two of the largest companies named in the suit settled out of court, agreeing to pay financial compensation for past sales and signing a licensing agreement for future sales (Accola 2002).

The International Center for Tropical Agriculture (CIAT) in Cali, Colombia, filed a formal protest with the USPTO on December 20, 2000. CIAT claims that it maintains some 260 bean samples with yellow seeds, and six accessions are "substantially identical" to claims made in Proctor's patent.[34] CIAT's annual report mentions that Pod-Ners has recently filed additional claims based on the original patent application.

Lessons

As with other cases, critics point to the Enola bean patent as a manifestation of overly broad IPR protection in industrial countries: the Enola bean is not truly distinct from varieties grown in Mexico nor is it novel—tests that plant varieties are required to meet to receive plant breeders' rights or patents. But unlike other cases, here the assertion of IPRs caused direct economic harm to existing producers.

The patent does not prevent poor farmers from growing the beans they have been growing for years (the patent applies only to sales and production in the United States), but it costs them export revenue—presumably more revenue than they would have lost simply through competition with unpatented production of yellow beans in the United States.

Why could Larry Proctor block yellow bean imports but RiceTec cannot block basmati imports? In other cases, one can easily argue that some innovation took place, innovation that should legitimately receive protection, but also that genuinely distinguishes the new product from existing products. Traditional basmati rice will not grow in the United States; new breeding must take place.

Another important element of this case is that the developing country had already succeeded in transforming the traditional plant into a commercially successful export crop. This is also true for basmati rice, but not for many traditional medicines or neem pesticides.

General Themes

What general lessons can one draw from these cases? First, it is important to observe that in only one case, that of yellow beans, did the awarding of an IPR actually block commercialization by a developing country. An industrial patent does not prevent people in developing countries from continuing to use medicinal plants or food crops in their traditional fashions. There is insult, but not injury, from biopiracy.

Second, all cases support the claim that industrial country governments are too quick to grant IPR protection on plants, products, and processes that already exist in developing countries. In part this flows from procedures that deny recognition to oral prior art. In part this reflects a move away from extensive examination by patent offices in rich countries, and a move toward an adversarial process to settle disputes after patents are granted. In most of the celebrated cases the patents have been contested by public interest advocacy organizations. In some cases they were overturned or substantially narrowed. Contesting patents is an expensive proposition, especially for the nonprofit organizations that have been most active in challenging these patents. One cannot view this adversarial process as a general solution to the problem of mismatched IPR laws.

One must recognize that simply awarding a patent or trademark in an industrial country generally does not cause economic harm to those who developed the traditional knowledge. In general, the patents awarded do not preclude existing uses of plants, medicines, and the like. The outstanding exception is the plant patent on the yellow bean. In that case the patent recipient sued existing importers of Mexican Mayacoba beans for patent infringement. In other cases, however, the patents covered products or uses that were purportedly in some way nontraditional: a new process for extracting active ingredients from neem, a new hybrid of basmati, new medicines, and so forth. In most celebrated biopiracy cases there is insult, but not injury.

Finally, the economic impact comes from commercialization of products using traditional knowledge rather than awarding IPR protection, and a patent is only one component of commercialization—and not always a necessary ingredient at that (the California Basmati Rice company has neither patent nor trademark protection on its Calmati strain of basmati rice). Commercialization of the new product in an industrial country can have a number of impacts on the source country. In none of these cases has the new product displaced the traditional product in the developing country.[35] Direct harm comes, rather, through loss of export markets. American-grown basmati rice competes in U.S. markets with traditional basmati rice imported from South Asia.

What do these cases tell us about channeling benefits from commercialization of traditional knowledge back to the originating communities? One might categorize solutions as follows:

1. **Harmonize IPR laws.** What might be called the "TRIPs solution" is to harmonize legal protections across countries, which implies introducing rich country IPR regimes into poor countries. From this point of view, uneven IP protection generates uneven commercialization—neem biopesticides are developed in industrial countries because that's where IP protections are the strongest.
2. **Reform rich country IPRs.** An alternative view is that IPR regimes in rich countries are the problem, and therefore all governments should eliminate patentability of plants ("no patents on life") and require disclosure of traditional knowledge used (and prior informed consent to use that knowledge).
3. **Place ethnobotanical knowledge in the public domain.** Given that USPTO officials are not familiar with ancient Ayurvedic texts, put that information into computer databases. Given that much traditional knowledge is oral tradition,

document it and publish it. This strives to ensure that nobody will commercialize traditional knowledge.

4. **Create knowledge-sharing contracts.** Introduce contracting mechanisms. Require prior informed consent. Try to create tollgates on the transfer of knowledge. This is agnostic about the quality of IPRs specifically, but it depends on the prior existence of high-quality legal institutions in general.

5. **Promote indigenous commercialization.** Promote commercialization at home, irrespective of industrial country property rights. Commercialization of traditional knowledge depends primarily on general commercial factors. Is there a market? Can companies bring new products to that market (and keep their returns)?

Points 1, 2, and 3 all place legal controls at the center. These legal issues are addressed in greater detail elsewhere in this volume (see chapters by Visser and Wüger). Point 4 relies on the existence of clearly identifiable choke points on the transmission of knowledge or genetic material from developing countries to industrial users. In most of the cases discussed in this chapter, an individual acquired the knowledge first-hand rather than through an existing institutional channel (such as research center germplasm banks or botanic gardens). The chapter by ten Kate and Laird discusses ways of implementing contractual arrangements in such circumstances. Indigenous commercialization is no trivial task. It depends on a country's business environment, capacity to conduct research and development, and presence of a well-functioning market—the basic economic problems facing all developing countries. Furthermore, ethnobotanical knowledge is often embodied in traditional products that are not easily sold in modern commercial markets. For example, traditional health remedies would require testing for efficacy and safety to be sold as medicines in industrial countries. This can be extremely costly. In addition, traditional products are made for traditional uses—neem was traditionally processed for immediate usage, not for future sale in distant locations. The challenge facing developing countries is to unpackage knowledge from traditional products and repackage it for commercial markets. The existence of IPRs is insufficient to meet this challenge.

Endnotes

1. I use "ethnobotanical knowledge" to refer to a community's knowledge about medicinal and alimentary uses of plants. This distinguishes the knowledge of the plants from the plant matter itself.

2. Rural Advancement Foundation International (RAFI), a Canadian advocacy organization (now called Action Group on Erosion, Technology, and Concentration [ETC]), coined the term in 1994 as a spin on bioprospecting. RAFI/ETC publishes annual Captain Hook awards for notable achievements in biopiracy.

3. The value of the original plant matter is far less than that of retail prescription drug sales. U.S. imports of Indian medicinal and cosmetic plants (Harmonized Tariff System category 1211) equaled US$37.8 million in 2001, one-quarter of total U.S. imports. Imports from China are roughly equivalent.

4. Simply knowing that gold is present in a mountain range does not make me rich; I first need to find it, then extract, process, and sell it.

5. Only these two patents have attracted much attention, although W.R. Grace also holds 12 other patents and registered trademarks on several neem products (Neemix, Neem Guard, Neemazad, and BioNeem), and a number of other companies also hold patents on neem-based products and processes. Grace sold its biopesticides division in 1996, a fact that has gone unnoticed in media and nongovernmental organization (NGO) accounts of this story, and filed for bankruptcy protection in 2001 as a consequence of asbestos-related product liability lawsuits.

6. Magda Aelvoet, on behalf of the Greens, the Research Foundation for Science, Technology and Natural Resource Policy (of India), and International Federation of Organic Agriculture Movements (INFOAM; Germany) challenged the European patent; Jeremy Rifkin joined them to challenge the U.S. patent.

7. W.R. Grace spokesperson quoted in an article by John F. Burns in the *New York Times*, September 15, 1995.

8. Europe Agri (June 9, 2000) says 1980; the firm's website states that it was founded in 1990.

9. Vandana Shiva identifies the businessman as Robert Larson; Marc Ketchel, a founder of several neem products companies, also claims to have discovered the ubiquitous uses of neem in India in 1971 in a December 1997 speech, and credits Larson with the laboratory testing (http://www.theoriginalneemcompany.com/Misc/historicoverview.htm).

10. Indian farmers traditionally soaked neem seeds in water and alcohol and then sprayed the emulsion on their plants. A drawback of the traditional process is that the fungicide begins to degrade if the emulsion is not used right away. Commercial production requires a more stable product.

11. In the area of pharmaceuticals manufacturing, one increasingly common feature is the multiplicity of patents and protections applied to commercial products. Even when one patent expires, generic drug manufacturers are still prevented from entering the market by the presence of many remaining patents.

12. Parry's Cuddalore plant has the capacity to manufacture 10 million tons annually; in 2000 output was 3.5 million tons, of which 1.5 million tons were exported to the United States and Europe.

13. The *CPL Worldwide Directory of Agrobiologicals* (2001) lists three manufacturers based in India: Wockhardt, SPIC Group, and Krishna Bio-Tech. None of these products have received EPA regulatory approval for sale as a pesticide in the United States.

14. Note that during this same period the rupee depreciated from Rs 10 per U.S. dollar to Rs 50 per dollar.

15. Since dietary supplements do not undergo the same tests for efficacy and safety as drugs, makers of dietary supplements are not permitted to make medical claims in their promotional literature.

16. Medline is operated by the U.S. National Institutes of Health and is generally considered to be the authoritative source for information on medical publications.

17. This amounts to about US$14,000 at spot exchange rates prevailing in 1996—not a large amount of money by the standards of U.S. corporate litigation, but presumably a sizable expenditure by a developing country research organization.

18. The issue of cultural degradation is taken up in the contribution to this volume by Daniel Wüger.   •

19. Other modern basmati varieties are not true hybrids (that is, offspring of genetically dissimilar parents), but rather pureline varieties developed through selective breeding of genetically similar parents.

20. RiceTec was founded in 1987 as a division of Farms of Texas. The company is solely owned by Prince Hans Adam II of Liechtenstein. It reportedly spent US$3 million to US$4 million to develop the localized basmati strains (http://pvgreens.org/pipermail/pvgreens-announce/2000-December/000147.html).

21. The USDA awards Plant Variety Protection Certificates to plant breeders, giving them monopoly rights over the use and sale of their new plant varieties, generally for a period of 20 years.

22. These are designated as RT1117, RT1121, and Basmati 867.

23. Physical characteristics include attributes such as size, color, chemical content, starch index, firmness when cooked, and so forth.

24. Chalkiness is deemed an undesirable property of traditional basmati.

25. Interestingly, there is no evidence that RiceTec contemplated pursuing patent infringement suits against the developers of Calmati or Dellmati, two other new basmati-type rice varieties bred to grow in the United States, even though the original patent would seem to enable such actions.

26. Letter from Donald Clark, secretary, Federal Trade Commission, to Charlotte Arnold Christin, Esq., et al., May 9, 2001.

27. Fifteen rice varieties are recognized by either Pakistan or India as basmati rice. The list includes both traditional "true-line" varieties as well as new, high-yield, semidwarf varieties.

28. Labels on boxes of Kasmati and Texmati identify the rice as basmati: Texmati is described as "Long Grain American Basmati Rice" and Kasmati as "Indian-Style Basmati Rice." Other companies also sell local hybrids as "basmati": Lundberg Family Farms in California sells "California White Basmati" and "California Brown Basmati" rice. The California Basmati Company began distributing the Calmati-201 variety of basmati to rice growers in 1999 and markets the rice as "California Grown Basmati Rice." Louisiana State University agronomists are less ambitious with Dellmati, which they began distributing in 2000; this is referred to as "basmati-type" rice.

29. The article did not cite the source of this estimate or provide any information about how this estimate was arrived at.

30. It is sometimes spelled mayocoba, and the yellow beans are also known as azufrado beans. It is a variety of *Phaseolus vulgaris*.

31. U.S. patent 5,894,079 and U.S. Plant Variety Protection Certificate 9700027.

32. Proctor once sent seeds down to a trade show in Mexico, and he notes that many of his field workers are Mexican.

33. American Radio Works, *A Bean of a Different Color* (broadcast in June 2001). The text of the program is posted at http://www.americanradioworks.org/features/food_politics/beans. Lawyers for a Colorado bean grower report that U.S. production of Enola beans represents only 20 percent of current U.S. yellow bean sales, however, suggesting that imports have not completely dried up in spite of the lawsuits (Accola 2002).

34. CIAT's submissions to the USPTO are posted at http://www.ciat.cgiar.org.

35. This differs from technology transfer in more traditional industrial products. Japan exports autos to the countries where autos were invented.

References

The word *processed* describes informally reproduced works that may not be commonly available through libraries.

Accola, John. 2000. "No Small Beans: Inventor Sues Growers over Seeds." *Rocky Mountain News*, November 20, 2000, Business section, p. 3C.

———. 2002. "Pod-Ners Drops Suit Stemming from Bean Patent." *Rocky Mountain News*, November 21, 2002.

AgJournal.com, December 4, 2001. Available at http://www.agjournal.com/story.cfm_story_id=1641.

Bangkok Post. 2001. "Experts May Register Rice as Trademark." November 27, 2001.

Burns, John F. 1995. "Tradition in India vs. a Patent in the U.S." *New York Times*, September 15, 1995, p. D4.

Business Line. 2001a. "EID Parry Opens U.S. Arm to Sell Bio-Pesticides." March 16, 2001.

Business Line. 2001b. India: No Specific Patent for Basmati to RiceTec." August 24, 2001.

Business Week. 1993. "A Tree Grows in India—and It's a Biotech Wonder." December 3, 1993, p. 85.

CPL Worldwide Directory of Agrobiologicals. 2001. Newbury, United Kingdom: CPL Scientific Publishing.

CSIR (Indian Council for Scientific and Industrial Research). n.d. Press release posted at http://www.rediff.com/news/aug/27haldi1.htm.

Deccan Chronicle. 2000. "India Has Not Lost Patent Case, Asserts Govt." May 12, 2000.

Denver Business Journal. 2001. "Bean Inventors Sue Greeley Growers." November 30, 2001.

Economic Times. 2000. "Texmatis, Casmatis to Keep Flooding US Marts." January 7, 2000.

EPO (European Patent Office). 2000. "'Neem Tree Oil' Case: European Patent No. 0436 257 Revoked." Press release, May 10, 2000.

Europe Agri. 2000. "W.R. Grace's Neem-Related Patent Withdrawn." June 9, 2000.

Food Standards Agency. 2002. "Use of the Name Basmati." Reference No. LSD 12/.

Friedland, Jonathan. 2000. "Litigation Sprouts Up over Claim to Invent Bean." *Denver Post,* March 21, 2000, p. C-1.

The Hindu. 1999. "Council for Scientific and Industrial Research Unlikely to Oppose U.S. Patent." July 20, 1999.

IFOAM (International Federation of Organic Agriculture Movements). n.d. "Background Paper on the Neem Patent Controversy." Available at http://www.ifoam.org/press/neem_back.html.

International Plant Medicine. n.d. Website at http://members.tripod.co.uk/jdunan/ipm2000/DEFAULT.HTML

Ivanovich, David. 2001. "RiceTec Sees Partial Win over Patents; Indian Government Angry that Basmati Types OK'd." *Houston Chronicle,* August 24, 2001, Business section, p. 1.

Jamil, Uzma. 1998. "Biopiracy: The Patenting of Basmati Rice by RiceTec." Commission on Environmental, Economic and Social Policy.

Kocken, Joris, and Gerda van Roozendaal. 1997. "The Neem Tree Debate." *Biotechnology and Development Monitor* No. 30.

NRC (National Research Council). 1992. *Neem: A Tree for Solving Global Problems.* Washington, D.C.: National Academy Press, p. 32.

PR Newswire. 1995. "Grace Issues Statement about Patent for Neem Pesticide." September 14, 1995.

Raabe, Steve. 1999. "Researcher Using His Bean Grower Claims Yellow Variety Will Change Industry." *Denver Post,* September 18, 1999, p. C-1.

RAFI (Rural Advancement Foundation International)/United Nations Development Programme. 1994. "Conserving Indigenous Knowledge—Integrating New Systems of Integration." Available at http://www.undp.org/csopp/CSO/NewFiles/dociknowledge1.html.

Rediff Business Interview, July 7, 1998. Posted at http://www.rediff.com/business/1998/jul/07rice.htm.

Sharma, Ashok B. 2001. "India's Battle over Basmati Patent Not Fully Lost Yet." *Financial Express,* October 1, 2001.

Shiva, Vandana. n.d. *The Neem Tree—A Case History of Biopiracy.* Available at http://www.twnside.org.sg/title/pir-ch.htm.

Srinivas, Nidhi Nath. 2000. "Texmatis, Kasmatis to Keep Flooding U.S. Marts." *Economic Times,* July 8, 2000.

SRISTI (Society for Research and Initiatives for Sustainable Technologies and Institutions). n.d. "Patents on Neem." Available at http://csf.colorado.edu/sristi/papers/patentonneem.html.

The Statesman. 1998. "Biocolonialism Patent Mightier than Sword." March 3, 1998.

The Sunday Pioneer. June 7, 1998. Posted at http://www.hvk.org/articles/0698/0085.html.

Wiser, Glenn. 2001. "U.S. Patent and Trademark Office Reinstates Ayahuasca Patent." Center for International Environmental Law. Processed.

Wiser, Glenn. n.d. "PTO Rejection of the 'Ayahuasca' Patent Claim." Center for International Environmental Law. Available at http://www.ciel.org/Biodiversity/ptorejection.html.

8

PREVENTION OF MISAPPROPRIATION OF INTANGIBLE CULTURAL HERITAGE THROUGH INTELLECTUAL PROPERTY LAWS

Daniel Wüger

Globalization has led to an increase in the flow of thoughts, commodities, and people to an extent that is unprecedented in history. Existing cultures face alternative cultures in increasing frequency and intensity. While some welcome this development, others do not. The designer who uses indigenous designs or art styles for his or her creations might be pleased about the new ideas resulting from cultural exchange. To the indigenous group, the "appropriation" of their intangible cultural property might be deeply offensive. Some indigenous groups might accept tourists as a welcome source of income while others do not want to be bothered by tourism. As a matter of fact culture in many forms has become a significant commodity in world markets today, a development that presents many new challenges to lawmakers.[1] Several chapters in this volume address ways in which developing countries and indigenous and local communities can better share in the benefits that are generated by the "world culture market." Yet, sometimes holders of intangible cultural property do not want increased economic benefits but are concerned with its devaluation through outside appropriations. Hence, unauthorized (commercial) uses of intangible cultural property might be offensive to them, and they might oppose commercialization completely, or approve it only under certain conditions. Misappropriations occur where the use of intangible cultural property occurs without the consent of its holders.

The Prevention of Misappropriations of Folklore

National legislators started to protect folklore in the framework of their copyright laws in the 1960s.[2] However, the adoption of a binding international instrument within the United Nations Educational, Scientific, and Cultural Organization (UNESCO) or the World Intellectual Property Organization (WIPO) failed, in contrast to efforts related to tangible cultural heritage that resulted in several international conventions within UNESCO.[3] Yet, work on the subject within the two organizations continued. In 1976, at a meeting organized jointly by WIPO and UNESCO, a panel of experts drafted the so-called "Tunis Model Law on Copyright for Developing Countries" (UNESCO/WIPO 1976) that provides for a copyright-based approach to protect folklore.[4] In 1982, WIPO and UNESCO jointly issued "Model Provisions for National Laws on the Protection of Expressions of Folklore against Illicit Exploitation and Other Prejudicial Actions" ("WIPO Model Provisions"; WIPO 1982). In 1989, UNESCO adopted a "Recommendation on the Safeguarding of Folklore" (UNESCO 1989). Today, several governments again have asked WIPO to sponsor a treaty to protect expressions of folklore.[5] More specifically, at its 26th session, in 2000, the WIPO General Assembly established a special body to facilitate activities among member states on intellectual property (IP) issues related to inter alia folklore: the Intergovernmental Committee on Intellectual Property and Genetic Resources, Traditional Knowledge and Folklore.[6]

The UNESCO Recommendation defines folklore or "traditional and popular culture" as the "totality of *tradition-based* creations of a cultural community, expressed by a group or individuals and recognized as reflecting the expectations of a community in so far as they reflect its cultural and social identity" (UNESCO 1989, § A). It encompasses a broad range of objects, such as folk tales, songs, instrumental music, dances, plays, artistic forms, rituals, drawings, paintings, carvings, sculptures, pottery, terracotta, mosaic, woodwork, metalware, jewelry, basket weaving, needlework, textiles, carpets, costumes, musical instruments, and architectural forms.[7]

Typically, folklore is handed down from generation to generation as part of an oral tradition. It can be part of the national cultural heritage or be intangible cultural property of indigenous or local communities. Often the latter is controlled by the indigenous or local group as a community and strongly interwoven in a net of customary obligations and rights of the individuals and the community.[8] Also, folklore can include sacred and secret tribal knowledge. An aboriginal artist, for instance, is not allowed to paint certain sacred symbols or stories until he or she undergoes an initiation procedure, and severe sanctions can be imposed if images are painted without permission of the tribe.[9] Meanwhile, some forms of folklore, like artisan arts and crafts, have become an important source of income in developing countries and for local and indigenous communities.[10] With the commercialization of folklore, the risk of misappropriation has heightened, and developing countries as well as local and indigenous communities are looking for means to protect their intangible cultural property.

Copyright Protection

The close analogy of many forms of folklore to literary and artistic works seems to make copyright the natural solution for the protection of folklore. Indeed, many forms of folklore prima facie fall under the category of literary and artistic works protected by copyright laws. These laws protect such works as verbal expressions, writings, musical expressions, choreographic expressions, drawings, paintings, sculptures, and even architectural forms.[11] However, only the particular expression is protected, not the underlying idea or a particular style. The only requirement that works have to fulfill, according to the Berne Convention, is that they must constitute intellectual creations. Yet, many national laws require that a work be original.[12] Furthermore, many countries, especially those following the Anglo-Saxon tradition, protect only works fixed in a tangible medium, such as writing or sound recording. The Berne Convention does not impose these requirements, and member countries following the civil-law tradition usually assign copyrights to oral or other "unfixed" works (Puri 1997, p. 53).

An author of a copyrighted work enjoys economic rights to his or her work and, in many countries, so-called "moral rights." The economic rights allow the author to directly control the use of the work. By means of a license, he or she can allow others to use the work in a certain manner or can cede the copyright. The moral rights protect the author's reputation by allowing him or her to prevent distortions and giving him or her the right to be named on copies of the work. Moral rights are independent of the economic rights and can endure longer, in some countries even in perpetuity. These rights may only be waived, not ceded. An author can decide not to publish a work because he or she enjoys complete control over its use. A country or local or indigenous community that owned a copyright to its folklore, thus, could decide to publish it or keep it secret.

An additional element of copyright laws, the so-called "neighboring rights," bears the potential to further the protection of folklore in that performers of folklore can get protection of their performance even though the actual work performed is not protected. However, many domestic laws require that the performed work must still be copyright protected for protection to be afforded to the performer.[13] WIPO has proposed to protect performers of expressions of folklore even if the particular work of folklore is not protected under the respective national law (WIPO 2001c, pp. 110–11), and many countries have amended their copyright laws accordingly.[14] Article 2(a) of the WIPO Performances and Phonograms Treaty goes a step further, explicitly extending neighboring rights protection to performers of expressions of folklore.[15]

Standard copyright laws do not account for the fact that folklore is frequently associated with community interest. Particularly, indigenous cultures often do not know the public-private distinction underlying the property conception in many industrial countries. As stated above, property in folklore is frequently based on a network of continued duties and rights between the individual and the community. Copyright laws, however, are based on a limited period of individual authorship as a reward for the creative act provided by the individual. After that period, the work falls into the public domain and can be used by anyone.[16] There is no communal ownership and perpetual protection of copyrights. As a result, folklore that has existed for a long time is usually part of the public domain.

The Pueblo of Santo Domingo Case[17]   On January 21, 1984, a photographer of the newspaper *The Santa Fe New Mexican* flew over the Pueblo of Santo Domingo and photographed a ceremonial dance. The photos were published at least two times and once described as a "pow-wow." In response, the Pueblo filed suit alleging trespass, violation of the Pueblo's ban on photography, and invasion of privacy. The dance was sacred and had to be kept secret according to the Pueblo's customary laws. By appropriating the image of the dance and publicizing it, the members of the Pueblo believed its intrinsic value was diminished because it rendered the dance "nothing more than commercial entertainment for the white man" (Scafidi 2001, p. 830). Though this loss could not be restored by postinjury remedies, the Pueblo intended to stop the use of the pictures to avoid future harm. There was no authoritative decision in this case as the parties settled out of court. Nevertheless, it provides an interesting example of a piece of folklore that does not enjoy copyright protection as such.

The sacred dance might have fit under the category of "choreographies" protected by U.S. copyright law.[18] Yet, the "choreography" was not fixed, and an author was not identifiable. The dance is part of the community's sacred, intangible cultural property but, for copyright purposes, is part of the public domain.

Furthermore, the Pueblos were prevented from seeking protection as performers as, in general, U.S. copyright laws do not afford protection to performers of uncopyrighted works.[19] Hence, the Pueblo had to resort to claims other than copyright infringements.

The Australian Experience with Aboriginal Art   Unlike Native Americans, Australian aborigines have in several cases successfully used copyright laws to prevent the unauthorized use of folklore. In *Milpurrurru v. Indofurn*,[20] Indofurn produced carpets in Vietnam using designs from paintings by aboriginal artists who had authorized the reproduction of their pictures in a publication that was designed for the education of members of the white community about aboriginal culture, but did not authorize other uses. The publications made it clear that the pictures depicted sacred stories, that aboriginal law strictly controlled the painting techniques as well as the images, and that errors in reproduction could cause deep offense (Blakeney 1995). The painters obtained permission to use the sacred symbols only after a procedure of initiation. Upon importation of the rugs into Australia, the plaintiffs (the individual artists) sought recourse that was granted by the Australian court.[21] The court recognized the specific aboriginal paintings as original artworks suitable for protection under Australia's copyright laws.

Initially, Australian courts had problems in finding ways to take into account communal interests. In *Yumbulul v. Reserve Bank of Australia*,[22] Yumbulul licensed one of his works, a morning star pole, to the Aboriginal Artists Agency that sublicensed the Reserve Bank of Australia to be included in a commemorative banknote. Yumbulul had consented to the sublicense without knowing who the customer was (Ragavan 2001, p. 49). Fellow clan members criticized this act as being contrary to their traditional law.[23] Subsequently, the artist tried but failed to set aside the assignment of his copyright in court, claiming that only the tribe could have assigned copyrights to the bank. The judge stated that Australian copyright law does not recognize communal rights that supersede the right of the individual author that would have given the clan a claim against the author, and suggested that the legislature deal with the issue.[24]

However, in *Bulun Bulun v. R & T Textiles*,[25] a case that was decided in 1998, the court under the law of equity constructed a fiduciary relationship between the aboriginal artist and his/her clan that obliges him/her not to exploit the artwork contrary to the customary law of the clan. R & T Textiles had printed Bulun Bulun's paintings on clothing fabrics without his permission.[26] The artist took action against the company, and the court granted a permanent injunction. At the same time a representative of Bulun Bulun's clan brought an action claiming that the traditional aboriginal owners of Ganalbingu country were the equitable copyright owners of Bulun Bulun's paintings.[27] Affirming its decision in *Yumbulul*, the court rejected the suggestion that the aboriginal clan had equitable ownership in the paintings.[28] Nevertheless, the fiduciary relationship between Bulun Bulun and the Ganalbingu people was acknowledged based on "trust and confidence" between the representatives of the Ganalbingu people who had granted permission to paint the sacred story and the artist.[29] As a fiduciary, Bulun Bulun was under an "overriding obligation to act to preserve the integrity of the Ganalbingu culture where action for that purpose is required," that is, he was obliged "not to exploit the artistic work in a way that is contrary to the laws and custom of the Ganalbingu people, and, in the event of infringement by a third party, to take reasonable and appropriate action to restrain and remedy infringement of the copyright in the artistic work."[30] The clan's primary right in this relationship is to be able to require the artist to take these actions. Hence, if the artist has undertaken all reasonable and appropriate action, as in the Bulun Bulun case, "there is no occasion for the intervention of equity to provide any additional remedy to the beneficiaries of the fiduciary relationship."[31] Yet, in an obiter the court held that had Bulun Bulun failed to fulfill his obligations "the Australian legal system will permit remedial action through the courts by the clan."[32]

Australian courts have recognized copyrights of aboriginal artists in their works even if such artists depict preexisting symbols.[33] Originality thus need not be a hurdle for the protection of folklore works. In fact, the transmission of preexisting symbols, paintings, and themes usually involves an amount of creativity on the side of the artist that allows the recognition of copyrights. In the *Yumbulul* case, the court recognized that "there is no doubt that the pole was an original artistic work, and that he [Yumbulul] was the author, in whom copyright subsisted."[34] In general, the lower the originality threshold, the easier it will be to get copyright protection for new works of folklore.[35] As has been said above, the Berne Convention does not mandate originality at all. A developing country legislature will have to weigh the interest at stake. The choice for a low originality threshold includes a choice for a smaller public domain. In general, commentators tend to suggest that developing countries need a large public domain from which the public can draw, as these countries, at least at the moment, lack the creative power for their cultural industry and their educational systems.[36]

Furthermore, the court's approach in *Bulun Bulun* provides a powerful tool for enforcing customary rules applying to the use of cultural property where such property enjoys protection under Australian copyright law. It represents a pragmatic way to enforce such customs in that community action is possible only where the individual artist fails to protect community interests. A feature of the *Milpurrurru* decision, in which the judge awarded damages for culturally based harm,[37] reinforces these remedies. The community will even be able to stop inappropriate uses once an aboriginal artist has licensed his or her work, as in the

Yumbulul case. The fiduciary construction leaves some gaps in the protection of aboriginal art, however. It does not apply to nonmembers of the community not bound by customary obligations (Weatherall 2001, p. 222). Furthermore, had R & T Textiles not used a copyrighted work, neither Bulun Bulun nor the clan would have had any claim.[38]

The Australian experience shows how flexible interpretation of existing legal instruments can be used to protect cultural property from misappropriations. There is one important gap, however. Nothing prevents a third party from making a copy of a piece of folklore that is part of the public domain or not copyrightable at all, as in the *Pueblo of Santo Domingo* case. Still, Australia's approach provides a model for other countries if no new legislation is enacted.

Folklore Music in Ethiopia   Several countries have amended their copyright acts by explicitly including folklore as one category of protected works and extending its term of protection compared with other works.

One example is provided by Ethiopia. Ethiopia requires prior authorization by the Ministries of Culture and Information for any reproduction or adaptation of folklore in exchange for the payment of a fee (Endeshaw 1996, p. 232). *Fikre Gebru v. Mohammed Awol,*[39] although not a case of misappropriation of cultural property, exemplifies Ethiopia's system. The ministry has authorized the Musician's Association to "license" the use of folklore music. Gebru had obtained permission from the Ethiopian Musicians' Association to use nine songs that were considered part of the Ethiopian folklore. Awol, meanwhile, claimed that he had written the nine songs but could not produce written evidence or sound recordings that proved his assertions. Only the members of his band were able to testify on his behalf. The court heard expert witnesses who confirmed the association's view that the songs were folklore and, hence, denied copyright protection to Awol.[40] The court did not consider whether the adaptations that Awol made of the traditional folklore songs constituted derivative works protected under copyright laws.[41]

In a system such as Ethiopia's, the protection of intangible cultural heritage from misappropriation depends on a central agency that has to safeguard the cultural interests of the parties involved.[42] Several other states have chosen similar constructions[43] or directly assigned copyrights to the central government.[44] However, nothing would prevent legislation that assigns copyrights in folklore directly to local or indigenous communities if such communities enjoy standing in a particular legal system. Few countries have done this, however.[45] Eventual benefits deriving from approved commercial uses can be used for promoting local and indigenous cultures.[46] Especially in countries where folklore is considered part of the national heritage, a centralized agency might be suitable for that task. In the case of intangible cultural property of indigenous or local communities, however, the decision on whether to "license" a piece of folklore should be "delegated" to the community itself. It is unthinkable that a central authority could safeguard the interests of an aboriginal tribe, for example. Only the indigenous or local group holding a particular object of intangible cultural property is able to decide on its use in accordance with its customary laws.[47]

If a legislature chooses to protect folklore as a special category of its copyright laws, several questions have to be addressed, such as who owns the copyright in folklore, who is entitled to represent the owner, and what is the relation of existing to new and derived works of folklore. Folklore should be clearly defined, preferably adding a list-style description, as in the WIPO Model Provisions,[48] and legislation should indicate if the term applies to certain ideas, too. Laws should also regulate whether they have a retroactive effect, that is, if such protection applies to expressions of folklore that have already fallen into public domain before the acts came into force.[49] When regulating the terms of protection, countries should be careful not to overprotect their folklore.[50]

Other IP Rights and the Protection of Folklore

Besides copyrights, trademarks, certification marks, and industrial designs[51] have been used to protect folklore. Appellations of origins have also been suggested for the protection of the authenticity of artwork.[52] Increasingly, local communities use trademarks and certification marks to protect their products. Certain states, such as Kazakhstan, have registered trademarks to protect characteristic national products[53] or sponsor programs that encourage indigenous and local communities to register trademarks (as in Australia or in the United States).[54] Trademarks have a certain potential to protect the integrity of intangible cultural property in that they can serve as a label for consumers to recognize which products have been produced by traditional artists, especially where copyrights do not provide protection for certain aspects of traditional culture, such as specific painting, cloth weaving, or carpet knitting techniques and designs.[55] Their potential to safeguard against misappropriations of intangible cultural property is limited, however. No producer can be forced not to use a certain design. He or she can only be barred from using designs that have been registered by a country or a local or indigenous community that designates a folklore article as genuine. Hence, in many situations (such as the Australian cases referred to above), trademarks do not provide a viable alternative.

Design or patent protection is problematic for safeguarding against cultural misappropriation, as it requires registration of the actual element of intangible cultural property. Registration includes disclosure, and that is exactly what communities like the Pueblo of Santo Domingo want to safeguard against. In cases where a property holder is not opposed to disclosure but intends to prevent distortions, designs or patents do provide an alternative route for protection of noncopyrightable, intangible cultural property. Countries should make sure, however, that registration procedures are not too burdensome or should provide special assistance or facilitation to indigenous or local communities.

The Use of Trademarks in Australia   Again, an Australian initiative can serve as an example of the use of trademarks to protect the authenticity of folklore. Some nonaboriginal producers of folklore products have started to imitate the style of aboriginal art (while not copying it specifically), for example, the popular dot painting style. Copyright laws do not protect such styles at all. Copyright laws do not protect musical instruments either. An example is the traditional aboriginal and Torres Strait Islander musical instrument, the didgeridoo, which is manufactured and exported by many nonaboriginal producers. In response, the Tiwi artists created an authenticity label. Registered as a trademark, it provides for rules for its use, management, and enforcement (WIPO 2001c, p. 73). Not only individual indigenous communities have registered trademarks or certification marks. The Australian government sponsors a program at the National Indigenous Arts Advocacy Association (NIAAA) that leads to the registration of a certification mark that certifies the authenticity of products and artwork claiming to be indigenous. The program also helps to raise general public awareness of indigenous IP issues and concerns.[56]

The Need for Sui Generis Protection of Folklore

The examples cited in the previous paragraph show that many countries have found solutions for protecting folklore within their existing IP framework that can prevent misappropriations of intangible cultural property. Copyright laws are widely used. Sometimes, to make sure that folklore enjoys comprehensive protection from misappropriation, countries have amended their copyright laws to include all works of folklore or even particular styles or ideas. Furthermore, terms of protection for folklore in most countries are different from regular terms of protection. Hence, copyright laws have to be stretched considerably to cover folklore comprehensively. Many countries might not be prepared to take such steps. A sui generis protection for folklore might then be the better alternative.[57]

   The term "sui generis IP rights" is used for protective systems that create new IP categories to protect folklore. Only a few examples exist, one of which is the 1982 WIPO Model Provisions[58] that prohibit any publication, reproduction, distribution, public recitation or performance, transmission, and any other form of communication to the public, of expressions of folklore without the authorization of a competent national authority or the community concerned.[59] The model provisions create a sui generis system closely related to copyrights but define a new IP category: "expressions of folklore."[60] The provisions contain criminal and civil remedies and provide for the protection of expressions of folklore of other countries subject to reciprocity.

An example of a protective regime that is based on an enumerative system is Guatemala's Cultural Heritage Protection Law.[61] It allows any natural person or legal entity owning a cultural good to register it in the "Cultural Goods Registry," which is part of the Ministry of Cultural Affairs. Cultural goods include intangible cultural heritage made up of institutions, traditions, and customs including oral, musical, medical, culinary, and religious traditions as well as dance, theater, and customs.[62] Once a cultural good is registered, the owner has the responsibility for conserving the cultural good. The ministry can require living proof of an existing cultural good and reject a good for registration, or revoke an existing registration for a good. There is no time limitation for the protection of the cultural good. Civil and criminal remedies are available, and the attorney general can enforce the rights.[63]

According to a recent UNESCO report, a comprehensive approach to protect expressions of folklore would have to protect "knowledge and values enabling their production, the creative processes that bring the products into existence and the modes of interaction by which these products are appropriately received and appreciatively acknowledged" (UNESCO 2001, § 4). There is still need for creative solutions to implement these goals. Until then, existing approaches might provide a workable environment for developing countries that wish to protect folklore.

"Technical" Traditional Knowledge and Patent Protection

As initially stated, the administration of traditional "technical" knowledge, such as plant medicine or agricultural knowledge, can be regulated by customary rules of indigenous or local communities. When examining whether protection through existing IP regimes is available, foremost, one has to look at patents. However, the protection of traditional knowledge under *patent regimes* is less readily available than copyright protection for folklore. Traditional knowledge is often not in a form that would allow the grant of a patent because it lacks the potential industrial application (Ragavan 2001, pp. 8–9, 13; WTO 2001a, § 29). Technological processes such as cloth-weaving, metal-working, construction of musical instruments, and some practices of herbal medicines might have the potential for commercial application in exceptional cases.[64] Furthermore, patent law requires an invention to be novel.[65] Traditional knowledge, as has been stated above, typically does not fulfill this requirement because it has been used by many previous generations. Nevertheless, traditional medicinal or agricultural knowledge can be strictly regulated by customary laws.

In addition, there are procedural requirements for obtaining patent protection. Unlike copyrights, patents are not granted automatically. The inventor must fulfill strict procedural requirements and file a patent application if he or she wants to protect an invention. Specifically, the invention must be disclosed in a manner sufficiently clear and complete for it to be carried out by a person skilled in the art.[66] Local communities often lack the capacity to file such patent applications. Moreover, certain aspects of traditional knowledge are not intended to be disclosed at all, or only under certain strict requirements.[67]

Even if a traditional knowledge holder fulfills all these requirements, the terms of protection under traditional patent laws are restricted, and community ownership is not reflected in patent laws. As a result, concerns similar to those analyzed under the copyright protection through folklore arise. Companies from industrial countries are conducting so-called "bioprospecting missions" to developing countries with the aim of finding plants with active ingredients that provide potential commercial applications. The missions rely on the knowledge of indigenous and local communities to find such plants. Several cases have arisen in which companies did not respect the customary rules of the local communities or did not pay an adequate remuneration in exchange for using their intangible cultural property.[68] The commercial side, the right to get an adequate benefit in exchange for the knowledge provided, has been addressed in other chapters of this volume.[69] Still, indigenous and local communities sometimes do not want to share their knowledge at all or only under certain restrictions.

The Revocation and Reaffirmation of the Ayahuasca Patent

In another case, the U.S. Patent and Trademark Office (USPTO) had granted a patent on a variation of a vine used by indigenous tribes throughout the Amazon basin to produce a ceremonial drink called Ayahuasca, which is used to treat sicknesses, contact spirits, and foresee the future. The preparation and administration of the drink are strictly regulated by customary law, and many indigenous Amazon peoples regard the vine as a sacred symbol of their religion. The drink can be prepared only under the guidance of a shaman (Fecteau 2001, pp. 70–71). The holder of the patent had obtained samples of the vine in the 1970s, brought it back to the United States, and claimed a patent on the newly discovered plant that was granted in 1986.[70]

When the Coordinating Body of Indigenous Organizations of the Amazon Basin (COICA) learned about the patent, it filed a request for reexamination mainly on grounds of nonnovelty because of the characteristics of the plant that were widely known in scientific literature and nonutility because of violation of religious beliefs of the indigenous peoples using the plant.[71] In a first procedural step USPTO rejected the patent, basing its rejection on the finding that the invention was identical to other specimens of Ayahuasca found in U.S. herbarium collections, that is, it was nonnovel.[72] The USPTO did not examine whether prior use by indigenous communities outside the United States constitutes prior art that would exclude the grant of a patent. Yet, U.S. patent law excludes the consideration of unpublished foreign sources as prior art anyway.[73] Furthermore, USPTO did not address the question of whether the fact that the vine was a sacred religious symbol precluded its patentability on grounds of nonutility. In the final decision, however, USPTO, after reviewing the response of the patent holder, affirmed the patent (USPTO 2001). A new review of the herbarium collections led the examiner to conclude that the variety discovered by the patent holder is not identical to the varieties documented in the collections.[74]

This case is an example in which a piece of traditional knowledge was patentable under a national law, because the United States recognizes patents on plants. However, the patent was granted not to the indigenous community but to a nonnative discoverer of the plant. In an effort to remedy such situations, India has enacted a Plant Variety and Farmer's Rights Protection Act that allows the registration of community rights in traditional agricultural plant knowledge.[75] Such innovative solutions are possible under international conventions because they do not mandate a certain system of protection. Article 27.3(b) of the TRIPS Agreement requires countries to establish either patent protection of plant varieties or a sui generis system.[76] With regard to plant patents, countries thus are free to enact a system of protection that suits their cultural needs and can provide protection of intangible cultural property against misappropriations.

In the *Ayahuasca* case, the local communities have not even managed to prevent IP protection of their knowledge on the basis that such patents are not novel. While the patent in this case was granted on "narrow grounds" because of plant characteristics formerly unknown in U.S. herbarium collections, in most situations documentation of traditional knowledge is not available at all. Most patent laws do not recognize foreign, unpublished sources as forms of prior art that would exclude novelty. Even if a national law accepts unpublished foreign sources as part of prior art, national authorities would not have the means for reviewing patent applications on that basis. As a response, many so-called defensive publication projects have been started in order to make traditional knowledge available for patent authorities to review patent applications.[77] Such projects also cover trademarks, designs, and even copyrights. Yet, again, such publications would not prevent the use of the intellectual creations collected.

Arogyapacha

Arogyapacha is a plant with tonic effects bred by the Kani, a tribe living mainly in the Kerala state of India.[78] The Tropical Botanic Garden and Research Institute (TBGRI), a governmental agency established to study plant genetic resources and their sustainable use, had "discovered" that the members of the tribe used to eat the seeds of the plant, giving them energy when they were tired. TBGRI started a research project, developed a product called Jeevani that contained active ingredients from Arogyapacha, obtained a patent, and sold it. The benefit from the patent was shared between the TBGRI and the Kanis.

Despite the TBGRI's efforts to guarantee an equitable sharing of the benefits with the tribe, the Kanis were divided over whether their tribal knowledge should be sold or not. The Kanis do not constitute a cohesive community. Their families are scattered over several areas in Kerala. TBGRI primarily interacted with only one group of Kanis, with the result that other groups opposed the deal with the institute (Anuradha 1998, p. 7). Furthermore, a number of tribal members regarded their knowledge as a sacred tribal secret (Ramani 2001, p. 1166). The younger tribals eagerly took part in the TBGRI project while the older generation regarded their knowledge as sacred and appealed to the younger generation to protect their tribal knowledge (Ramani 2001, p. 1172). A group of nine medicine men even wrote a letter to the chief minister of Kerala, objecting to the sale of their knowledge to "private companies" (Anuradha 1998, p. 8). They were supported by another government agency, the Kerala Institute for Research, Training and Development of Scheduled Castes and Scheduled Tribes (KIRTADS). The institute, devoted to the protection of traditional knowledge, insisted that "the tribal medical knowledge should not be diluted by crass commercialization" (Meetali 1999–2000, pp. 808–11), and subsequently was even pushing for legislation that would give IP rights (IPRs) to the tribes.[79]

The traditional knowledge of the Kanis would not have been suitable for a patent. Although the "world did not know about this unique plant until the Kani people led us to it,"[80] a TBGRI research team isolated the active ingredient in the plant, developed an herbal formulation suitable for medicinal application, and patented the discovery (Ramani 2001, p. 1154). As India did not have any legislation that protected the tribe's knowledge,[81] TBGRI was under no obligation to share the benefits with the Kanis or to seek formal consent before starting its research project. The tribals who initially disclosed the information were two guides hired by a team of researchers and were not official representatives of the

Kanis (Ramani 2001, pp. 1166–67). The tribe would not have had any legal means to pursue its claims either. In such cases, only sui generis protection would give an indigenous community an enforceable right to prevent third parties from using their knowledge in a way detrimental to their customary law. Article 8(j) of the Convention on Biological Diversity (CBD) thus calls for national legislation requiring prior informed consent of holders of "knowledge, innovations and practices of indigenous and local communities embodying traditional lifestyles" before their knowledge can be used by third parties.[82] Its scope, however, is limited to traditional knowledge relevant for the conservation of biological diversity. Contrarily, the draft Declaration on the Rights of Indigenous Peoples calls for the "full ownership, control and protection of their [Indigenous Peoples] cultural and intellectual property."[83]

Several countries have enacted restricted access systems to indigenous intangible cultural property, thus creating a sui generis IP right of indigenous communities to their intangible cultural property. The Philippines' Indigenous Peoples Rights Act allows prospecting for genetic resources within ancestral lands and domains of indigenous cultural communities only "with the prior informed consent of such communities, obtained in accordance with the customary laws of the concerned community."[84] Costa Rica's Biodiversity Law[85] recognizes the "right of local communities and indigenous peoples to oppose any access to their resources and associated knowledge, be it for cultural, spiritual, social, economic or other motives …"(WIPO 2001d, Annex I, article 66). It also establishes "sui generis community intellectual rights" that protect "knowledge practices and innovations of indigenous peoples and local communities related to the use of components of biodiversity and associated knowledge." These rights are recognized by their "mere existence" and do not "require prior declaration, explicit recognition nor official registration."[86]

Another means to enforce prior informed consent with regard to patents that has been proposed several times is to require patent filers to prove that where traditional knowledge has been used it was acquired legally and, thus, to disclose its source.[87] Such a measure might be feasible to ensure that companies that file patent applications for inventions with input stemming from traditional knowledge share their benefits with the indigenous or local communities. However, it does not afford control over the use of intangible cultural property other than for patent purposes. Furthermore, there are concerns that such a requirement is in violation of the TRIPS Agreement.[88]

Apart from the actual recognition of community interests, there are more practical problems, as the Kani example shows. Communities are not always identifiable. There might be no clear identification mark of a community, or a community might be spread over different parts of a country or even over different countries.

There are not always mechanisms that could represent the community.[89] A central authority or clear legislation may help to alleviate these problems.

Conclusion

There is no single feasible, legal way to alleviate concerns about the misappropriation of intangible cultural heritage. Developing countries that consider using legal means to protect their intangible cultural heritage should carefully evaluate their needs before deciding what legislative action they want to take. Careful drafting of IP laws can prevent many problems from developing. In addition, sui generis protective systems are available to provide more comprehensive protection and protection adapted to the specific needs of a country. However, legislators have to be aware of the fact that "overprotection" can be detrimental to other cultural, social, or economic interests. IPRs should not be understood as a fixed set of rules, but merely as a toolbox from which the adequate tools can be chosen and combined. Finally, cultural disintegration is also about social and economic opportunities.[90] An intangible cultural asset will be preserved only if the lifestyle embodying these assets provides valuable economic prospects. Eventually, commercialization of certain aspects of intangible cultural property can contribute to the preservation of cultural heritage as a whole. IP laws can contribute such opportunities in a limited way, but countries have to consider a holistic approach that combines prohibitive action with support initiatives. Capacity building and promoting understanding on IP issues, especially within indigenous and local communities, have to be a further important component of that policy.

Notes

1. In a recent submission to the World Intellectual Property Organization (WIPO), Zambia stated: "Traditional knowledge systems, traditional knowledge and innovations are manifested through traditional practices and lifestyles. The introduction of foreign values, foreign religions, changing lifestyles and the legacy of colonialism have contributed greatly to lowering the status of traditional knowledge systems, traditional knowledge and innovations in Zambia" (WIPO 2001g, Annex, p. 2).

2. These states included Tunisia in 1967, Bolivia in 1968, and Chile and Morocco in 1970. See WIPO 2001c, p. 173.

3. At the WIPO Stockholm Conference of 1967, India proposed to include folklore as one category of protected works in article 2.1 of the Berne Convention. However, member states could not agree on this approach. Finally, article 15(4) was included, allowing countries to task a national authority with representing authors of anonymous works. See Ricketson 1987, p. 314. The WIPO Performances and Phonograms Treaty, adopted on December 20, 1996, available at http://www.wipo.int/treaties/ip/wppt/index.html (visited June 30, 2002), is the first international text that contains binding obligations on folklore. Member states have to protect performers of "expressions of folklore" without providing a definition of the term. Currently, 34 countries are a party to that convention. Apart from several Eastern European states, the United States is the only industrial country that has ratified the treaty so far. The treaty entered into force on May 20, 2002.

4. The Tunis Model Law affords protection to folklore by extending traditional copyright regimes through perpetual protection, exemption from the fixation requirement, and introduction of moral rights to prevent destruction and desecration. The rights are vested in a competent authority. See Berryman 1994, p. 313; Githaiga 1998, § 68.

5. See the web page of the Intellectual Property Policy Directorate at http://strategis.ic.gc.ca/SSG/ip01078e.html (visited June 30, 2002).

6. See, for example, the WIPO Statement on Intellectual Property, Biodiversity and Traditional Knowledge (WTO WT/CTE/W/182 and IP/C/W/242); submission by WIPO to the Committee on Trade and Environment of the WTO (WTO WT/CTE/W/196 and IP/C/W/297).

7. See § 2 of the WIPO Model Provisions. § A of the UNESCO Recommendation recognizes "among others, language, literature, music, dance, games, mythology, rituals, customs, handicrafts, architecture and other arts" as forms of folklore.

8. See, for example, a statement by the aboriginal artist Bulun Bulun before a court: "A painting such as this is not separate from my rights in my land. It is a part of my bundle of rights in the land and must be produced in accordance with Ganalbingu custom and law. Interference with the painting or another aspect of the Madayin associated with Djulibinyamurr is tantamount to interference with the land itself as it is an essential part of the legacy of the land, it is like causing harm to the spirit found in the land, and causes us sorrow and hardship." *John Bulun Bulun & Anor v. R & T Textiles Pty Ltd.* 1998. 1082 FCA (September 3, 1998).

9. See the *Yumbulul* case below. See also Puri 1997, p. 47.

10. See chapter 5 of this volume. See also Weatherall 2001, p. 220. Significant markets for arts and crafts exist in industrial countries too. A 1985 study by the U.S. Department of Commerce estimated the U.S. market in U.S. Indian arts and crafts at US$400 million to US$800 million. About 20 percent of this market, the study continued, was occupied by "fake" imports, mainly from Mexico, the Philippines, and Taiwan, China. See Hapiuk 2001, p. 1017.

11. See article 2.1 of the Berne Convention (Ricketson 1987, pp. 238–53). Several scholars emphasize that copyright laws are apt to protect folklore. See Gavriolov 1984, p. 78; Long 1998, pp. 262–77. In a submission to WIPO, the Group of Countries of Latin America and the Caribbean (GRULAC) suggested that "[f]olklore could be protected by means of a system similar to copyright that took into account essential particularities such as collective ownership and the moral rights of authorship and integrity, the lack of a fixed form and the exclusion of styles from protection, and which at the same time introduced remedies against abuse, improper use and unauthorized exploitation. Those rights could, but need not, be made subject to temporary limitations in particular cases" (WIPO 2001d, Annex I, p. 7).

12. The Berne Convention does not mandate originality, though. See Ricketson 1987, pp. 158, 231–32.

13. There is no necessity to do so under article 14 of the Trade-Related Aspects of Intellectual Property Rights (TRIPS) Agreement. Hence, Woodward (1996, p. 279) suggests that developing countries may especially stand to benefit from TRIPS Agreement article 14. Contrarily, article 3 of the Rome Convention for the Protection of Performers defines performers as "actors, singers, musicians, dancers, and other persons who act, sing, deliver, declaim, play in, or otherwise perform *literary or artistic works...*" (Rome Convention for the Protection of Performers, Producers of Phonograms and Broadcasting Organizations, adopted on October 26, 1961, available at http://www.wipo.int/treaties/ip/rome/index.html [emphases added, visited June 30, 2002]).

14. For example, § 2 of Antigua and Barbuda's Copyright Bill of 2000 (WTO IP/N/1/ATG/C/1); article 5.XIII of Brazil's Law 9.610 (WTO IP/N/1/BRA/C/2); article 2.3 of Lithuania's Law on Copyright and Related Rights (WTO IP/N/1/LTU/C/1); article 2.2 of Paraguay's Law No. 1328/98 (WTO IP/N/1/PRY/C/1); article 118(1) of Slovenia's Copyright and Related Rights Act (WTO IP/N/1/SVN/1/Add.2); and article 4 of Thailand's Copyright Act (Weeraworawit 1997, p. 111).

15. See note 3 above. This extension of the categories of protected performers was proposed by Argentina. See "Basic Proposal for the Substantive Provisions of the Treaty for the Protection of the Rights of Performers and Producers of Phonograms to be Considered by the Diplomatic Conference," WIPO CRNR/DC/5, notes on article 2, 2.04.

16. See, for example, Heald 1996; Litman 1990.

17. The case is documented in Scafidi 2001, pp. 828–30.

18. For the purposes of this chapter, it is not important if ceremonial dances constitute "social dance steps and simple routines," which are not protected under U.S. Copyright Law (Skojec 1987).

19. U.S. state common law rights in live performance, however, can afford a certain amount of protection to the performer. See Teller 1990, pp. 777–79.

20. *Australian Law Reports* 130 (1994):659. The case is available online at http://www.austlii.edu.au/au/cases/cth/federal_ct/unrep7290.html (last visited October 8, 2003).

21. During the proceedings, according to aboriginal custom, the names of deceased aboriginal artists were not used. The court awarded additional damages for culturally based harm, and the damages were awarded as a lump sum to enable aboriginal clans to take account of collective ownership. See Puri 1997, p. 46.

22. *Intellectual Property Reports* 21 (1991):481. The case is available online at http://www.austlii. edu. au/au/cases/cth/federal_ct/unrep4955.html (last visited October 8, 2003).

23. *Intellectual Property Reports* 21 (1991):481. See also Haight Farley 1997, p. 32.

24. The district judge concluded that "Australia's copyright law does not provide adequate recognition of Aboriginal community claims to regulate the reproduction and use of works which are essentially communal in origin" (*Intellectual Property Reports* 21 [1991]:481). However, the court took into account the effect of the unauthorized reproduction of artistic works under customary aboriginal laws in quantifying the damage. The case against the Federal Reserve Bank settled out of court, but the case against the agent of the Aboriginal Artists Agency continued until its dismissal. See Haight Farley 1997, p. 32.

25. *John Bulun Bulun & Anor v. R & T Textiles Pty Ltd.* (*Australian Law Reports* 157 [1998]:193). The case is available online at http://www.austlii.edu.au/au/cases/ cth/federal_ct/1998/1082.html (last visited October 8, 2003).

26. See Puri 1997, p. 45.

27. Despite the permanent injunction granted to Bulun Bulun, the clan representative argued "that copyright infringements of artworks such as the artistic work affect interests beyond those of the copyright owner, and that the Ganalbingu people considered it to be of great importance that the Court recognise the rights of the Ganalbingu people and the injury caused to them by the respondent's infringement." *John Bulun Bulun & Anor v. R & T Textiles Pty Ltd.* (*Australian Law Reports* 157 [1998]:193).

28. The court held that as copyright was entirely governed by the Australian copyright act of 1968, aboriginal laws and customs could not be incorporated. The copyright act does not provide a basis for collective ownership either. *John Bulun Bulun & Anor v. R & T Textiles Pty Ltd.* (*Australian Law Reports* 157 [1998]:193).

29. The court emphasized that its finding did "not treat the law and custom of the Ganalbingu people as part of the Australian legal system" but "as part of the factual matrix which characterises the relationship as one of mutual trust and confidence." *John Bulun Bulun & Anor v. R & T Textiles Pty Ltd.* (*Australian Law Reports* 157 [1998]:193).

30. *John Bulun Bulun & Anor v. R & T Textiles Pty Ltd.* (*Australian Law Reports* 157 [1998]:193).

31. *John Bulun Bulun & Anor v. R & T Textiles Pty Ltd.* (*Australian Law Reports* 157 [1998]:193).

32. *John Bulun Bulun & Anor v. R & T Textiles Pty Ltd.* (*Australian Law Reports* 157 [1998]:193).

33. See, for example, a statement by the aboriginal artist Bulun Bulun before a court: "Paintings, for example, are a manifestation of our ancestral past. They were first made, in my case by Barnda [creator ancestor of the clan]. Barnda handed the painting to my human ancestors. They have been handed from generation to generation ever since." *John Bulun Bulun & Anor v. R & T Textiles Pty Ltd.* (*Australian Law Reports* 157 [1998]:193).

34. *John Bulun Bulun & Anor v. R & T Textiles Pty Ltd.* (*Australian Law Reports* 157 [1998]:193).

35. The Ethiopian Civil Code does not require originality at all (Ethiopia is not a member of the WTO or the Berne Convention, however). See Endeshaw 1996, pp. 229–30.

36. Otieno-Odek, 1995, pp. 16–26. In addition, a low originality threshold might fail to protect a specific set of cultural property. The *Ayahuasca* case, cited below, is an example in point. A U.S. patent holder was able to get protection because the patent was granted on very narrow grounds, recognizing novelty for even minor variations in plant varieties. The indigenous peoples did not succeed in getting a revocation of the patent on a plant that they consider sacred because known varieties of the same plant were slightly different.

37. See above, note 21.

38. See Haight Farley 1997, p. 32.

39. Case cited in Endeshaw 1996, pp. 232–34.

40. See Endeshaw 1996, pp. 232, 233. This author submits that the Ethiopian court relied unduly on the association's claim (p. 233).

41. Artists who are unable to protect their works will not be able to live from their profession. Endeshaw (1996, p. 234) describes the choice as one between an "effort to make authors pay for any folklore content" and "the quality of any new element in adaptation of songs."

42. Paraguay's Law No. 1328/98 on Copyright and Related Rights explicitly tasks the Dirección Nacional del Derecho de Autor to defend folklore, as part of the national patrimony against abusive exploitation and violations of its integrity (article 83). See WTO 2000a, p. 20.

43. Central agencies installed to administer folklore "licenses" include Nigeria's Copyright Commission (see WTO 2001b, p. 3); Sri Lanka's Minister in charge of the subject culture (§ 12(2) of the Sri Lanka Code of Intellectual Property, see note 49 below), who can seek injunctions and damages from the infringing entity (§ 22(c), criminal sanctions for copyright violations are regulated in § 144); and Tunisia's Ministry of Culture (article 7 of the Copyright Act [Law No. 94-36 of February 1994]) makes the commercial exploitation of expressions of folklore dependent on an express authorization by the Ministry of Culture (WIPO 2001e, Annex, p. 5). See also several other African countries referenced in Kuruk 1999, pp. 799–806.

44. Barbados (see note 49), Ghana (WIPO 2001e, Annex, p. 5), and St. Vincent and the Grenadines (see note 49).

45. In Egypt, legislation was proposed to assign property in expressions of folklore collectively to local communities and the state (WIPO 2001e, Annex, p. 5). In some instances, countries protect a sort of moral community right to prevent mutilations and deformations of works of folklore and a right of the community to be named on copies of works derived from folklore. See Paraguay's Law No. 1328/98 "De Derecho de Autor y Derechos Conexos," articles 83 and 84. Available at http://www.sice.oas.org/int_prop/nat_leg/Paraguay/L132898in.asp.

46. For example, in Ghana, benefits from governmental licenses are paid into a fund to be used for the promotion of institutions for the benefit of authors, performers, and translators of expressions of folklore (WIPO 2001e, Annex, p. 5).

47. Still, problems might arise, especially in communities that are not cohesive. See the Kani example below.

48. See note 7.

49. This question already gave rise to concerns at the Stockholm Conference of the Berne Convention (see Ricketson 1987, p. 314). Existing national copyright laws only partly address these questions. The Copyright and Related Rights Laws and Treaties Copyright Act (1998) of Barbados, after defining folklore as "all literary and artistic works that a) constitute a basic element of the traditional and cultural heritage of Barbados; b) were created in Barbados by various groups of the community; and c) survive from generation to generation," assigns the rights to the crown and entitles the attorney general to enforce the rights of the crown. However, the act does not specify what happens with newly emerging works of folklore, and if works can cease being folklore (§ 22.5 and 6 of the act, available at http://www.sice.oas.org/int_prop/nat_leg/Barbados/Ca98-1e.asp#toc, visited June 30, 2002). Sri Lanka's Code of Intellectual Property does not specifically assign the ownership of copyrights in folklore but states that works of Sri Lanka folklore shall be protected without limitation in time (§ 12.2) and that the economic and moral rights shall be exercised by the minister in charge of the subject of culture (§ 22.1). The act also stipulates that works derived from folklore shall be protected as original

works (§ 8.1(c)) (see WTO 2001c). In this law, too, it is not clear what happens with the original owners, and if folklore refers only to ancient knowledge. § 16 of the Copyright Act of St. Vincent and the Grenadines (No. 53 of December 27, 1989), similarly to the Barbadian act, vests the author's rights in folklore in the crown and entitles the attorney general to enforce these rights. In addition, the act explicitly extends protection in perpetuity (see http://www. sice.oas.org/int_prop/nat_leg/St_Vincent/ ca1989_i.asp, last visited October 8, 2003).

50. Litman 1990; Long 1998, p. 274 (stating that the term of protection should not be longer than required to protect the cultural element); Weatherall 2001, pp. 233–35. The regulation of the terms of protection is also related to the required originality threshold.

51. In Kazakhstan, for instance, such designs as "head dresses (saykele), carpets (tuskiiz), decorations of saddles, national dwellings (yurta) ... women's decorations in form of bracelets (blezik), national children's costs-crib-cradles and table wares (piala, torcyk)" are protected as industrial designs (WIPO 2001b, Response of Kazakhstan, 2001, p. 1). Available at http://www.wipo.int/globalissues/ questionnaires/ic-2-7/index.html (last visited October 8, 2003).

52. See, for example, WIPO 2001d, Annex I, p. 7.

53. See WIPO 2001b, Response of Kazakhstan, 2001, p. 1.

54. See the Indian American Arts and Crafts Act, 25 U.S.C. 305 (2002). Section 305a(g)(1) of the act tasks the Indian Arts and Crafts Board, created under the act, to "create for the Board, or for an individual Indian or Indian tribe or Indian arts and crafts organization, trademarks of genuineness and quality...." For the Australian example, see note 56 below.

55. As an example, aboriginal tribes control certain painting techniques, such as the well-known dot painting style.

56. See WIPO 2001b, Response of Australia, 2001, p. 3. Available at http://www. wipo.int/globalissues/ igc/survey/index.html (visited June 30, 2002). In the United States, Native American tribes have started to register their names as trademarks.

57. UNESCO, in a 2001 report, concluded that recent meetings organized by UNESCO and WIPO suggested that IP does not give appropriate protection to expressions of folklore and that a sui generis regime needed to be developed (UNESCO 2001, § 13). With respect to copyright, the report emphasizes that copyrights serve a different purpose than the protection of folklore and proved to be inadequate to guarantee necessary protection. UNESCO specifically refers to the requirements of originality of the work, the final artistic form of the work and its fixation, the identification of the author, and the duration of the protection (UNESCO 2001, § 14).

58. See WIPO 1982.

59. For its definition of folklore, see text, p. 4.

60. See introductory observations to the WIPO Model Provisions (WIPO 1982), § 14.

61. Law No. 26-97 as amended by decrees No. 39-98 and 81-98. See WIPO 2001b, Response of Guatemala, p. 5. Available at http://www.wipo.int/globalissues/questionnaires/ic-2-7/index.html (last visited October 8, 2003). The law extends protection to intangible cultural property that is not protected under the existing IP rights laws of Guatemala. See also article 14 of the Ley de Derecho de Autor y Derechos Conexos (Law No. 33-98), available at http://www.sice.oas.org/ int_prop/ ipnale.asp#GUA (last visited October 8, 2003).

62. Law No. 26-97 as amended by decrees No. 39-98 and 81-98. See WIPO 2001b, Response of Guatemala, p. 5. Available at http://www.wipo.int/globalissues/questionnaires/ic-2-7/index.html (last visited October 8, 2003).

63. Similar systems have been proposed in scholarly works. Nuno Pires Carvalho has suggested a sui generis database protection that would protect not only the collection as such, but also undisclosed and disclosed works within the collection. See Nuno Pires Carvalho, *From the Shaman's Hut to the Patent Office: How Long and Winding Is the Road*, cited in WIPO 2001d, Annex I, p. 9.

64. Sodipo 1997, p. 38. For an example of a country protecting techniques attributed to traditional knowledge, see Kazakhstan protecting "the method of producing kumis (mare's milk)," "the method of producing shubat (female camel's milk)," or the "method of Kuskon of manufacturing relief picture of leather" (WIPO 2001b, Response of Kazakhstan 2001, p. 1).

65. International conventions do not mandate a certain degree of novelty though (Long 1998, p. 265, note 155). The patents issued by Kazakhstan based on traditional knowledge and cited in the previous footnote are probably possible only under a low novelty threshold (Kazakhstan is neither a member to the Paris Convention nor to the WTO TRIPS Agreement). Yet, a low threshold of novelty generally is not seen as in the interest of developing countries, as this narrows down the public domain. A large public domain is important for developing countries to create their own scientific and technological industries. See, for example, Otieno-Odek 1995, pp. 16–26.

66. See, for example, article 29.1 of the TRIPS Agreement.

67. See below, the *Ayahuasca* case and the *Arogyapacha* case.

68. Such cases have frequently been referred to as "biopiracy." See, for example, Fecteau 2001, p. 71.

69. See especially the chapter in this volume, "Biopiracy and Commercialization of Ethnobotanical Knowledge," by Philip Schuler.

70. The United States Plant Patent Act under 35 U.S.C. 161 (2002) recognizes patents for plant varieties with novel characteristics discovered in a cultivated state if they can be reproduced asexually.

71. A claim was also raised with regard to the well-known patent on a pesticide derived from the Neem tree held by the U.S. company W.R. Grace & Co. See Marden 1999, pp. 285–86. WIPO too suggested that the moral exception could be interpreted so as to prohibit the protection of intellectual creations that are "culturally offensive." See WIPO 2001c, p. 74.

72. See CIEL press release, November 4, 1999, available at http://www.ciel.org/Biodiversity/ ayahuascapatentcase.html (visited June 30, 2002) and Fecteau 2001, p. 86.

73. 35 U.S.C. § 102 (a) and (b) (2002). However, § 25(a)(k), 65(a)(iv)(q) of India's 1999 Patents (Second Amendment) Act, if adopted, would prevent the registration of a patent if the invention "is anticipated having regard to the knowledge, oral or otherwise, available within any local or indigenous community in any country." Available at http://www.iprlawindia.org/iprlaw.

74. USPTO at the same time emphasized that the "claim in a United States Plant Patent is among the very narrowest in scope granted by the United States Patent and Trademark Office, as it is specific to a single plant and its identical asexually reproduced progeny" (USPTO 2001).

75. See Sahai 2001a, p. 4.

76. Under that provision, countries do not have to provide patents or any other protection for animal species at all.

77. For example, in India a project to establish a traditional knowledge digital library (TKDL) for Ayurveda was started recently with the aim of preventing patents from being granted on nonoriginal inventions. See *Business Line* 2001. See also WIPO's work on IP aspects of the documentation of public domain traditional knowledge and its inclusion in the patent examination process as part of searchable prior art. See WIPO 2001a. See also Gupta 2001.

78. The case is documented by Anuradha 1998; Martin 1999; and Meetali 1999–2000.

79. Meetali 1999–2000. See also note 84. Ultimately, there was no collective body that could speak for all Kanis.

80. Ramani (2001), p. 1153, citing one of the researchers who "discovered" the plant.

81. Only limited protection for plant species is provided in the Plant Variety Protection and Farmers' Rights Act adopted in September 2001, which requires prior consent for species essentially derived from species "owned" by local communities. See Sahai 2001b. The proposed Biodiversity Bill focuses on sovereign rights on access to biodiversity and does not recognize rights of traditional knowledge holders. See *The Telegraph* 2001.

82. The CBD text is available online at http://www.biodiv.org (visited June 30, 2002). Article 9.2 of the Treaty on Plant Genetic Resources for Food and Agriculture adopted by the Food and Agriculture Organization of the United Nations (FAO) Conference on November 3, 2001, contains a similar but nonbinding provision. Available at http://www.fao.org/ag/ magazine/ITPGRe.pdf (visited June 30, 2002).

83. Article 29 of the draft Declaration on the Rights of Indigenous Peoples, available at http://www.unhchr.ch/indigenous/main.html (last visited October 8, 2003). The General Assembly

declared the period between 1995 and 2004 as the International Decade of the World's Indigenous Peoples (Resolution 48/163, adopted December 21, 1993, A/RES/48/163) and the UN Human Rights Commission has mandated the establishment of the Working Group on the draft Declaration on the Rights of Indigenous Peoples (Resolution 1995/32 endorsed by ECOSOC Resolution 1995/32). See also Lipszyc 1999, p. 100. The Venezuelan Constitution contains a similar commitment: "The collective intellectual property of indigenous knowledge, technology and innovations is guaranteed and protected. Any work on genetic resources and the knowledge associated therewith shall be for the collective good. The registration of patents in those resources and ancestral knowledge is prohibited." See WIPO 2001d, Annex I, p. 5. Furthermore, the draft Free Trade Area of the Americas (FTAA) Agreement requires each party to "recognize that the customs, traditions, beliefs, spirituality, religiosity, worldview, expressions of folklore, artistic expressions, traditional knowledge and any other form of traditional expression of indigenous peoples and local communities are part of their cultural patrimony," that "may not be subject to any form of exclusivity on the part of third parties not authorized through the intellectual property rights system, unless application is made by the indigenous peoples and local communities or by third parties authorized by them." Provisions contained in the subparagraph "Relationship between the Protection of Traditional Knowledge and Intellectual Property" (articles not numbered), text available at http://www.ftaaalca.org/ftaadraft/eng/ngip_e.doc (visited June 30, 2002).

84. 1997 Indigenous Peoples' Rights Act. See Philippines Executive Order, No. 247, 1995, Section 2(a), cited in WIPO 2001b. In response to the Arogyapacha controversy, KIRTADS initiated the drafting of a state-level bill that would have given exclusive rights to tribal communities over their tribal IPRs. A tribal IPR council would oversee action to prevent exploitation and misuse of tribal IPRs. An infringement of tribal IPRs could lead to imprisonment and a fine. See Martin 1999.

85. See WIPO 2001d, Annex I, p. 8. The law is based on Decision 391 of the Andean Community establishing a Common Regime on Access to Genetic Resources (see WIPO 2001f, Annex III). Article 7 of the decision recognizes "the rights and decision-capacity of indigenous, Afro-American and local communities with regard to their traditional practices, knowledge and innovations connected with genetic resources and their derivatives" (WTO 2000b, p. 6). See also ten Kate and Laird 1999, pp. 28–29. The decision introduced the so-called "intangible components" defined as "knowledge, innovation or individual or collective practices, of actual or potential value, that are associated with genetic resources or their derivatives or the biological resource containing them, whether or not protected by intellectual property regimes." See WTO 2000b, p. 6. The concept was included in order "to give local and indigenous communities legal protection against misappropriation of their knowledge and to facilitation of access contracts" (WTO 2000b, p. 6). Peru, too, has enacted a national law that requires prior informed consent of indigenous groups for the use of their traditional knowledge. See WTO 2000b, p. 3. See also GRULAC, Annex I, pp. 8–9.

86. See also WIPO 2001d, Annex I, p. 8, article 82.

87. The system would also work with trademarks, industrial designs, and geographical indications. See WIPO 2001, pp. 73–74. Peru during the negotiations of the Patent Law Treaty under the auspices of WIPO suggested the inclusion of a provision that required such disclosure (see de Carvalho 2000, p. 377); the proposal was largely disputed by industrial countries. In the discussions on the revision of article 27.3(b) of the TRIPS Agreement, several countries mandated that a requirement should be added "which would oblige patent applications to provide an official certificate of the source and origin of the genetic material and the related traditional knowledge used, evidence of fair and equitable benefit sharing and evidence of prior informed consent from government or local communities for the exploitation of the subject matter of the patent." See WTO 2001a, § 22. Many industrial states opposed such an inclusion because the patent authorities should not be used to enforce the access to genetic resources. Only a few countries have enacted biodiversity laws that could provide appropriate certification. See, for example, WTO 2001a, § 22. The European Community proposed, at the same time, the establishment of a "multilateral system and/or other solutions for disclosing and sharing information about the geographical origin of biological material relied on in patent applications" (WTO 2001a, § 23).

88. See de Carvalho 2000, pp. 379–89.

89. The two problems have been referred to as the problem of effective agency and clear identity. See Weatherall 2001, p. 230; see also ten Kate and Laird 1999, p. 30 (citing a Peruvian example in which not all local communities agreed with a benefit-sharing agreement, but because of a lack of rights were not able to oppose it, p. 29).

90. See UNESCO 2001 Annex § 4, wherein UNESCO emphasizes "the fact that many intangible cultural heritage manifestations are threatened with disappearance mainly because the well-being of the creators of this heritage is endangered by economic, political and social forces such as socio-economic marginalization, a global entertainment industry, religious intolerance and ethnic wars. . . ."

References

Anuradha, R. V. 1998. "Sharing with the Kanis. A Case Study from Kerala, India." Convention on Biodiversity Case Study. Available at http://www.biodiv.org/doc/case-studies/.

Berryman, Cathryn A. 1994. "Toward More Universal Protection of Intangible Cultural Property." *Journal of Intellectual Property Law* 1:293.

Blakeney, Michael. 1995. "Milpurrurru & Ors. v. Indofurn Pty Ltd & Ors.—Protecting Expressions of Aboriginal Folklore under Copyright Law." *Murdoch University Electronic Journal of Law* 2(1).

Business Line. 2001. "India: Traditional Knowledge Digital Library on Anvil." *The Hindu,* January 25, 2001. 2001 WL 3982065.

de Carvalho, Nuno Pires. 2000. "Requiring Disclosure of the Origin of Genetic Resources and Prior Informed Consent in Patent Applications without Infringing the TRIPS Agreement: The Problem and the Solution." *Washington University Journal of Law and Policy* 2:371.

Endeshaw, Assafa. 1996. *Intellectual Property Policy for Non-Industrial Countries.* Dartmouth: Aldershot, Brookfield, USA.

Fecteau, Leanne M. 2001. "The Ayahuasca Patent Revocation: Raising Questions about Current U.S. Patent Policy." *Boston College Third World Law Journal* 21:69.

Gavriolov, E. P. 1984. "The Legal Protection of Works of Folklore." *Copyright: Monthly Review of the World Intellectual Property Organization* 20:76.

Githaiga, Wambugu. 1998. "Intellectual Property Law and the Protection of Indigenous Folklore and Knowledge." *Murdoch University Electronic Journal of Law* 5(2).

Gupta, Anil K. 2001. "IP for Traditional Knowledge On-line: Recognizing, Respecting and Rewarding Creativity and Innovation at Grassroots." Available at http://ecommerce.wipo.int/meetings/2001/conference/program/index.html (last visited October 8, 2003).

Haight Farley, Christine. 1997. "Protecting Folklore of Indigenous Peoples: Is Intellectual Property the Answer?" *Connecticut Law Review* 30:1.

Hapiuk, Wiliam J. 2001. "Of Kitsch and Kachinas: A Critical Analysis of the Indian Arts and Crafts Act 1990." *Stanford Law Review* 53:1009.

Heald, Paul J. 1996. "Reviving the Rhetoric of the Public Interest: Choir Directors, Copy Machines, and New Arrangements of Public Domain Music." *Duke Law Journal* 46:241.

Kuruk, Paul. 1999. "Protecting Folklore under Modern Intellectual Property Regimes: A Reappraisal of the Tension between Individual and Communal Rights in Africa and the United States." *American University Law Review* 48:769.

Lipszyc, Delia. 1999. *Copyright Neighbouring Rights.* United Nations Educational, Scientific, and Cultural Organization, Paris.

Litman, Jessica. 1990. "The Public Domain." *Emory Law Journal* 39:965.

Long, Doris Estelle. 1998. "The Impact of Foreign Investment on Indigenous Cultures: An Intellectual Property Perspective." *North Carolina Journal of International Law and Commerce Regulation* 23:229.

Marden, Emily. 1999. "The Neem Tree Patent: International Conflict over the Commodification of Life." *Boston College International and Comparative Law Review* 22:279.

Martin, Max. 1999. "How To Sell a Wonder Herb." *DownToEarth* (7)12.

Meetali, Jain. 1999–2000. "Global Trade and the New Millennium: Defining the Scope of Intellectual Property Protection of Plant Genetic Resources and Traditional Knowledge in India." *Hastings International and Comparative Law Review* 22:777–819, 808–11.

Otieno-Odek, James. 1995. "Public Domain in Patentability after the Uruguay Round: A Developing Country's Perspective with Specific Reference to Kenya." *Tulane Journal of International and Comparative Law* 4:15.

Puri, Kamal. 1997. "The Experience of the Pacific Region." In *United Nations Education, Scientific, and Cultural Organization-World Intellectual Property Organization World Forum on the Protection of Folklore.* UNESCO Publication No. CLT/CIC/98/1, WIPO Publication No. 758, p. 39.

Ragavan, Srividhya. 2001. "Protection of Traditional Knowledge." *Minnesota Intellectual Property Review* 2:1.

Ramani, Rekha. 2001. "Market Realities v. Indigenous Equities." *Brooklyn Journal of International Law* 26:1147.

Ricketson, Sam. 1987. *The Berne Convention for the Protection of Literary and Artistic Works 1886–1986.* London: Kluwer.

Sahai, Suman. 2001a. India's Plant Variety Protection and Farmers Rights Act. Available at http://www.ciroap.org/food/documents/PVP_SUNS.PDF (last visited October 8, 2003).

———. 2001b. "India: Protect Farmers' Rights under WTO." *The Hindu,* September 16, 2001.

Scafidi, Susan. 2001. "Intellectual Property and Cultural Products." *Boston University Law Review* 81:793.

Skojec, Sheila A. 1987. "Annotation, Copyright of Dance or Choreography." *American Law Reports Federal* 85:par. 906.

Sodipo, Bankole. 1997. *Piracy and Counterfeiting: GATT, TRIPS and Developing Countries.* London: Kluwer Law International.

Teller, Bonnie. 1990. "Toward Better Protection of Performers in the United States: A Comparative Look at Performers' Rights in the United States, under the Rome Convention and in France." *Columbia Journal of Transnational Law* 28:775.

ten Kate, Kerry, and Sarah Laird. 1999. *The Commercial Use of Biodiversity, Access to Genetic Resources and Benefit-Sharing.* London: Earthscan.

The Telegraph. 2001. "India Advised to Learn Lessons from U.S. Patenting of Basmati Rice." Calcutta, India, August, 23, 2001, p. 10.

UNESCO (United Nations Educational, Scientific, and Cultural Organization). 1989. "Recommendation on the Safeguarding of Traditional Culture and Folklore." Adopted by the UNESCO General Conference at its 25th Session, Paris, November 15, 1989. Available at http://www.unesco.org/culture/heritage/intangible/.

———. 2001. "Report on the Preliminary Study on the Advisability of Regulating Internationally through a New Standard-Setting Instrument, the Protection of Traditional Culture and Folklore." 161 EX/15. Paris.

UNESCO/WIPO (United Nations Educational, Scientific, and Cultural Organization/World Intellectual Property Organization). 1976. "Model Provisions for National Laws on the Protection of Expressions of Folklore against Illicit Exploitation and Other Prejudicial Actions." WIPO/GRTKF/IC/3/10, Annex III.

USPTO (U.S. Patent and Trademark Office). 2001. "Notice of Intent to Issue Reexamination Certificate for Patent PP05751." Control Number 90/005,307. January 26, 2001.

Weatherall, Kimberlee. 2001. "Culture, Autonomy and Djulibinjamurr: Individual and Community in the Construction of Rights to Traditional Designs." *Modern Law Review* 64:215.

Weeraworawit, Weerawit. 1997. "Protection by Copyright and Neighboring Rights." In *United Nations Educational, Scientific, and Cultural Organization-World Intellectual Property Organization World Forum on the Protection of Folklore.* UNESCO Publication No. CLT/CIC/98/1, WIPO Publication No. 758, p. 107.

———. 1982. "WIPO Model Provisions for National Laws on the Protection of Expressions of Folklore against Illicit Exploitation and Other Prejudicial Actions." Available at http://www.wipo.int/globalissues/tk/pdf/1982-folklore-model-provisions.pdf (visited June 30, 2002).

WIPO (World Intellectual Property Organization). 1997. *Introduction to Intellectual Property Theory and Practice.* London.

_____. 2001a. "Progress Report on the Status of Traditional Knowledge as Prior Art." WIPO/GRTKF/IC/2/6.

_____. 2001b. "Survey on Existing Forms of Intellectual Property Protection for Traditional Knowledge." Submitted to the Intergovernmental Committee on Intellectual Property and Genetic Resources, Traditional Knowledge and Folklore's second meeting in December 2001. WIPO/GRTKF/IC/2/5.

_____. 2001c. "Intellectual Property Needs and Expectations of Traditional Knowledge Holders." WIPO Report on Fact Finding Missions on Intellectual Property and Traditional Knowledge (1998–2000). Geneva.

_____. 2001d. "Traditional Knowledge and the Need to Give It Adequate Intellectual Property Protection." Documents submitted by GRULAC [Group of Countries of Latin America and the Caribbean] to the Intergovernmental Committee on Intellectual Property and Genetic Resources, Traditional Knowledge and Folklore, First Session, Geneva, April 30–May 3, 2001. WIPO/GRTKF/IC/1/5.

_____. 2001e. Proposal presented by the African Group to the First Meeting of the Intergovernmental Committee on Intellectual Property and Genetic Resources, Traditional Knowledge and Folklore, First Session, Geneva, April 30–May 3, 2001. WIPO/GRTKF/IC/1/10.

_____. 2001f. Document submitted by the Member States of the Andean Community, Intergovernmental Committee on Intellectual Property and Genetic Resources, Traditional Knowledge and Folklore, First Session, Geneva, April 30–May 3, 2001. WIPO/GRTKF/IC/1/11, Annex III.

_____. 2001g. Document submitted by the Delegation of Zambia to the Intergovernmental Committee on Intellectual Property and Genetic Resources, Traditional Knowledge and Folklore, First Session, Geneva, April 30–May 3, 2001. WIPO/GRTKF/IC/1/12.

Woodward, Martin, D. H. 1996. "TRIPS and NAFTA's Chapter 17: How Will Trade-Related Multilateral Agreements Affect International Copyright?" *Texas International Law Journal* 31:369.

WTO (World Trade Organization). 2000a. "Main Dedicated Intellectual Property Laws and Regulations Notified under Article 63.2 of the Agreement, Council for Trade-Related Aspects of Intellectual Property Rights." WTO IP/N/1/PRY/C/1.

_____. 2000b. "Peru's Experience of the Protection of Traditional Knowledge and Access to Genetic Resources." Committee on Trade and Environment. WT/CTE/W/176. Geneva, Switzerland.

_____. 2001a. "Review of the Provisions of Article 27.3(b) of the TRIPS Agreement, Communication from the European Communities and Their Member States." Council for Trade-Related Aspects of Intellectual Property Rights. IP/C/W/254. Geneva, Switzerland.

_____. 2001b. "Checklist of Issues of Enforcement, Responses from Nigeria, Council for Trade-Related Aspects of Intellectual Property Rights." WTO IP/N/6/NGA/1.

_____. 2001c. "Main Dedicated Intellectual Property Laws and Regulations Notified under Article 63.2 of the Agreement, Council for Trade-Related Aspects of Intellectual Property Rights." WTO IP/N/1/LKA/C/1.

9

MAKING INTELLECTUAL PROPERTY LAWS WORK FOR TRADITIONAL KNOWLEDGE

Coenraad J. Visser

Without entering into the debate about the precise definition of the term "traditional knowledge,"[1] or about whether such a definition is a prerequisite to any legal protection of traditional knowledge, I should merely note that for the purposes of this Chapter, I use the term in its widest possible sense, to include traditional and tradition-based[2] literary, artistic, and scientific works; performances, inventions, scientific discoveries, and designs; marks, names, and symbols; undisclosed information; and all other innovations and creations resulting from intellectual activity in the industrial, scientific, literary, or artistic fields.[3] So categories of traditional knowledge include agricultural knowledge; scientific knowledge; technical knowledge; ecological knowledge; medicinal knowledge, including knowledge relating to medicines and remedies; knowledge relating to biodiversity; and traditional cultural expressions[4] in the form of music, dance, song, handicrafts, designs, stories, artworks, and elements of languages (such as names, geographical indications, and symbols; WIPO 2001).

International Framework: The TRIPS Agreement

Internationally, the Agreement on Trade-Related Aspects of Intellectual Property Rights (in short, the TRIPS Agreement)[5] mandates the level of protection of intellectual property rights (IPRs)[6] in national law. As a basic premise, the TRIPS

Agreement requires that all countries, whether they are developed or developing,[7] adopt the same level of protection for IPRs.

Complying formally with the TRIPS Agreement imposes enormous costs on developing countries. Not only do they have to set up industrial property registries that many of them did not have before, but they also have to comply with the extensive enforcement obligations of the agreement (articles 41–61), which include border measures (articles 51–60) and criminal sanctions to combat piracy and counterfeiting (article 61). The high economic cost of compliance is, of course, compounded by the fact that these countries are net importers of intellectual property. In hard currency terms, then, compliance with the TRIPS Agreement brings about an outflow of foreign currency from developing countries.

Why did developing countries, then, agree to the TRIPS Agreement in Uruguay?

In the first instance, it has been argued that during the TRIPS negotiations, developing countries were often not party to bilateral negotiations between the United States and Europe, and so did not have access to the same level of information as those two negotiating parties (Drahos and Braithwaite 2002). Also, all negotiating parties were ignorant about the likely effects of the TRIPS Agreement in information markets—the real world costs of extending intellectual property rights and their effects on barriers to entry in markets were not clear at all. In a sense, "TRIPS was less a negotiation and more a 'convergence of processes'" (Drahos and Braithwaite 2002).

Second, developing countries and less developed countries (LDCs)[8] have longer time frames within which to comply with the TRIPS Agreement (articles 65.1 and 66.1, respectively), and there are minor exceptions in their favor, most notably in respect of patent protection (article 65.4).[9] (These exceptions are not relevant to this chapter.)

Third, the TRIPS Agreement imposes an obligation on developed countries to provide incentives to enterprises and institutions in their territories to promote and encourage technology transfer to LDCs "in order to enable them to create a sound and viable technological base" (article 66.2).[10] Also, developing countries were persuaded that strong intellectual property protection would lead to increased foreign investment. Unfortunately, figures for foreign direct investment (FDI), for example, show that this vaunted benefit has not materialized.[11]

Fourth, developed countries are enjoined to assist developing countries and LDCs by means of technical and financial cooperation in favor of these countries. But the focus of such cooperation is narrow—it includes by name only "assistance in the preparation of laws and regulations on the protection and enforcement of IPRs as well as on the prevention of their abuse, and shall include support regarding the establishment or reinforcement of domestic offices and agencies relevant to these matters, including the training of personnel" (article 67). So the focus of international assistance rendered by organizations such as the World Trade Organization (WTO) itself and the World Intellectual Property Organization (WIPO)[12] is only on the implementation of the TRIPS Agreement.

Fifth, as the TRIPS Agreement was negotiated as part of an international trade agreement, developing countries were also persuaded that the costs of implementing the TRIPS Agreement would be offset by gains in international trade generally. The Doha Ministerial Declaration likewise repeats the truism that "[i]nternational trade can play a major role in the promotion of economic development and the alleviation of poverty" (§ 2). The World Bank has estimated that increasing access by developing countries to world export markets could generate an additional US$1.5 trillion in income over 10 years and raise their annual gross domestic product growth rates by 0.5 percent (World Bank 2002). A major hurdle to be cleared by developing countries, though, is that the barriers to international trade are at their most impenetrable precisely in those economic sectors where developing countries can compete most effectively in international trade, especially in agriculture. In the Doha Ministerial Declaration, members of the WTO weakly committed themselves to comprehensive negotiations, "without prejudging the outcome of the negotiations," to improve market access, and to reduce subsidies and other trade-distorting domestic support practices for agricultural products (§ 13). For the foreseeable future, then, it seems unlikely that developing countries will be able to compete effectively in the agricultural export sector of the world market and that they will be able to offset the costs of implementing the TRIPS Agreement against gains in international trade in commodities that have traditionally been their strength in this context.

Sixth, developing countries were told that strengthening their domestic intellectual property protection would benefit their own creators and inventors.

Developing Countries: A Clash of IPR Paradigms

When we concern ourselves with intellectual property protection in developing countries, we have to be conscious that we are effectively dealing with two systems of legal protection. The first is the system of IPRs enshrined in the TRIPS Agreement. These rights are characterized by the fact that they are individualized—they attach to their holders in the romantic liberal traditional of rights that attach to individual citizens. Roht-Arriaza, for example, writes of patents (one of the categories of intellectual property protected by the TRIPS Agreement):

"... the individual nature of patent law is reinforced in the trade-related intellectual property rights (TRIPS) agreement ... which recognizes intellectual property rights only as private rights. Rights belonging to the public, or a sector of it, do not fit easily" (Roht-Arriaza 1997).

Coexistent with this system of individual IPRs are indigenous knowledge systems—traditional knowledge, including, as I have indicated at the outset, traditional cultural expressions and traditional ecological knowledge (sometimes called ethnobotanical knowledge).

Gudeman (1996) explains further:

> Built upon the Cartesian duality of mind and body, intellectual property rights are aligned with practices of rationality and planning. The expression "intellectual property rights" makes it appear as if the property and rights are products of individual minds. This is part of a Western epistemology that separates mind from body, subject from object, observer from observed, and that accords priority, control, and power to the first half of the duality. The term "intellectual" connotes as well the knowledge side and suggests that context of use is unimportant.... In contrast to this modernist construction, in a community economy innovations are cultural properties in the sense that they are the product and property of a group.

In the same vein, it has been argued (Berkes, Folke, and Gadgil 1995) that

> indigenous [*viz* traditional] knowledge differs from scientific knowledge in being moral, ethically-based, spiritual, intuitive and holistic; it has a large social context. Social relations are not separated from relations between humans and non-human entities. The individual self-identity is not distinct from the surrounding world. There often is no separation of mind and matter. Traditional knowledge is an integrated system of knowledge, practice and beliefs.

The communal nature of traditional knowledge is recognized expressly in legislation in the Philippines and República Bolivariana de Venezuela, for example.

The Philippine Constitution of 1987 expressly mandates the recognition, respect, and protection of the rights of indigenous cultural communities and indigenous peoples (section 17, article XIV). In discharge of this mandate, the Indigenous Peoples Rights Act (Republic Act No. 8371) was enacted in October 1997. It protects the following "community intellectual property rights" of indigenous peoples: past, present, and future manifestations of their cultures, such as archeological and historical sites, designs, ceremonies, technologies, visual and performing arts, literature, and religious and spiritual properties; science and technology, such as "human and other genetic resources, seeds, medicines, health practices, vital medicinal plants, animals, minerals, indigenous knowledge systems and practices, resource management systems, agricultural technologies, knowledge of the properties of fauna and flora, and scientific discoveries"; and "language, music, dance, script, histories, oral traditions, conflict resolution mechanisms, peace building processes, life philosophy and perspectives and teaching and learning systems" (Rules and Regulations Implementing Republic Act No. 8371, section 10, rule VI). The extent of these rights appears from section 34:

> Indigenous cultural communities/indigenous peoples are entitled to the recognition of the full ownership and control and protection of their cultural and intellectual rights. They shall have the right to special measures to control, develop and protect their sciences, technologies and cultural manifestations, including human and other genetic resources, including derivatives of these resources, seeds, traditional medicines and health practices, vital medicinal plants, animals and minerals, indigenous knowledge systems and practices, knowledge of the properties of flora and fauna, oral traditions, literature, designs and visual and performing arts.

Article 124 of the Constitution of the República Bolivariana de Venezuela of 1999 states succinctly:

> The collective intellectual property of indigenous knowledge, technology and innovations is guaranteed and protected. Any work on genetic resources and the knowledge associated therewith shall be for the collective good. The registration of patents in those resources and ancestral knowledge is prohibited.

This distinction between individual IPRs and communal traditional knowledge rights is a slight oversimplification, of course. While many indigenous and local communities generate and transmit knowledge from generation to generation collectively, there are situations in which individual members of these communities can distinguish themselves and be recognized as informal creators or inventors distinct from their community (Gupta 1999). Also, collective marks[13] are known to trademark law, and the TRIPS Agreement itself recognizes geographical indications (article 22)—both types of IPR protect the interests of a collective.[14]

When these rights paradigms clash, who will emerge the winner? Shiva (1997) asks:

> When indigenous systems of knowledge and production interact with dominant systems of knowledge and production, it is important to anticipate whether the future options of the indigenous system or the dominant system will grow. Whose knowledge and values will shape the future options of diverse communities?

Given the reality of economic power, it is not hard to predict that the system of individual IPRs as sanctioned by the TRIPS Agreement will hold sway. But it is precisely its superimposition on traditional knowledge systems that challenges developing countries in two very different ways—to protect their traditional knowledge holders[15] against the operation of the IPR systems as embodied in the TRIPS Agreement and, at the same time, to use those IPRs to protect their traditional knowledge holders, no matter whether they hold individual or communal rights.

Protecting Traditional Knowledge in Developing Countries: Two Goal Posts

So we should look at intellectual property from the point of view of, first, the protection of traditional knowledge against IPRs and, then, the protection of traditional knowledge by IPRs. At first blush, this distinction seems to mirror the distinction between the "positive" and "defensive" protection of traditional knowledge (Wendland 2002). Some indigenous peoples and traditional communities want *positive* protection of their traditional cultural expressions—they want to benefit from the commercialization of these expressions. But some members of these groups and communities are concerned with the cultural, social, and psychological harm caused by the unauthorized use of their traditional cultural expressions. To these people, such use deprives these expressions of their original significance, which, in turn, may disrupt and dissolve their culture. So this group argues for the *defensive* protection of these cultural expressions.

These are not watertight categories, of course. The protection of traditional knowledge for the purposes of exploitation by its holders also entails the protection of such knowledge against misappropriation by "outsiders," against exploitation of traditional knowledge, in other words.

Note also that at the World Summit on Sustainable Development (WSSD; 2002), the participants recognized, "[s]ubject to national legislation, ... the rights of local and indigenous communities who are holders of traditional knowledge, innovations and practices, and, with the approval and involvement of the holders of such knowledge, innovations and practices, develop and implement benefit-sharing mechanisms on mutually agreed terms for the use of such knowledge, innovations and practices" (WSSD ¶ 42(j)).

Goal Post 1: Protection against Exploitation of Traditional Knowledge

Patents

The following are two illustrations of the appropriation of traditional knowledge without the consent of the holders of such knowledge, and the subsequent use of such knowledge to obtain patents. Turmeric is an Indian plant that has been used for thousands of years for controlling pests and healing wounds and rashes. The United States Patent and Trademark Office (USPTO) granted a patent for turmeric to be used to heal wounds. The patent was assigned to the University of Mississippi Medical Center. It claimed that the administration of an effective amount of turmeric through local and oral routes enhances the wound-healing process. This patent was revoked for anticipation (lack of novelty) after the Indian

Council for Scientific and Industrial Research presented an ancient Sanskrit text that witnessed the traditional use of the plant.[16]

Likewise, the neem tree grows in India and other parts of Southeast Asia. Neem extracts can be used as a pesticide for pests (such as the white fly) and fungus diseases. Besides, the oil extracted from its seeds can be used to relieve various human diseases, such as malaria, skin diseases, and even meningitis. The European Patent Office granted a patent to an American corporation for an insecticide and a fungicide derived from a neem seed extract comprising neem oil. The patent was later revoked, again mainly for lack of novelty—the invention claimed was not new because of prior public use by farmers in India.[17]

Many of the instances of the appropriation and exploitation of traditional knowledge in this manner involve the use of both genetic resources and traditional ecological knowledge about the properties of such resources. The protection of the genetic resources as such falls outside the scope of this chapter. But while, at first blush, the genetic resources that are used in a patented invention may seem economically to be the most important factor, the economic significance of the traditional ecological knowledge should not be overlooked. It has been claimed that of the 120 active compounds derived from plants that are widely used in contemporary medicines, 75 percent were already known within traditional knowledge systems (McLeod 2001). Using those knowledge systems increases 400-fold the ability to locate plants that have specific medicinal uses (Shiva 1997). According to another estimate, "bioprospectors can increase the success ratio in trials for useful substances from one in ten thousand samples to one in two" (Roht-Arriaza 1997).

The problem facing developing countries in this context is multidimensional. First, no financial benefits from the exploitation of traditional knowledge in this way reach the holders of such knowledge. The United Nations has estimated that developing countries lose at least US$5 billion annually in unpaid royalties to multinational corporations that appropriate traditional knowledge (McLeod 2001). Second, the existence of an earlier patent bars the registration of a patent by the holders of traditional knowledge—they are excluded from obtaining patents for their inventions that utilize their traditional knowledge. Third, a patent confers on its holder a monopoly to exploit the patented invention in the territory for which it is registered. So the holders of traditional ecological knowledge may well find themselves unable to use their own knowledge, since that may infringe the rights conferred by a related patent registered for their territories. Fourth, although most patents using indigenous knowledge may be open to revocation on the basis that the inventions should not have been patented since they had not been new at the time of application (as in the turmeric and neem cases), the legal processes of opposition and revocation are costly and so often beyond the financial means of the communities concerned. Fifth, in some legal systems the claim for revocation must be backed up by written evidence of prior art.

As far as protection against exploitation under patent law is concerned, then, three complementary approaches can be taken.

Prior Informed Consent   Patent applicants can be required or encouraged to furnish information relating to genetic resources and/or traditional ecological knowledge used in the development of inventions claimed in patent applications. This approach may involve disclosing the source of the material and providing information about the legal basis of access to it, such as an indication or evidence of prior informed consent. Various proposals along these lines have been made in international fora such as the WTO, the Convention on Biological Diversity (CBD), United Nations Conference on Trade and Development (UNCTAD), and WIPO. Examples of such a consent requirement can be found in Decision 391 (1996) of the Andean Community, which introduces the Common System to regulate access to Genetic Resources, and the Biological Diversity Law No. 7788 (1998) of Costa Rica.

The Conference of Parties of the CBD invited governments "to encourage the disclosure of the country of origin of genetic resources in applications for intellectual property rights, where the subject matter of the application concerns or makes use of genetic resources in its development, as a possible contribution to tracking compliance with prior informed consent and the mutually agreed terms on which access to those resources was granted" and "to encourage the disclosure of the origin of relevant traditional knowledge, innovations and practices of indigenous and local communities relevant for the conservation and sustainable use of biological diversity in applications for intellectual property rights, where the subject matter of the application concerns or makes use of such knowledge in its development" (CBD 2002).

The WIPO Intergovernmental Committee on Intellectual Property and Genetic Resources, Traditional Knowledge and Folklore[18] (WIPO-IGC) is responding to a request from the Secretariat of the CBD to prepare a technical study on various requirements for disclosure related to genetic resources and traditional knowledge in patent examinations (CBD 2002). An initial report was presented to the WIPO-ICG in December 2002 (WIPO 2002c).

It is controversial whether prior informed consent, as envisaged by the CBD, can be introduced as an additional substantive requirement for patentability within the framework of the TRIPS Agreement (WTO 2002). The debate turns on whether the statement that "patents shall be available for any inventions, whether products or processes, in all fields of technology, provided that they are new, involve an inventive step and are capable of industrial application" (TRIPS Agreement, article 27.1) effectively closes the list of substantive requirements of patentability.[19]

The debate also touches on the scope of the provisions of the agreement relating to disclosure[20] and compliance with "reasonable formalities and procedures ... consistent with the provisions of this Agreement" (TRIPS Agreement, article 69.1).

If a lack of prior informed consent is introduced as a ground for the revocation of a patent, as opposed to prior informed consent as a substantive requirement of patentability, most of these objections fall away. But serious practical problems remain to be addressed. They relate mainly to the fact that the same genetic resource can be found in the territories of any number of countries, or that the same traditional ecological knowledge can be held independently by any number of indigenous or local communities. So it may well be prohibitively difficult to prove misappropriation of any such resource from a certain territory, or such knowledge from a given community. This problem can be solved by a reverse burden of proof:[21] where an applicant for the revocation of a patent for lack of prior informed consent can prove that the invention uses or derives from a genetic resource found within its territory, or from traditional ecological knowledge held by a local or indigenous community in it, it is presumed that the patentee has taken such resource or knowledge without the prior informed consent of the relevant indigenous or local community. This rebuttable presumption then requires the patentee to carry the burden of proving the contrary.

Also, where a lack of prior informed consent is proved, the question arises as to whether revocation of the patent in question is necessarily the most desirable remedy. I believe not. Rather, patent legislation should allow the relevant administrative or judicial authority to order the transfer of the patent to the successful applicant, effective from the filing date of the patent application. There is good precedent for such a remedy elsewhere in intellectual property law: a competent authority is allowed to order the transfer of a domain name in appropriate circumstances.[22] This remedy in patent law would be fair and equitable and would deter future action without prior informed consent.

Searchable Prior Art   The second approach is to prevent the unauthorized (improper) acquisition of industrial property rights (especially patents) over traditional knowledge by documenting and publishing traditional knowledge as searchable prior art, should the holders of the traditional knowledge concerned want this. Once such knowledge becomes part of the prior art, that mere fact destroys the novelty of any invention based on such knowledge. Even if a patent is obtained, it may be revoked on this ground. This procedure may involve an application launched by the holders concerned (which would involve substantial legal costs), or by a rival pharmaceutical company that wants to exploit the knowledge for its own gain (and at its own cost).

The WIPO-IGC has been examining the integration of public domain traditional knowledge documentation into searchable prior art. This has involved drawing up inventories of publicly available periodicals and databases relating to traditional knowledge and setting up a WIPO Portal of Traditional Knowledge Databases.[23]

Morality   The third approach is built on the optional morality requirement in article 27.2 of the TRIPS Agreement:

> Members may exclude from patentability inventions, the prevention within their territory of the commercial exploitation of which is necessary to protect *ordre public* or morality ... provided that such exclusion is not made merely because the exploitation is prohibited by their law.

The current approach to the application of the morality requirement in a similarly worded provision in the European Patent Convention[24] is very limiting—morality relates only to the exploitation of the invention, and not to the morality of the appropriation of the invention, or the genetic resources or traditional ecological knowledge on which it is based. In my view, immorality of appropriation taints whatever exploitation occurs after such appropriation.

But the morality requirement can be read differently, too, to protect traditional knowledge. In New Zealand, for example, the Intellectual Property Office has developed guidelines for patent examiners concerning patent applications that are significant to Maori (WIPO 2002c). The guidelines concern inventions relating to, using, or derived from indigenous flora and fauna, Maori individuals or groups, indigenous microorganisms (such as viruses, bacteria, fungi, and algae, where any line of research resulted from any traditional knowledge), and indigenous material derived from an inorganic source, where the research resulted from any traditional knowledge. If an application meets one of these criteria, an examiner is required to assess whether it is appropriate to raise an objection to registration under section 17 of the Patents Act of 1953, which provision allows the commissioner of patents to refuse an application where the use of the invention in question would be contrary to morality. In making this assessment, examiners are directed to consider the extent to which the application may have special cultural or spiritual significance for Maori, and whether or not the application is likely to be considered culturally offensive. Where an application may reasonably be considered to fall under section 17, applicants should be advised accordingly, and be given the opportunity to obtain the consent of the competent Maori authority.

Trademarks

Trademark law may prohibit the registration of distinctive signs and so on as trademarks where such registration may offend sections of the community (including indigenous and local communities), or where it falsely suggests a connection between such sign and an indigenous or a local community.

In New Zealand, for example, a new Trade Marks Bill proposes that the commissioner of trademarks be allowed to refuse to register a trademark where its use or registration will be likely to offend a significant section of the community, including the Maori.

In the United States, a proposed trademark may be refused registration and a registered trademark canceled if the mark consists of or comprises matter that may disparage, or falsely suggest a connection with, persons (living or dead), institutions, beliefs, or national symbols, or bring them into contempt or disrepute (Trade Marks Act of 1946, section 2(a)). The USPTO may refuse to register a proposed trademark that falsely suggests a connection with an indigenous tribe or beliefs held by that tribe. According to the USPTO, this provision protects not only Native American tribes but also those of "other indigenous peoples worldwide" (WIPO 2001). Also, the Trademark Law Treaty Implementation Act of 1998 required the office to complete a study on the official protection of insignia of federally and state recognized Native American tribes. As a direct result of this study, the office established, on August 31, 2001, a searchable Database of Official Insignia of Native American Tribes that may prevent the registration of a mark confusingly similar to official insignia. (The term "insignia" connotes "the flag or coat of arms or other emblem or device of any federally or State recognized Native American tribe as adopted by tribal resolution," but it does not include matter consisting only of words.) The database is included within the USPTO's database of material that is not registered but is searched to make a determination regarding the registrability of a proposed trademark.

Goal Post 2: Protection for Exploitation of Traditional Knowledge

Protection for Traditional Cultural Expressions

These are some examples of traditional cultural expressions for which legal protection has been sought: (a) Traditional cultural artistic expressions (such as paintings) have been reproduced without authority on carpets, printed fabric, T-shirts, dresses and other garments, and greetings cards, and have subsequently been distributed and offered for sale. Body paintings and rock paintings (petroglyphs) have also been photographed without authority, and the photos distributed and offered for sale (WIPO 2002b). (b) Traditional cultural musical expressions have been recorded, adapted, and arranged, performed in public, and communicated to the public, among other means, by the Internet. Traditional music can be downloaded from some free music archives, stored as sound files, and then manipulated in whatever manner one creatively sees fit (Sandler 2001). A major concern is that music that was originally recorded for ethnographic purposes can now be sampled and used in new compositions protected by copyright. Much of this music was recorded at live performances, often without the knowledge of the performers. A well-known example is the *Deep Forest* compact disc produced in 1992—it fused digital samples of music from Ghana, the Solomon Islands, and African "pygmy" communities with "techno-house" dance rhythms (Mills 1996). A related issue is the composition of original music that may be mistaken for traditional music, in that it treats traditional subject matter or is accompanied by a rhythmic pattern associated with traditional music (Sandler 2001). (c) Traditional cultural oral literary expressions (such as stories and poems) have been written down, translated, and published without authority. (d) Designs embodied in handwoven or handmade textiles, weavings, and garments have been copied and exploited commercially without authority. Examples include the *amauti* in Canada, the *saris* of South Asia, the "tie and dye" cloth in Nigeria and Mali, *kente* cloth in Ghana and some other West African countries, traditional caps in Tunisia, the Mayan *huipil* in Guatemala, the Kuna *mola* in Panama, and the *wari* woven tapestries and textile bands from Peru (WIPO 2002b). (e) Traditional cultural expressions (such as stories, plays, and dances) have been recorded, adapted, and performed in public without authority. Examples include the *sierra* dance of Peru and the *haka* dance of the Maori in New Zealand (WIPO 2002b). (f) Sacred or secret traditional cultural expressions have been used, disclosed, and reproduced without authority. Examples include the sacred Coroma textiles of Bolivia (Lobo 1991) and sacred songs that can be performed only at a special place and for a specified purpose (Sandler 2001). (g) Words from the vernacular of indigenous and local communities have been registered as trademarks by people who were not members of these communities. Examples include Pontiac, Cherokee, billabong, tomahawk, boomerang, tohunga, mata nui, piccaninny, and tairona (WIPO 2002b).

Copyright   Original traditional cultural expressions may be protected by copyright as literary and artistic works, without any need for registration or compliance with any formality. Such informal acquisition of copyright is mandated by the Berne Convention for the Protection of Literary and Artistic Works (article 5(2)), most of the substantive provisions of which have been incorporated by reference into the TRIPS Agreement (article 9.1). The Berne Convention extends to authors of original works economic (exploitation) and moral rights. The economic rights comprise the exclusive right to authorize any reproduction of the work, the right to broadcast the work or to perform it in public, and the right to make an adaptation of the work (which includes translating it). Two moral rights are protected—the right to claim authorship of the work (known as the "paternity" right) and the right to object to any distortion, mutilation, or other modification of, or other derogatory action in relation to, the work that would prejudice the author's honor or reputation (known as the "integrity" right) (article 6bis).

The strongest advantage of copyright law is, of course, that, on the basis of the principle of national treatment, it transcends national borders and so protects authors in all member states of the Berne Union and WTO.

Many developing countries regulate the use of traditional cultural expressions within the framework of their copyright laws.[25] These countries do so by taking advantage, expressly or implicitly, of a special provision in the Berne Convention that states that, with unpublished works, where the identity of an author is unknown, but there is "every ground" to presume that he or she is a national of the country concerned, legislation in that country may designate the competent authority to represent the author and to protect and enforce his or her rights (article 15(4)(a)).[26] (Sometimes, of course, works that appear to be traditional cultural expressions can actually be traced back to their original authors. Then the author, or the author's successors in title, can recover royalties.) So traditional cultural expressions are assimilated into original literary and artistic works, so that the economic rights in respect of such expressions can be exercised by the designated authority.

But traditional cultural expressions fit uncomfortably into the copyright paradigm. For one, they are often the result of a continuing and slow process of creative activity exercised by a certain community by consecutive imitation, whereas works protected by copyright traditionally should show some individual originality. In short, copyright is author centric; with traditional cultural expressions, by contrast, any notion of an author in the copyright sense is generally[27] absent (Ficsor 1997). Also, since the term of copyright protection is usually determined with reference to an identifiable author,[28] the lack of such author in the context of traditional cultural expressions makes them square pegs in the copyright round hole. Traditional cultural expressions continue to evolve, and have done so over centuries, and so any notion of a fixed term of protection in respect of folklore denies this essential feature.

The originality and identifiable author requirements of copyright law need not prevent the copyright protection of tradition-based cultural expressions made by the current generation of traditional knowledge holders (WIPO 2002b).

Some national laws require fixation in some or other material form as a prerequisite for copyright protection—this prevents the copyright protection of intangible traditional cultural expressions, such as songs, poetry, and stories that have not been reduced to material form. The Tunis Model Law[29] allows countries to exclude traditional cultural expressions (there termed "folklore") from the fixation requirement (section 5bis).[30] The authors of the Model Law state that if fixation were required, copyright in such expressions may well vest in the person who takes the initiative of fixing them (paragraph 20 of the commentary).

As far as preexisting traditional cultural expressions are concerned, they remain for copyright purposes in the public domain (WIPO 2002b). So for them a different regime of protection is needed.

UNESCO-WIPO Model Provisions   The directors general of UNESCO and WIPO convened a meeting of a Committee of Governmental Experts on the Intellectual Property Aspects of the Protection of Expressions of Folklore in Geneva, from June 28–July 2, 1982. The committee adopted the Model Provisions for National Laws on the Protection of Expressions of Folklore Against Illicit Exploitation and Other Prejudicial Actions (Model Provisions).

The key term "expressions of folklore" connotes productions consisting of characteristic elements of the traditional artistic heritage developed and maintained by a community in the country, or by individuals reflecting the traditional artistic expressions of such a community (section 2). The reference to "artistic" heritage excludes, for example, traditional beliefs, traditional ecological knowledge, and merely practical traditions as such, separate from possible traditional artistic forms of their expression. To the definition of "expressions of folklore" is added an illustrative enumeration of the most typical kinds of expressions of folklore according to the form of the "expression": expression by words ("verbal"), expressions by musical sounds ("musical"), expressions "by action" (of the human body), and expressions incorporated in a material object ("tangible expressions"). The first three kinds of expression need not be "reduced to material form"—the words need not be written down, the music need not exist in the form of musical notation, and the bodily action (such as dance) need not exist in a written choreographic notation. But tangible expressions must be incorporated in a permanent material, such as stone, wood, textile, or gold.

The following considerations were taken into account when the committee had to decide what kinds of utilization of expressions of folklore should be subject to authorization: whether there is gainful intent; whether the utilization is made by members or nonmembers of the community from which the expression utilized comes; and whether the utilization occurs outside the traditional or customary context. The committee agreed that utilizations made both with gainful intent and outside their traditional or customary context should be subject to authorization. This means, among other things, that a utilization—even with gainful intent—within the traditional or customary context is not subject to authorization. But a utilization, even by members of the relevant community of the expression, requires authorization if it is made outside that context and with gainful intent. The term "traditional content" is understood to connote the way of using an expression of folklore in its proper artistic framework based on continuous use by the community. By contrast, the term "customary context" connotes rather the utilization of expressions of folklore according to the practices of the everyday life of the community, such as the usual ways of selling copies of tangible expressions of folklore by local craftsmen.

Section 3 then specifies the acts of utilization that require authorization where these circumstances exist. In doing so, it distinguishes between instances where copies of the expressions are involved, on the one hand, and instances where copies of such expressions are not necessarily involved, on the other. With the former, the acts requiring authorization are publication, reproduction, and distribution; with the latter, public recitation, public performance, transmission by wireless means or by wire, and "any other form of communication to the public."

The utilizations listed in section 3 are subject to authorization by a "competent authority" or the "community concerned." States may designate a competent authority, if they prefer to do so (section 9). (They may also designate a "supervisory authority" with certain special functions.) The functions of the competent authority are to grant authorizations for certain kinds of utilization of expressions of folklore (section 3), receive applications for authorization of utilizations, decide on them, and, where authorization is granted, to fix and collect a fee, where required (section 10). Any decision of the competent authority should be subject to an appeal (sections 10.3 and 11.1).

Authorization need not be obtained where the utilization is for the purposes of education or by way of illustration, where expressions of folklore are "borrowed" to create an original work, or in the case of "incidental utilization" (section 4), such as for reporting on current events, or where the expression of folklore is an object permanently located in a public place. These exceptions are important as counterweights to the strong protection of traditional cultural expressions. By overprotecting such expressions, the public domain shrinks, which means that there are fewer works to build new ones with. So artists from indigenous and local communities who want to develop their artistic traditions by reinterpreting traditional themes and motifs in nontraditional ways may be inhibited by overprotection (Wendland 2002). The danger is that overprotection may "freeze" traditional culture at a historic moment and so deny traditional cultural expressions a contemporary voice (Farley 1997).

The Model Provisions were drafted well before the digital era, and so should be reconsidered carefully to see if they meet the demands of this era. In the case of the Berne Convention, for example, the WIPO Copyright Treaty was adopted to update copyright law to meet the special challenges to copyright law posed by the Internet (see below).

Also, these are model provisions for national laws—they have not been drafted as a model international treaty for the protection of traditional cultural expressions.

The Digital Environment: The WIPO Copyright Treaty   The emergence of global information networks—such as the Internet—and electronic commerce raises a number of key issues in the field of copyright. Those relevant to this chapter include the following: (a) The use of computers requires that works be transformed from their traditional material form into digital form. Digitization has two main advantages: transmission of a digitized work occurs without any degradation (every copy is perfect), and copies of such a work can be made quickly and cheaply. Unfortunately, though, these advantages also mean that copyright may be infringed with ease and on a scale previously unknown. (b) Material stored or made available for access on hosts, or transmitted through the Internet, may be the subject of copyright owned by a third party who has not consented to these activities. (c) To protect their works against these first two risks, authors have often resorted to technical protection measures. These measures usually operate at one of two levels—access control[31] and copy control.[32] These measures can remain effective, of course, only if their unauthorized circumvention is prohibited. (d) With works in digital form, it is easy to remove any rights management information. If this is done, it may become difficult to prove copyright ownership.

These issues have been addressed at the international level in the WIPO Copyright Treaty (WCT), adopted on December 20, 1996, at the Diplomatic Conference on Certain Copyright and Neighboring Rights Questions, organized in Geneva under the auspices of WIPO. In the first instance, the WCT confirms an author's exclusive right, in the digital environment, to reproduce his or her work in any manner or form (Agreed Statement Concerning Article 1(4)).[33] It is also understood that the storage of a protected work in digital form in an electronic medium constitutes a reproduction of that work. Second, the WCT grants an exclusive right to authors to authorize that their works be made available through interactive, on-demand services (article 8). The relevant act of exploitation is making the work available to the public: the act "commences, and is completed by providing public access to the work" (Hugenholtz 2001). Third, for the first time in an international instrument, the WCT recognizes that in a digital environment any new rights in respect of digital uses of works would, for the rights to be effective, require the framework support of provisions dealing with technical measures of protection and electronic rights management information. To this end, the WCT obliges contracting parties to provide adequate legal protection and effective remedies against the circumvention of measures to protect the rights of authors (article 11),[34] and to provide, under certain conditions, adequate remedies against the removal or alteration of electronic rights management information (article 12).[35]

Paying Public Domain Professor Adolf Dietz has proposed the payment of remuneration for the use of works and performances in the public domain—the creation of a community right of authors and performers (Dietz 2000). The underlying notion is that the community of living authors and performers should benefit from the use of works and performers of their predecessors that are no longer protected, as the term of protection had expired. Such a remuneration right can be established by legislation, in favor of an authors' and performers' fund administered by a foundation or nonprofit corporation. Such foundation or corporation, in turn, should largely be managed and administered by the authors' and performers' organizations themselves. Existing collecting societies, where they exist, can collect the remuneration in the same way as they do for the use of protected works and performances. The money will then not be distributed according to the individual distribution schemes, though, but will rather be forwarded to the foundation or corporation concerned.

For developing countries, this is an attractive proposal.[36] Of course, nothing prevents the extension of this proposal to include traditional cultural expressions, which would then attract a similar right of remuneration. The notion of a paying public domain ("domaine public payant") for traditional cultural expressions is not new, of course—it is proposed in the Tunis Model Law (section 17). The money collected should be used "to protect and disseminate national folklore." Such remuneration right can be made subject to an obligation to acknowledge the source of the traditional cultural expressions used, and an obligation not to use such expressions outside their traditional or customary context in a manner that offends the local or indigenous community concerned.

Related Rights: Performers Since 1961, performers of literary and artistic works have been protected within the framework of the International Convention for the Protection of Performers, Producers of Phonograms and Broadcasting Organizations (the Rome Convention). For historical reasons, this protection was weak—performers do not acquire exclusive rights, but should merely be able to prevent certain acts from being performed in respect of their recorded performances, or their live performances from being recorded or broadcast.

The TRIPS Agreement similarly states that performers should "have the possibility of preventing" a limited number of acts (article 14.1).

Like the WCT, the WIPO Performances and Phonograms Treaty (WPPT) addresses issues relating to the protection of performers' rights in the digital context. It greatly enhances their position.

For the first time, it grants performers certain exclusive rights of authorization in respect of their live and recorded performances. In respect of their live performances, performers have the exclusive right to authorize the broadcasting and communication to the public of such performances and the recording (fixation) of such performances (article 6). In respect of their recorded performances, performers have the exclusive right to authorize their reproduction (article 7), their distribution (article 8), their rental (article 9),[37] and their availability so that "members of the public may access them from a place and at a time individually chosen by them" (article 10).

Performers are also entitled to remuneration for broadcasting and communication to the public of commercial recordings of their performances (article 15).

Another first: performers are given moral rights on similar terms to those extended to authors (article 5). So they also enjoy paternity and integrity rights.

Developing countries seeking international protection of traditional cultural expressions should note an important step forward in the WPPT. Unlike the Rome Convention, which limits the definition of "performers" to those who perform "literary or artistic works" (article 3), the WPPT extends this definition to apply also to those who perform "expressions of folklore" (article 2). Certain traditional cultural expressions—such as folk tales, folk poetry, folk songs, instrumental folk music, folk dances, and folk plays—live through performance. To the extent that these performances are protected against unauthorized recording and broadcasting and communication to the public, the traditional cultural expressions being performed are indirectly protected. This is a fairly efficient means for an indirect protection of these traditional cultural expressions (Ficsor 2002).

The WPPT grants coextensive rights to the producers of sound recordings (articles 11 through 15). Obviously, they do not enjoy any moral rights in respect of their recordings.

If the balance between authors (including composers), performers, and producers of sound recordings in the WCT and the WPPT is maintained, and it is not disturbed by the existence of the "iron triangles" of the sort outlined above, multinational record companies can become "partners and not predators." Then FDI, as well as domestic direct investment by local musicians, can contribute toward alleviating poverty.

Designations of Authenticity: Certification Marks   In Australia, for example, the preferred legal technique to protect against nonindigenous people who manufacture and sell indigenous artifacts at the expense of the indigenous artistic community is through the use of certification marks,[38] which serve as labels of authenticity (Wiseman 2001). The National Indigenous Arts Advocacy Association (NIAAA) registered the first of two proposed national indigenous labels of authenticity as certification marks in Australia. These labels are applied to goods[39] and services[40] of aboriginal or Torres Strait Islander origin, which makes it more difficult for nonaboriginal people to pass off their works as if they were authentically aboriginal.

The first mark—the label of authenticity—is applied to "products or services that are derived from a work of art created by, and reproduced or manufactured by Aboriginal or Torres Strait Islander people who satisfy the definition of 'authenticity'" (NIAAA 2001). An artist who has successfully applied to use this label is referred to as a certified indigenous creator. The second mark—the collaboration mark—is applied to "products or services derived from a work of art which has been created by an Aboriginal or Torres Strait person or people who satisfy the definition of 'authenticity'" (NIAAA 2001). This mark recognizes that products and services are often produced, reproduced, or manufactured under licensing agreements with indigenous people. The collaboration mark is applied to such products and services, provided that the licensing arrangements are "fair and legitimate."

It has to be recognized that although these labels of authenticity will raise the profile of indigenous artists and help to make sure that they are properly remunerated, they will provide only limited protection to these artists. It is unlikely that, by themselves, the marks will prevent the production, import, or export of forgeries (Wiseman 2001). Also, since the marks are registered in a national registry, their effect is limited to that national territory, unless, of course, in the rare situation where they qualify for protection as well-known marks.[41]

In New Zealand, Te Waka Toi (the Maori Arts Board of Creative New Zealand) is utilizing trademark protection through the development of the "Maori Made Mark." This mark is intended to be a mark of authenticity and quality, which will indicate to consumers that the creator of the mark is of Maori descent and produces work of a particular quality.

In India, too, the Policy Sciences Center is implementing, with the Indian commissioner for handicrafts, a certification system for products labeled "Handmade in India" (Penna and Visser 2002).

As certification marks require registration, they suffer from territoriality—they are enforceable only in the territories for which they have been registered.

Trade Dress At a workshop at the World Bank on the crafts industry in India, Professor Jerome Reichman suggested using trade dress protection in this context (Reichman 2001). This type of protection relates to product packaging:[42] if such packaging is inherently distinctive, it qualifies for trademark protection, (potentially) forever. Professor Reichman's advice:

> The package. Make a fancy package. Make not just the India mark, but the way that it comes in, per company and per product and per region. Those are strongly protectable in national law and in international law under the TRIPS Agreement, which requires all sorts of international trademark protections and is very strong now.

Again. the problem is that the protection is territorial only, based on national legislation, with the only possible exception being in respect of well-known marks.

Unfair Competition: Misleading the Public   Using misleading indications of origin may constitute unfair competition.

The Paris Convention, for example, requires countries to grant protection against "indications or allegations the use of which in the course of trade is liable to mislead the public as to the nature, the manufacturing process, the characteristics, the suitability for their purpose, or the quantity, of the goods" (article $10^{bis}(3)3$).

The WIPO Model Provisions on Protection Against Unfair Competition are more explicit. They state that any act or practice, "in the course of industrial or commercial activities, that misleads, or is likely to mislead, the public with respect to an enterprise or its activities, in particular, the products or services offered by such enterprise," constitutes unfair competition (article 4(1)). They add that "[m]isleading may arise out of advertising or promotion and may, in particular, occur with respect to "the geographical origin of products or services" (article 4.2).

The main problem with protection against unfair competition is that it is confined to the national level and so differs from country to country. While this kind of protection may protect indigenous and local artists against misappropriation within their national states, it offers no protection at the international level.

Geographical Indications   One of the intellectual property issues for developing countries is the unauthorized use of a geographical indication on noncompeting goods, such as Taj Mahal for a hotel in Nevada. It is a complex issue. It has been noted that the issue "here is not necessarily a question of misleading consumers" but "also a question of the reputation of the geographical indication" (Baeumer 1989). At the same time, the protection should not overreach—it has been argued that while the protection of geographical indications against unauthorized use on all types of goods is excessive, protection should be given against "a blatant misuse of reputation" (Bienaymé 1989).

In terms of the Paris Convention, goods in respect of which a false indication of source is used should be seized upon importation (article 9(1)), or seized in the country into which they are imported, if the false indication[43] had been applied in that country (article 9(2)), or barred from importation (article 9(5)), or subject to such other actions and remedies as are available in such cases to nationals of the country in question (article 9(6)). Any producer or manufacturer engaged in the production or manufacture of the goods to which the geographical indication refers can take action against the use of a false indication (article 10(2)).

The Madrid Agreement for the Repression of False or Deceptive Indications of Source on Goods extends this protection to "deceptive" indications of source. Although a deceptive indication may literally be true, it is still misleading. For example, where two geographical areas in different countries have the same name, but only one of them has been used to indicate the source of certain products, and such indication is then used for goods originating from the other area in a way that leads members of the public to believe that they originate from the first area, such use is deceptive—the public believes that the products originate from the geographical area in respect of which the indication traditionally has been used (Baeumer 1997).

The Lisbon Agreement for the Protection of Appellations of Origin and Their International Registration provides strong protection for certain geographical indications, called "appellations of origin."[44] This protection is based on an international registration of an appellation of origin, effected by WIPO. The main factor limiting the scope of application of this agreement is the requirement that an appellation of origin be protected as such in its country of origin before it can be registered as such with WIPO (article 1(2)).

The TRIPS Agreement defines "geographical indications" as "indications which identify a good as originating in the territory of a Member [of the WTO], or a region or locality in that territory, where a given quality, reputation or other characteristic of the good is essentially attributable to its geographical origin" (article 22.1).[45] The scope of protection also expressly extends deceptive indications within the meaning of that term in the Madrid Agreement (article 22.4). Protection should be available against misleading use of a geographical indication and against acts of unfair competition (article 22.2), and against the registration of a trademark that contains, or consists of, a geographical indication relating to goods not originating in the territory indicated, if use of such a trademark is of such a nature as to mislead the public about the true place of origin (article 22.3). Geographical indications in respect of wines and spirits enjoy additional protection (article 23).

Members of the WTO have agreed to enter into negotiations to raise the level of protection of individual geographical indications (article 24). Some developing countries have argued in the TRIPS context that the work mandated in respect of the establishment of a notification and registration system of geographical indications for wines be extended to other products recognizable by their geographical origins, such as handicrafts and agrofood products (WTO 1999).

Protection for Traditional Ecological Knowledge

Patents   Holders of traditional knowledge can be given access to the industrial property system, to enable them to obtain patents (or utility models or "petty patents" where provision is made for these) where appropriate. One basic problem with doing so is that a patent protects active ingredients that have been isolated and tested. Such isolation and testing cost hundreds of millions of dollars and so are possible only for multinational pharmaceutical companies, not for the developing countries, or certainly not for their indigenous peoples. A further problem is that it may not be possible to obtain a patent because the novelty of the invention may have been destroyed by prior use of the invention by the local community itself.[46] It is possible, of course, to exclude such use from the prior art for the purposes of determining the novelty of an invention, much like certain disclosures are excused for these purposes. An example is article 54(1)(a) of the European Patent Convention (the provision is headed "Non-prejudicial disclosures"): it states that a disclosure will not be taken into account if it occurred in consequence of "an evident abuse in relation to the applicant or his legal predecessor."

Patents depend on registration and so are subject to the principle of territoriality—they are enforceable only in the territory for which they have been registered.

Transfer of Technology   A variety of transfer of technology approaches can be considered. These approaches assume for their effective operation an organized body of knowledge and an identifiable entity to administer such transfer.

One such approach is illustrated by the contract signed in 1991 between Merck and Costa Rica's Instituto Nacional de Biodiversidad (INBio), a nonprofit organization. In terms of this agreement, over a two-year period, Merck received some 10,000 plant samples. Merck was supplied with information about their traditional use. Merck paid a reported US$1.35 million to INBio for these samples and has agreed to pay a royalty of between 2 percent and 3 percent. If one of the samples becomes a billion-dollar drug, Merck has agreed to pay INBio between US$20 million and US$30 million in royalties. Conceivably, the royalties from these samples could earn INBio more than US$100 million every year. (Admittedly, this agreement seems to relate more to genetic resources than traditional ecological knowledge, but I have demonstrated earlier the link between such resources and knowledge.)

Of course, an obvious problem with this approach is that if the royalties are paid to an official body, and not to a nongovernmental organization (NGO) or private corporation, they may disappear into the general state revenue account and may not "trickle down" to the relevant communities or individuals.

An alternative approach relies on the law relating to the protection of trade secrets: the trade secret is disclosed (licensed) to someone in exchange, among other things, for an undertaking of confidentiality and remuneration (usually, a royalty).

The Policy Sciences Center has piloted a trade secret approach for communities to use so that they can derive revenue from traditional ecological knowledge (Penna and Visser 2002). The center has made a grant to the NGO Otro Futuro in Venezuela, to assist it in helping the Yekuana Indians to develop an *Archive and Atlas* and to protect their IPRs. Those rights range from copyright for myths, stories, legends, and music to traditional ecological knowledge that can be patented. A community foundation[47] has been established with a board of directors composed of representatives of the 12 Yekuana tribes, inhabiting some 2 million square acres. The Yekuana perceive of their intellectual property as being communally owned. Such property now vests in the community foundation. To protect traditional ecological knowledge, it would be treated as a trade secret by the community foundation not to be disclosed to a pharmaceutical company or others unless such an "outsider" agreed to pay royalties to the foundation.

This approach is not free from pitfalls, either.

Trade secret protection usually depends on the legal rules of each country, and international attempts at harmonization have not yielded much. The TRIPS Agreement, for example, simply states that "[n]atural and legal persons shall have the possibility of preventing information lawfully within their control from being disclosed to, acquired by, or used by others without their consent in a manner contrary to honest commercial practices" (article 39.2).[48] The protected information should be secret in the sense that it is not, as a body or in the precise configuration and assembly of its components, generally known among or readily accessible to persons within the circles that normally deal with the kind of information in question; has commercial value because it is secret; and has been subject to reasonable steps under the circumstances, by the person lawfully in control of the information, to keep it secret. One problem with traditional ecological knowledge often may be that the steps to keep the information secret may not be sufficient under the existing common or civil law rules—secrecy often flows only from the fact that few people have access to the information concerned, based on customary law and practices (Gervais 2001).

The WIPO Model Provisions on Protection Against Unfair Competition do not take the matter much further. A proposal relating to unfair competition in respect of secret information[49] simply states that "[a]ny act or practice, in the course of industrial or commercial activities, that results in the disclosure, acquisition or use by others of secret information without the consent of the person lawfully in control of that information ... and in a manner contrary to honest commercial practices shall constitute an act of unfair competition" (article 6(1)). The examples of such unfair competition include secret information acquired in breach of contract or of confidence (article 6(2)). The same conditions as in the

TRIPS Agreement have to be satisfied in order for information to qualify as "secret" (article 6(3)). In determining whether reasonable steps have been taken to keep the information secret, account should be taken of the amount of effort and money spent by the rightful holder[50] on developing the secret information, the value of that information to him or her and to his or her competitors, the extent of the measures taken by the rightful holder to keep the information secret, and the ease or difficulty with which it could be lawfully acquired by others (note 6.20 on article 6). Also, the secret information has to be identifiable (for example, in documents, or through storage in a database).

So, to protect traditional ecological knowledge not only in the country of origin but also in foreign countries, the legal rules relating to trade secret protection may have to be reviewed and strengthened internationally.

The fact that the secret information has to be identifiable (in this context, usually in a database such as the *Archive and Atlas* of the Yekuana Indians) raises a further issue: the protection of nonoriginal compilations of data. Essentially, two main approaches to such protection can be discerned.

The first approach grants the maker of the database strong sui generis intellectual property protection in the form of exclusive rights. For example, in terms of the European Database Directive (1996 *O.J.* (L 77)), the maker of a database obtains an exclusive "right to prevent extraction and/or reutilization of the whole or of a substantial part Y of the contents of that database" (article 7(1)). This approach usually results in a rights regime of almost unlimited duration, subject to few, if any, public policy limitations. For this reason it has been argued persuasively that this type of protection jeopardizes basic research, eliminates competition in the markets for value-added products and services, and converts existing barriers to entry into insuperable legal barriers to entry (Reichman and Samuelson 1997). Economic efficiency, in contrast, demands low prices for such use and favors minimum incentives to provide the needed investment and services.

The second approach favors a weak intellectual property right to overcome the risk of market failure[51] without creating legal barriers to entry. A modest adoption of this approach calls for a misappropriation model based on simple unfair competition principles. Courts could use market-oriented factors to determine whether there has been an "unfair extraction" from a database. Useful factors include the extent of the data appropriation by the user; the nature of the data appropriated; the purpose for which the user appropriated the data; the degree of investment initially required to bring the data into being; the degree of dependence, or independence, of the user's own development effort and how substantial the user's own investment in such an effort has been; the degree of similarity between the contents of the database and a product developed by the user; the proximity or remoteness of the markets in which the database maker and the user are operating;

and how quickly the user was able to come to the market with his or her own product as compared with the time required to develop the original database (Reichman and Samuelson 1997). Obviously, any such protection has to be balanced with limitations and exceptions favoring science and education.

Of these two approaches, the second is obviously of more benefit to developing countries. While it allows makers of databases to be protected against the risk of market failure, it does not create real barriers to market entry at the expense of the scientific and educational sectors.

Legal Hybrid I: Compensatory Liability   In a different context, Professor Jerome Reichman (1994) has suggested a "third intellectual property paradigm," loosely derived from classical trade secret law and from antitrust principles that apply to two-party transfers of unpatented industrial know-how. The proposed regime

> … aims to avoid market failure without introducing the market distortions characteristic of intellectual property rights and without forfeiting the pro-competitive social benefits that result from trade secret laws under optimum conditions. It solves the free-rider problem facing growing numbers of investors in applied know-how by directly linking the prospects for short-term returns on investment to the stipulation of a standard, multi-party set of default rules applicable to eligible forms of innovation.

The proposed "compensatory liability" regime is inspired by the Italian neighboring right that protects engineering projects. In terms of article 99 of the Italian Copyright Law of 1941, authors of engineering projects, or other analogous productions, who contribute novel (but not obvious) solutions to technical problems are entitled to a reasonable royalty from third parties who commercially exploit their technical contributions *without authorization*. This right to "equitable compensation" subsists for 20 years from registration. An appropriate notice must appear on copies of the plans.

Reichman (2000) has argued that this regime could solve some pressing needs of developing countries:

> As with small-scale innovations, the goal is to reward both first comers (in this case, the relevant indigenous community), and second comers (those who build on the community's cultural heritage), without impeding access to the public domain or the flow of new products. With small amounts of tinkering, a compensatory liability regime could be adapted to encourage use of traditional knowledge without denying the relevant indigenous communities the right to a fair share of the proceeds.

This regime could best be extended to traditional ecological knowledge. Legislation can allow "second comers" commercially to exploit such knowledge without prior authorization, subject to an obligation to pay a reasonable royalty to a designated person or institution. At the international level, the legal framework for this regime can be established either by an express provision in a future trade instrument or by incorporation within article 10bis of the Paris Convention.

Legal Hybrid II: A Global Biocollection Society   An alternative hybrid form of protection has been proposed by Professor Peter Drahos: a global biocollecting society (GBS), possibly under the auspices of the World Bank. Membership would be open on a voluntary basis to both companies and groups that had claims to traditional ecological knowledge and genetic resources. The GBS would act as the repository for community registers of such knowledge and as the custodian of these registers under strict obligations of confidentiality. It could also assist in negotiations between companies and groups for the use of genetic resources, set standards for such contracts, and provide a dispute-resolution mechanism. The advantage of such a system is that it obviates the need for negotiating an international treaty on IPRs for genetic resources (Subramanian 2002). It can also create an incentive for pharmaceutical companies to join the GBS, as transaction costs of dealing with the GBS would be lower than those associated with national bureaucracies that administer national laws.

Conclusions and Recommendations

Copyright and Related Rights

1. In the interest of developing their traditional cultural industries, countries should adopt the WCT and the WPPT. Doing so will establish strong regimes of copyright and related rights protection for tangible, contemporary traditional cultural expressions and indirect protection for all performance-based traditional cultural expressions. Countries should pay careful attention, though, to exceptions and limitations in favor of education and research. They should also be careful not to overextend the sanction of technical protection measures.
2. Countries with a fixation requirement for copyright protection should abolish such requirement for traditional cultural expressions, in order to also protect intangible cultural expressions. This is especially important for traditional musical cultural expressions.
3. Countries may consider adopting a sui generis system of protection for traditional cultural expressions along the lines of the UNESCO-WIPO Model Provisions, but again with careful consideration of exceptions and limitations to such protection, so as to allow the continuing artistic development of traditional cultural expressions.

4. While the sui generis protection of nonoriginal databases (those that do not meet the requirement of originality in copyright law) is important for the protection and exploitation of traditional technical and ecological knowledge, developing countries should study the possible negative impact of a strong exclusive rights regime on science, technology, and education in their countries.

Trademarks and Geographical Indications

1. Countries should refuse to register trademarks (or cancel their registration at any time) where their registration or use is likely to offend a significant section of indigenous or local communities, or where such trademarks consist of or comprise matter that falsely suggests a connection with such communities, or bring them into contempt or disrepute.
2. The protection of geographical indications should be strengthened. Developing countries should argue strongly for extending a notification and registration system of geographical indications for wines to other products that can be recognized by their geographical origins and that are economically and culturally important to these countries, such as handicrafts and agrofood products.
3. Countries should allow the registration of designations of authenticity in the form of certification marks.

Patents

1. Countries should use the (optional) morality requirement in the TRIPS Agreement to refuse the registration of a patent where the invention to which the application relates has special cultural or spiritual significance for indigenous or local communities, or where the application is likely to be considered culturally offensive to such communities.
2. Patent statutes should provide that where an applicant for the revocation of a patent for lack of prior informed consent can prove that the invention uses or derives from a genetic resource found within its territory, or from traditional ecological knowledge held by a local or indigenous community in it, it is presumed that the patentee has taken such resource or knowledge without the prior informed consent of the relevant indigenous or local community. Also, instead of revocation, patent statutes can allow the transfer of the patent to the successful applicant, effective from the filing date of the patent application.
3. Patent statutes should state that prior use by a local community of an invention that utilizes such community's traditional technical knowledge does not anticipate (or destroy the novelty of) such invention.

Unfair Competition

1. As an alternative to an exclusive rights regime for the protection of nonoriginal databases, countries can instead adopt an expropriation model of protection.
2. As an alternative to extending the protection of geographical indications, countries can strengthen the protection against misleading the public as a form of unfair competition.
3. To protect traditional ecological knowledge against misappropriation, trade secret protection should be strengthened.

Notes

1. Alternative terms in international instruments include, for example, "knowledge, innovations and practices of indigenous and local communities embodying traditional lifestyles relevant for the conservation and sustainable use of biological diversity" (Convention on Biological Diversity, article 8(j)); "indigenous knowledge (systems and practices)" (United Nations Draft Declaration on the Rights of Indigenous Peoples, preamble); "indigenous cultural and intellectual property" (United Nations Draft Declaration on the Rights of Indigenous Peoples, article 29); "community knowledge" (the Organization of African Unity's Model Legislation for the Protection of the Rights of Local Communities, Farmers and Breeders, and for the Regulation of Access to Genetic Resources); "local and traditional knowledge" (United Nations Convention to Combat Desertification in Those Countries Experiencing Drought and/or Desertification, Particularly in Africa, article 16(g)); and "traditional and local technology, knowledge, know-how and practices" (United Nations Convention to Combat Desertification, articles 17.1(c) and 18.2(a) and (b)).

2. The terms "traditional" and "tradition-based" refer to knowledge systems, creations, innovations, and cultural expressions that have, generally, been transmitted from generation to generation, are generally regarded as pertaining to a particular people or its territory, and continuously evolve in response to a changing environment (World Intellectual Property Organization [WIPO] 2002a).

3. This is in line with the use of the term by the WIPO. So knowledge systems, properties, and other materials that are not the result of intellectual creativity in the industrial, scientific, literary, or artistic fields are excluded. Examples are burial sites, languages, spiritual beliefs, and human remains (WIPO 2001).

4. Sometimes called "folklore" or "expressions of folklore." These terms have been argued to carry negative and Eurocentric connotations, suggestive of "something dead to be collected and preserved, rather than as part of an evolving living tradition" (Janke 1997). To Spanish-speaking countries, especially, "folklore was an archaism, with the negative connotation of being associated with the creations of lower or superseded civilizations" (Blakeney 2000).

5. The TRIPS Agreement is not a freestanding agreement but is Annex 1C of the Agreement Establishing the World Trade Organization (WTO). This agreement reflects the outcome of the Uruguay round of General Agreement on Tariffs and Trade (GATT) negotiations that lasted from 1986 through 1994. On April 15, 1994, the agreement was signed by ministers from most of the 125 participating governments at a meeting in Marrakesh, Morocco. It entered into force on January 1, 1995.

6. The following intellectual property rights are covered specifically by the TRIPS Agreement: copyright, related rights (the rights of performers, broadcasters, and producers of sound recordings), patents, trademarks, geographical indications of origin, semiconductor chip topographies, and unfair competition.

7. There are no WTO definitions of "developed" and "developing" countries. Members announce for themselves whether they are "developed" or "developing" countries. But other members can challenge the decision of a member to make use of provisions aimed at assisting developing countries.

8. The WTO recognizes as LDCs those that have been designated as such by the United Nations. Today there are 49 LDCs on the UN list, 30 of which have become WTO members. They are Angola, Bangladesh, Benin, Burkina Faso, Burundi, Central African Republic, Chad, Democratic Republic of the Congo, Djibouti, The Gambia, Guinea, Guinea Bissau, Haiti, Lesotho, Madagascar, Malawi, Maldives, Mali, Mauritania, Mozambique, Myanmar, Niger, Rwanda, Senegal, Sierra Leone, Solomon Islands, Tanzania, Togo, Uganda, and Zambia. Nine LDCs are in the process of acceding to the WTO: Bhutan, Cambodia, Cape Verde, Lao People's Democratic Republic, Nepal, Republic of Yemen, Samoa, Sudan, and Vanuatu. Ethiopia and São Tomé and Principe are WTO observers.

9. At the Ministerial Conference in Doha, Qatar, the conference agreed that LDCs will not be obliged, with respect to pharmaceutical products, to implement or apply certain TRIPS provisions, or to enforce rights provided for in these provisions, until January 1, 2016.

10. In Doha, the Ministerial Conference reaffirmed that "that the provisions of Article 66.2 ... are mandatory, [and] ... agreed that the TRIPS Council shall put in place a mechanism for ensuring the monitoring and full implementation of the obligations in question" (Decision on Implementation-Related Issues and Concerns, adopted on November 14, 2001, at the Ministerial Conference, Fourth Session, in Doha, November 9–14, 2001 (WT/MIN(01)/17) § 11.2).

11. FDI refers, in a nutshell, to an investment involving management control of an entity resident in one economy by an enterprise resident in another economy. FDI involves a long-term relationship that reflects an investor's lasting interest in a foreign entity. FDI increased by 18 percent in 2000, but was expected to decline in 2001 (United Nations Conference on Trade and Development [UNCTAD] 2001). Although the flow of FDI to developing countries increased to US$240 billion, more importantly, these countries' share of the global inflows has decreased over three consecutive years to 19 percent, the lowest since 1991. FDI inflows to LDCs increased, too, but with only 0.3 percent of the global total, these inflows remain negligible.

12. In terms of article 4 of the Agreement between the WIPO and the WTO concluded in Geneva on December 22, 1995, which entered into force on January 1, 1996.

13. A collective mark does not distinguish the goods or services of one enterprise from those of other enterprises. Rather, it distinguishes the origin or common characteristics of the goods or services of different enterprises that use the mark under the control of its owner (WIPO 2001).

14. It is wrong, of course, to claim that "not all [intellectual property rights] are individualistic," since "[i]ncreasingly, invention and creation take place in firms where groups or persons may be cited as co-inventors or co-authors, concepts recognized by the [intellectual property] system" (WIPO 2001). Coinventors and coauthors jointly still hold individual rights—the content and nature of the right of a patentee or an author do not change by virtue of the fact that such is held jointly by two or more people.

15. WIPO uses the term "traditional knowledge holders" to refer to all persons who create, originate, develop, and practice traditional knowledge in a traditional setting and context. Although indigenous communities, peoples, and nations are traditional knowledge holders, not all traditional knowledge holders are indigenous (WIPO 2002a).

16. In terms of the Patents Act, an invention cannot be patented if "(a) the invention was known or used by others in this country, or patented or *described in a printed publication* in this or a foreign country, before the invention thereof by the applicant for patent," or "(b) the invention was patented or *described in a printed publication* in this or a foreign country or in public use or on sale in this country more than one year prior to the application for patent in the United States" (35 USC § 102, emphasis added).

17. Article 52(1) of the European Patent Convention requires a patentable invention to be "new." An invention is new if it does not form part of the state of the art (article 54(1)). The "state of the art" comprises "everything made available to the public by way of a written or oral description, by use, or in any other way" before filing an application for a European patent (article 54(2)).

18. This committee was established at the 26th Session of the WIPO General Assembly in Geneva, September 26–October 3, 2000.

19. For example, one can argue that a substantive consent or disclosure requirement violates the principle of nondiscrimination as to subject matter, which is implicit in article 27.1 of the TRIPS Agreement.

20. Article 29.1 of the TRIPS Agreement stipulates disclosure of the patented invention and the best method to perform it. In addition, member states are allowed to request information about foreign patent applications and grants (article 29.2).

21. This mechanism is known to the TRIPS Agreement: see article 34 in respect of the reverse burden of proof in civil proceedings relating to process patents.

22. In terms of the Uniform Domain-Name Dispute-Resolution Policy (UDRP) of the Internet Corporation for Assigned Names and Numbers (ICANN), available at http://www.icann.org/udrp/. For an example of a statutory provision authorizing the transfer of a domain name to a trademark owner in the event of cyberpiracy, see 15 USC § 1125(d)(2)(C).

23. Available at http://www.wipo.int/globalissues/databases/tkportal/index.html.

24. Article 53(a) of the convention states that "European patents shall not be granted in respect of … inventions the publication or exploitation of which would be contrary to 'ordre public' or morality, provided that the exploitation shall not be deemed to be so contrary merely because it is prohibited by law or regulation in some or all of the Contracting States."

25. For example, Tunisia, 1967 and 1994; Bolivia, 1968 and 1992; Chile, 1970; Islamic Republic of Iran, 1970; Morocco, 1970; Algeria, 1973; Senegal, 1973; Kenya, 1975 and 1989; Mali, 1977; Burundi, 1978; Côte d'Ivoire, 1978; Sri Lanka, 1979; Guinea, 1980; Barbados, 1982; Cameroon, 1982; Colombia, 1982; Madagascar, 1982; Rwanda, 1983; Benin, 1984; Burkina Faso, 1984; Central African Republic, 1985; Ghana, 1985; Dominican Republic, 1986; Zaire, 1986; Indonesia, 1987; Nigeria, 1988 and 1992; Lesotho, 1989; Malawi, 1989; Angola, 1990; Togo, 1991; Niger, 1993; and Panama, 1994. The Tunis Model Law on Copyright for Developing Countries (1976) and the Bangui text of 1977 of the Convention Concerning the African Intellectual Property Organization did the same. In China, the Copyright Law of 1999 indicates its intention to protect expressions of folklore by copyright. But article 6 of the Law states merely that "[r]egulations for the protection of copyright in expressions of folklore shall be established by the State Council." The Copyright Ordinance of 1994 of Vietnam states likewise: "Protection of copyright granted to folklore works shall be prescribed by the Government."

26. Article 15(4) forms part of the Stockholm (1967) and Paris (1971) Acts of the Convention. According to the intention of the revision conference, this article implies the possibility of granting protection to traditional cultural expressions (Ficsor 1997).

27. An interesting exception to this general observation has been noted in respect of the traditional Onge people of the Andaman Islands in the Bay of Bengal (Norchi 2000). Songs are composed for certain occasions, and their performance may be requested again later. Only the original composer is then allowed to sing the song. Should anyone else try to do so without his or her permission, that act is treated as theft.

28. For example, the "life plus 70" rule (copyright ceases to subsist 70 years after the death of the author) introduced for Europe by article 1.1 of the Council Directive 93/98 of October 29, 1993, harmonizing the terms of protection of copyright and certain related rights [1993] O.J. L290/9.

29. The Tunis Model Law on Copyright was adopted by the Committee of Governmental Experts convened by the Tunisian government in Tunis from February 23–March 2, 1976, with the assistance of WIPO and the United Nations Educational, Scientific and Cultural Organization (UNESCO). Its provisions are compatible with the Paris Act of the Berne Convention.

30. This provision is optional, as the fixation requirement is typically part of the Anglo-Saxon copyright approach, unlike the Francophone *droit d'auteur* approach where fixation is not required.

31. For example, through the use of passwords and encryption.

32. For example, through the use of software that limits the number of copies that can be made of a digital work.

33. The inclusion of temporary ("ephemeral") copies within the reproduction right had the potential of defeating the entire treaty (Vinje 1997). Even this Agreed Statement, unlike the other Agreed Statements, was adopted not by consensus but by majority vote.

34. This general obligation leaves an important degree of flexibility to the contracting parties when drafting their domestic legislation to choose the types of technological measures that should be protected, the types of sanctions that should be imposed, and the actual activities that should be targeted (Reinbothe, Martin-Prat, and Von Lewinsky 1997).

35. This provision reflects the general agreement on the need to protect certain types of information attached to works in order to provide some security for their identification and tracking in open information networks (Reinbothe, Martin-Prat, and Von Lewinsky 1997).

36. Some may argue that this proposal amounts to a new form of (indirect) taxation, which may make its adoption politically difficult in countries such as the United States (Gervais 2001).

37. This right is subject to the impairment test also found in respect of the limited (copyright) rental right in the TRIPS Agreement (article 11).

38. A certification mark, in terms of the Trade Marks Act of 1995 (Cth), is a sign used, or intended to be used, to distinguish goods or services dealt with or provided in the course of trade, and certified in relation to quality, accuracy, or some characteristic (such as origin, material, or mode of manufacture), from other goods or services dealt with or provided in the course of trade, but not so certified (section 169). Certification marks symbolize and promote the collective interests of certain groups of traders—by preventing traders whose goods do not comply with the certification process from using the mark, the integrity of those traders whose goods are certified is maintained (Wiseman 2001).

39. The goods may include a wide range, such as fabrics, boomerangs, coolamons, nets, traps, seed and shell necklaces, didgeridoos, musical recordings, sticks, and sculptures (Wiseman 2001).

40. The services may include activities such as theater, dance, concerts, and educational and tourism programs (Wiseman 2001).

41. The special protection of well-known marks is based on article 6bis of the Paris Convention, as extended by articles 16.2 and 16.3 of the TRIPS Agreement. This protection is further extended by the adoption of the Joint Recommendation Concerning Provisions on the Protection of Well-known Marks, by the Assembly of the Paris Union for the Protection of Industrial Property and the General Assembly of WIPO, September 20–29, 1999. The recommendation raises clearly the level of protection beyond that of the TRIPS Agreement and extends the scope of the substantive subject matter by dealing, for example, also with business identifiers and domain names (Kur 2000).

42. For an analysis of the key United States Supreme Court decision in *Two Pesos v Taco Cabana* 505 US 763 (1992), in which case the court protected the ambience and décor of a Mexican fast-food restaurant, see Dinwoodie (1997).

43. A "false indication" does not correspond to the facts—an indication relating to a geographical area for goods not originating in that area. An indication is false only where it is understood as such by the public in the country where the indication is used for such products (Baeumer 1997).

44. The term "appellation of origin" connotes "the geographical name of a country, region, or locality, which serves to designate a product originating therein, the quality or characteristics of which are due exclusively and essentially to the geographical environment, including natural and human factors" (article 2(1)).

45. Although this definition is based on that of an "appellation of origin" in the Lisbon Agreement, it is broader in one respect: the TRIPS Agreement protects goods that derive a reputation from their place of origin without their having a quality or other characteristic that is due to that place (Baeumer 1997).

46. Whether such prior use would actually destroy the novelty of the invention for which a patent is sought will depend on the patent law of the country in which protection is sought. Under the Patents Act of 1977 in the United Kingdom, for example, use founds an attack on novelty if it effects a public release equivalent to publication (Cornish 2003). The question is whether a skilled worker, by observation or analysis, could discover and reproduce the invention (*Stahlwerk Becker's Patent* (1919) 36 R.P.C. 13 (HL)).

47. Another option is to establish a not-for-profit corporation (Norchi 2000).

48. The phrase "a manner contrary to honest commercial practices" connotes "at least practices such as breach of contract, breach of confidence and inducement to breach, and includes the acquisition

of undisclosed information by third parties who knew, or were grossly negligent in failing to know, that such practices were involved in the acquisition" (note 10).

49. The use of the expression "secret information" as opposed to "undisclosed information" in the TRIPS Agreement does not imply any difference in substance: it merely indicates that the rightful holder of the information must take certain measures or must behave in a certain way to keep the information unknown to third parties (note 6.01 on article 6).

50. The "rightful holder" of secret information is the natural or legal person who is lawfully in control of such information (note 6.03 on article 6).

51. It has been argued that traditional intellectual property models, as supplemented by classic trade secret law, often fail to afford those who produce the current most commercially valuable information goods enough lead time to recoup their investments. The risk of market failure inherent in this "state of chronic under-protection tends to keep the production of information goods at suboptimal level" (Reichman 1994).

References

Baeumer, L. 1989. "Considerations Concerning a Definition of Geographical Indications." Paper presented to the WIPO Symposium on the International Protection of Geographical Indications, Santenay, France, September 9–10, 1989.

———. 1997. "Protection of Geographical Indications under WIPO Treaties and Questions Concerning the Relationship between Those Treaties and the Trips Agreement." Paper presented to the WIPO Symposium on the International Protection of Geographical Indications in the Worldwide Context, Eger, Hungary, October 24–25, 1997.

Berkes, F., C. Folke, and M. Gadgil. 1995. "Traditional Ecological Knowledge, Biodiversity, Resilience and Sustainability." In C. A. Perrings, K.-G. Mäler, C. Folke, C. S. Holling, and B.-O. Jansson, eds., *Biodiversity Conservation: Problems and Policies.* Dordrecht, Netherlands: Kluwer Academic Publishers, pp. 281–301.

Bienaymé, M.-H. 1989. "The Possible Content of a New Treaty on the Protection of Geographical Indications at the Multilateral Level (Part I)." Paper presented to the WIPO Symposium on the International Protection of Geographical Indications, Santenay, France, September 9–10, 1989.

Blakeney, M. 2000. "The Protection of Traditional Knowledge under Intellectual Property Law." *European Intellectual Property Review* 22:251–61.

CBD (Convention on Biological Diversity). 2002. "Access and Benefit Sharing as Related to Genetic Resources." Decision VI/20 adopted by the Conference of the Parties to the Convention on Biological Diversity at its Sixth Meeting, The Hague, April 7–19, 2002.

Cornish, W. R. 2003. *Intellectual Property: Patents, Copyright, Trade Marks and Allied Rights,* 5th ed. London: Sweet & Maxwell.

Dietz, A. 2000. "Term of Protection in Copyright Law and Paying Public Domain: A New German Initiative." *European Intellectual Property Review* 22:506–11.

Dinwoodie, G. B. 1997. "Reconceptualizing the Inherent Distinctiveness of Product Design Trade Dress." *North Carolina Law Review* 75:471–606.

Drahos, P., and J. Braithwaite. 2002. *Information Feudalism: Who Owns the Knowledge Economy?* London: Earthscan.

Farley, C. H. 1997. "Protecting Folklore of Indigenous Peoples: Is Intellectual Property the Answer?" *Connecticut Law Review* 30:1–57.

Ficsor, M. 1997. "Attempts to Provide International Protection for Folklore by Intellectual Property Rights." Paper presented to the United Nations Educational, Scientific, and Cultural Organization–World Intellectual Property Organization World Forum on the Protection of Folklore, Phuket, Thailand, April 8–10, 1997.

———. 2002. *The Law of Copyright and the Internet: The 1996 WIPO Treaties, Their Interpretation and Implementation.* New York: Oxford University Press.

Gervais, D. J. 2001. "Traditional Knowledge: A Challenge to the International Intellectual Property System." Paper presented to the Ninth Annual Conference in International Intellectual Property Law and Policy, Fordham University School of Law, New York, April 19–20, 2001.

Gudeman, S. 1996. "Sketches, Qualms, and Other Thoughts on Intellectual Property Rights." In S. B. Brush and D. Stabinsky, eds., *Indigenous Peoples and Intellectual Property Rights*. Washington, D.C.: Island Press, pp. 102–21.

Gupta, A. 1999. Statement at WIPO Roundtable on Intellectual Property and Traditional Knowledge, Geneva, November 1–2, 1999.

Hugenholtz, P. B. 2001. "Caching and Copyright: The Right of Temporary Copying." *European Intellectual Property Review* 23:482–93.

Janke, T. 1997. "UNESCO-WIPO World Forum in the Protection of Folklore: Lessons for Protecting Indigenous Australian Cultural and Intellectual Property." *Copyright Reporter* 15:105–18.

Kur, A. 2000. "The WIPO Recommendations for the Protection of Well-Known Marks." *International Review of Industrial Property and Copyright Law* 31:824–45.

Lobo, S. 1991. "The Fabric of Life: Repatriating the Sacred Coroma Textiles." *Cultural Survival Quarterly* 15:40–41.

McLeod, K. 2001. *Owning Culture: Authorship, Ownership and Intellectual Property Law*. New York: Peter Lang Publishing.

Mills, S. 1996. "Indigenous Music and the Law: An Analysis of National and International Legislation." *Yearbook for Traditional Music* 28:57–58.

Ministerial Declaration adopted on November 14, 2001, at the Ministerial Conference, Fourth Session, in Doha, November 9–14, 2001 WT/MIN(01)/DEC/1.

NIAAA (National Indigenous Arts Advocacy Association, Inc.). 2001. "NIAAA and the Label of Authenticity." Available at http://www.niaaa.com.au/label.html.

Norchi, C. H. 2000. "Indigenous Knowledge as Intellectual Property." *Policy Sciences* 33:387–98.

Penna, F. J., and C. J. Visser. 2002. "Cultural Industries and Intellectual Property Rights." In B. Hoekman, A. Mattoo, and P. English, eds., *Development, Trade and the WTO: A Handbook*. Washington, D.C.: World Bank.

Reichman, J. H. 1994. "Legal Hybrids between the Patent and Copyright Paradigms." *Columbia Law Review* 94:2432–558.

_____. 2000. "Of Green Tulips and Legal Kudzu: Repackaging Rights in Subpatentable Invention." *Vanderbilt Law Review* 53:1743–98.

_____. 2001. "IPR as Related to Crafts in India; Compensatory Liability Legislation." Paper presented to the Crafts Workshop: India, World Bank, Washington, D.C., January 9, 2001.

Reichman, J. H., and P. Samuelson. 1997. "Intellectual Property Rights in Data?" *Vanderbilt Law Review* 50:51–166.

Reinbothe, J., M. Martin-Prat, and S. Von Lewinsky. 1997. "The New WIPO Treaties: A First Résumé." *European Intellectual Property Review* 19:171–76.

Roht-Arriaza, N. 1997. "Of Seeds and Shamans: The Appropriation of the Scientific and Technical Knowledge of Indigenous and Local Communities." In B. Ziff and P. V. Rao, eds., *Essays on Cultural Appropriation*. pp. 255–87. Piscataway, N.J.: Rutgers University Press, pp. 255–87.

Sandler, F. 2001. "Music of the Village in the Global Marketplace: Self-Expression, Inspiration, Appropriation, or Exploitation?" PhD thesis, University of Michigan.

Shiva, V. 1997. *Biopiracy: The Plunder of Knowledge and Nature*. Cambridge, Mass.: South End Press.

Subramanian, A. 2002. "Proprietary Protection of Genetic Resources and Traditional Knowledge." In B. Hoekman, A. Mattoo, and P. English, eds., *Development, Trade and the WTO: A Handbook*. Washington, D.C.: World Bank.

UNCTAD (United Nations Conference on Trade and Development). 2001. *World Investment Report 2001*. New York: United Nations.

Vinje, T. C. 1997. "The New WIPO Copyright Treaty: A Happy Result in Geneva." *European Intellectual Property Review* 19:230–36.

Wendland, W. 2002. "The Legal Protection of Traditional Knowledge." Paper delivered at the International Bar Association Conference 2002, Durban, October 22, 2002.

WIPO (World Intellectual Property Organization). 2001. "Intellectual Property Needs and Expectations of Traditional Knowledge Rights Holders: WIPO Report on Fact-Finding Missions on Intellectual Property and Traditional Knowledge." World Intellectual Property Organization, Geneva.

———. 2002a. "Traditional Knowledge—Operational Terms and Definitions." Document prepared by the Secretariat for the Third Session of the Intergovernmental Committee on Intellectual Property and Genetic Resources, Traditional Knowledge and Folklore, Geneva, June 13–21, 2002. WIPO/GRTKF/IC/3/9.

———. 2002b. "Preliminary Systematic Analysis of National Experiences with the Legal Protection of Expressions of Folklore." Document prepared by the Secretariat for the Fourth Session of the Intergovernmental Committee on Intellectual Property and Genetic Resources, Traditional Knowledge and Folklore, Geneva, December 9–17, 2002. WIPO/GRTKF/IC/4/3.

———. 2002c. "Initial Report on the Technical Study on Disclosure Requirements Related to Genetic Resources and Traditional Knowledge." Document prepared by the Secretariat for the Fourth Session of the Intergovernmental Committee on Intellectual Property and Genetic Resources, Traditional Knowledge and Folklore, Geneva, December 9–17, 2002. WIPO/GRTKF/IC/4/11.

Wiseman, L. 2001. "The Protection of Indigenous Art and Culture in Australia: The Labels of Authenticity." *European Intellectual Property Review* 23:14–25.

World Bank. 2002. *Global Economic Prospects and the Developing Countries 2002.* Washington, D.C.: World Bank.

WSSD (World Summit on Sustainable Development). 2002. Plan of Implementation. Last revised on September 23, 2002. Available at http://www.un.org/jsummit/html/documents/summit_docs/2309_planfinal.htm.

WTO (World Trade Organization). 1999. "The TRIPS Agreement." Communication submitted by Kenya on behalf of the African Group to the General Council of the WTO, Geneva, August 6, 1999. WT/GC/W/302.

———. 2002. "The Relationship between the TRIPS Agreement and the Convention of Biological Diversity: Summary of Issues Raised and Points Made." Note prepared by the Secretariat of the World Trade Organization, Geneva. IP/C/W/368.

INDEX

Use of italic b or t denotes box or table.

Abeita, Andy, 119–20, 121
aboriginal arts and crafts
  Australia, 16–17, 35, 116–18, 187–89, 191,
    224–25
  Canada, 121–23
  New Zealand, 28–29, 30, 216, 217, 225
ACAA (Asociacion Cubana de Artesanos Artistas), 90–91
Africa Music Project, 13–16, 95–112
  achievements of, 104–8
  administration and accountability, building
    of, 35, 110–11
  communication among musicians enabled
    by, 110
  e-commerce's potential for, 111–12
  legal and business training provided by, 110
  Nashville as model for, 32–33, 97
  objectives of, 96–97
  plan for Senegal, 99–100
  tourism and, 108
  town hall meetings to identify problems and
    possible solutions for, 98–99
African crafts, 126
African music
  See also Africa Music Project; Ethiopia;
    Ghana
  business structure of, 97–104
  future opportunities of, 109–12
  illegal immigrants in, 104
  "iron triangle" and, 84, 103

opportunities for, 84, 95
public appearances, payment for, 102
radio stations' payments for, 101–2
taxes on, 34, 102
Agenda 21, 135
Agreement on Trade-Related Aspects of Intel-
  lectual Property Rights. *See* TRIPS
Agridyne, 164*b*7.1, 165
Ahiagble, Gilbert "Bobbo," 18, 126–27
AIPO (Australian Intellectual Property Organi-
  zation), 118
Ajay Bio-Tech, 163, 165
alternative trading organizations (ATOs). *See*
  Northern ATOs; Southern ATOs
amauti (Inuit woman's parka), 122, 218
Amazon Basin
  See also Yekuana
  Ayahuasca from and patent challenge, 25,
    138, 169–71, 193–95
  as biological hot spot, 37
  organizations working to protect, 42–46
  Yekuana's history in, 39–42
American Crafts Project, 128
Andean Community's Decision 391, 139, 214
Andrews, Robin, 172
animation industry, 11, 84, 87
Arogyapacha plant, 150, 153*b*6.4, 195–97
Artesanias de Colombia, 125
Artisan Advocacy Network, 83
Artisan Enterprise Network, 83

art of indigenous people. *See* crafts; *specific culture, country, or region*
Asia. *See specific countries*
Asociación Agricultores de Rio Ruerte Sur, 174, 175
Asociacion Cubana de Artesanos Artistas (ACAA), 90–91
Asociación Otro Futuro, 5, 41, 43, 229
Australia and aboriginal rights, 16–17, 35, 116–18, 187–89, 191, 224
Australian Institute of Aboriginal and Torres Strait Islander Commission (ATSIC), 17, 118
Australian Intellectual Property Organization (AIPO), 118
authenticity. *See* certificates of authenticity and certification marks
Ayahuasca (plant) and patent challenge, 25, 138, 169–71, 193–95

Baaba Maal, 33, 98
Bank-Netherlands Partnership Program, 13, 104
basmati rice and patent controversy, 23, 171–74, 173*t*7.2, 176
beans, yellow, and patent controversy, 23–24, 174–76, 177
benefit-sharing arrangements. *See* bioprospecting agreements
Berne Convention, 29, 185, 218, 219, 221
Bernstein, Martin, 72
Biodiversidad, Derechos Colectivos y Regimen Sui Generis de Propiedad Intelectual (COICA), 45
biopesticides. *See* neem trees and biopesticides
biopiracy, 1, 22–24, 159–81, 212–13, 227–32
    Ayahuasca, 25, 138, 169–71, 193–95
    basmati rice, 23, 171–74, 176
    Hoodia, 19, 143–46, 146*b*6.2, 154–55
    neem products, 22, 161–66, 164*b*7.1, 213
    negative effects of, 176–77
    solutions to, 27, 177–78
    turmeric, 22–23, 166–68, 168*t*7.1, 212–13
    yellow beans, 23–24, 174–76, 177
bioprospecting agreements, 19–22, 147–55
    constraints on, 155–56
    negotiating process, 149–50
    sharing of benefits in, 150–55
    structure of, 135, 148, 150, 151*b*6.3, 155
    terms and conditions of, 149
    transfer of technology agreements, 228–31
    types of, 147–48
Bolcher, Hans, 79
Bolivia

access to genetic resources, law governing, 139
registry of artisans in, 125
Bonn Guidelines on Access and Benefit-Sharing as Related to Genetic Resources, Monetary and Non-monetary Benefits, 135, 150, 151*b*6.3, 155
Brazil
    coffee crisis, 82
    council to protect genetic resources and traditional knowledge, 141
Bulun Bulun v. R&T Textiles (1997), 17, 117–18, 187–89
Bureau Senegalais du Droits d'Auteur (BSDA), 98, 104–6

Cama, Mansour, 100
Cameroon
    International Cooperative Biodiversity Groups (ICBGs) in, 154
    Limbe Botanic Garden, 142
Canadian indigenous artisans and crafts, 121–23
carpets, 89–90
"Carpets" case (*Milpurrurru v. Indofurn* 1994), 17, 117, 187
CBD. *See* Convention on Biological Diversity
Center for International Environmental Law (CIEL), 138, 170
Central Interregional de Artesanos del Peru (CIAP), 125
centralized bureaucracy and cultural diversity, 47
certificates of authenticity and certification marks, 30, 116, 120, 123, 124, 125, 127, 128, 190, 191, 224–25, 233
Chavez, Hugo, 44
Christian missionaries in Yekuana region, 38, 39
CIAC. *See* Council for Indigenous Arts and Culture
CIAP (Central Interregional de Artesanos del Peru), 125
CIAT. *See* International Center for Tropical Agriculture
CIEL. *See* Center for International Environmental Law
clothing designs, 58, 122, 126, 218
codes of ethics, 141–42, 155
coffee crisis, 82–83
COICA. *See* Coordinating Body of Indigenous Organizations of the Amazon Basin
collection societies
    for African music, 101, 103, 110

global biocollection society, proposal of, 232
for India craftspeople, 62–63
Collier, Paul, 13, 95
Collins, John, 33, 34
Colombia
access to genetic resources, law governing, 139
Foreign Trade Institute, 125
commercialization
of ethnobotanical knowledge, 159–81
See also biopiracy
of folklore, 185
See also folklore
indigenous, 178
compensatory liability regime for unpatented
industrial know-how, 231–32
compound P57. See Hoodia plant
comunitas, 46
Congolese designers and model/gift VW bugs,
11–12, 35, 89
Conquest of the South program
purpose of, 41
Yekuana region and, 39
Consejo Nacional Indio de Venezuela
(CONIVE), 45–46, 49
contracts
See also bioprospecting agreements
knowledge-sharing contracts, 178
Latin American–ICBGs contracts, 152
structure of, 135, 148, 150, 151b6.3, 155
Convention on Biological Diversity (CBD), 133,
135–36, 149, 196, 214
Working Group on 8j, 136
Convention on Desertification and Drought, 135
Coordinating Body of Indigenous Organizations of the Amazon Basin (COICA), 6, 26,
44–46, 138, 170, 194
copying and piracy, 16–19, 24–27, 113–31
See also biopiracy; copyright protection
of African copyrighted works, 127
of African music, 101, 104–5, 110
of clothing designs, 58, 122, 126, 218
of folklore, 184–92, 218
Indian cultural perspective on, 61–62, 65
Native American crafts copied in Asia, 113
of words from vernacular of indigenous people, 218
copyright protection, 29, 114–15, 185–90
See also World Intellectual Property Organization (WIPO)
of aboriginal designs, 35, 117, 187–89
of African music, 105, 108, 189–90
in Australia, 117–18, 187–89

costs associated with as barrier to pursuing, 128
in Ghana, 126
incompatibility of traditional cultural
expression with fixation requirement, 185,
219–20, 232
in India, 63–64
moral rights included, 185, 219
in Panama, 123–24
recommendations for developing countries,
232–33
traditional knowledge and, 90, 218–20
corporate policies, 142
Costa Rica
Biodiversity Law, 196, 214
Instituto Nacional de Biodiversidad (INBio)
agreement with Merck, 228
costs as barrier in developing countries to
enforcement of IP rights, 19, 85, 90, 208,
213, 228
Council for Indigenous Arts and Culture
(CIAC), 119, 120, 121
counterfeit craft designs, 16–19, 113–31
See also copying and piracy
country music industry in U.S., 32–33, 97
crafts
See also specific culture, country, or region
background of industry, 114
certification. See certificates of authenticity
and certification marks
counterfeit designs. See copying and piracy
fair trade of, 77–83
legal protection for, 30, 217–27
See also copyright protection
as type of traditional knowledge, 55
creativity
Indian cultural perspective on, 61–62, 65–66
licensing and export of outputs of, 75–76
CSIR. See Indian Council for Scientific and
Industrial Research
Cuba's artists' association, 90–91

dances of indigenous people, 186–87, 218
Darjeeling tea, 64
database protection, 28, 230–31
Deep Forest (music on cd), 218
de Soto, Hernando, 86
Dieng, Aziz, 99, 105, 106, 107
Dieng, Mbaye, 110
Dietz, Adolf, 223
Dioup, Mokhtar, 97
DISA, 91
Doha Ministerial Declaration, 209

Drabos, Peter, 232
Dread Africa, 103
Duer, Kreszentia, 96, 107, 108

ecological knowledge. *See* biopiracy
e-commerce
  African music and, 15, 111
  copyright protection and, 222
Ecuador's law governing access to genetic
  resources, 139
E.I.D. Parry, 165
enforcement procedures for IP laws
  See also copyright protection; patents; trade-
    mark protection
  African music and, 110
  costs as barrier. *See* costs as barrier in devel-
    oping countries to enforcement of IP rights
  developed countries able to protect rights of
    developing countries, 91
  Indian traditional crafts, 63–64
  Native American crafts, 118–21
  priorities for developing countries and, 85–86
Enola. *See* yellow beans and patent controversy
entrepreneurship and African music industry,
  109
Equal Exchange, 81
Erala Institute for Research, Training and
  Development of Scheduled Castes and
  Scheduled Tribes (KIRTADS), 195
Esperando a Kuyujani, 5, 41, 49
  See also Kuyujani Originario
Ethiopia
  folklore music in, 26, 33, 189–90
  pulses and grains, 84
ethnobotanical knowledge and biopiracy,
  159–81, 192–97, 227–32
  See also biopiracy; medicinal plants
European Database Directive, 230
European Fair Trade Association's fair trade
  impact evaluations, 79
European Patent Office on neem product
  patents, 22, 162, 166, 213
European Union
  green paper on corporate social responsibil-
    ity, 82
  handicrafts protection, 68
  export of intellectual property products, 83–87
  See also fair trade
  capacity building for, 90–91
  differences from physical product exports,
    76–77
  key factors for success in, 86–87

fair trade, 10–12, 75–93
  coffee crisis and, 82–83
  defined, 75–76
  impact evaluations of, 79–80
  in IP products, 77, 80–81, 83–88
  IP sectors that could benefit from, 88–89
  in physical goods, 77–83, 88–89
  value of, 83
Fair Trade Federation, 78, 83
  on value of global fair trade, 78
Fairtrade Labelling Organizations International
  (FLO), 78
  on coffee market, 82
farmers' rights, 136–37
Faye, Lamine, 112
Fikre Gebru v. Mohammed Awol (1996), 189
Finger, Michael, 95, 96
FLO. *See* Fair Trade Labeling Organization
  International
folklore
  copyright protection and, 185–86
  defined, 184
  misappropriation of, 26, 184–92, 218
  patent protection and, 190–91
  trademark protection and, 190–91
  UNESCO/WIPO Model Provisions, sui generis
    protection of, 29, 191–92, 220–22, 232
Ford Foundation and handicrafts protection, 68
Forest exploitation in Venezuela, 41
Fortune Biotech, 165

Galabingu and ownership of traditional
  designs, 117–18, 187–88
garment designs. *See* clothing designs
genetic resources, protection of, 133–58, 212–13
  See also biopiracy; bioprospecting agree-
    ments
geographical indications, unauthorized use of,
  23, 61, 64–65, 90, 138, 174, 226–27, 233
Ghana
  cultural industries in Bank strategy agree-
    ment with, 108
  IP protection in, 18, 126–27
  music business in, 34, 104
GlaxoSmithKline Policy Position on the CBD,
  142, 143
global biocollection society, proposal of, 232
Gollin, M.A., 148
Guatemala's Cultural Heritage Protection Law,
  25, 192
Guayaki, 90
Gudeman, S., 210

handmade certification. *See* certificates of
authenticity
herbal tea, 90
Hirshberg, Charles, 32–33
hologram stickers to protect copyright musical
products, 104
homeopathy. *See* medicinal plants; pharmaceuticals
Hoodia plant, 19, 143–46, 146*b*6.2, 154–55

ICBGs. *See* International Cooperative Biodiversity Groups
ICC (Inuit Circumpolar Conference), 123
IDB (International Development Bank), 56
ILO. *See* International Labour Organization
India
    basmati rice and trademark controversy, 23,
        171–74, 176
    Biological Diversity Bill, 139–40
    biopesticides from neem trees in, 22, 161–66,
        213
    chronology of commercialization of neem
        biopesticide, 164*b*7.1
    certification of authenticity, 225
    Copyright Act of 1957, 64
    Geographical Indications of Goods (Registration and Protection) Act of 1999, 64–67
    Kani-Tropical Botanic Garden and Research
        Institute (TBGRI) agreement, 20, 26–27,
        32, 150, 153*b*6.4, 195–97
    pharmaceutical use of plants from, 160
    Plant Variety and Farmer's Rights Protection
        Act, 194
    Tea Board, 64
    Trademarks Act, 64
    traditional crafts, 53–73
    See also India's traditional crafts
    turmeric from, 22–23, 166–68, 168*t*7.1,
        212–13
Indian (American) art and crafts. *See* Native
    American crafts and folklore
Indian Arts and Crafts Act of 1990, 119
Indian Council for Scientific and Industrial
    Research (CSIR), 22–23, 167, 168, 212–13
India's traditional crafts, 2–3, 7–10, 53–73
    changing market patterns, 57–59
    copying and creativity, cultural perspectives
        on, 61–62, 65–66
    credit problems associated with, 59
    Development Commissioner for Handicrafts
        and Development Commissioner for
        Handlooms, 67

educational problems associated with, 59
enforcement procedures for infringement,
    63–64
"fusion" products, 66
handicrafts, statistics of, 54*t*2.1
lack of professional respect for, 60
legislative protection, 64–67
nature of craft communities, 62
newer designers working with artisans, 68–69
ownership issues, 60–64
price spread in export markets and, 57,
    71–72
protection of, 55–57
solutions to IPR problems, 67–70
supply-side constraints, 59–60
tourism, effect of, 9, 69–70
types of ownership, 65–66
unorganized nature of, 60
informed consent. *See* prior approval provisions
insignia, USPTO's searchable database of Native
    Americans' and other indigenous peoples',
    30, 217
integrity right of copyright protection, 219,
    224
intellectual property laws. *See specific type of law
    (e.g., copyright protection), international
    agreements, or country*
International Center for Tropical Agriculture
    (CIAT), 24, 175–76
International Convention for the Protection of
    Performers, Producers of Phonograms and
    Broadcasting Organizations (Rome Convention), 223, 224
International Cooperative Biodiversity Groups
    (ICBGs), 20–21, 143, 150, 152
    African project, 154–55
    Latin American contracts, 152
International Development Bank (IDB), 56
International Federation for Alternative Trade,
    83
International Labour Organization (ILO), 56
    Convention 169 Concerning Indigenous Peoples, 135
International Plant Medicine Corp., 169
International Trade Centre (ITC), 56
International Treaty (IT) on Plant Genetic
    Resources for Food and Agriculture, 133,
    136–37, 149, 155
Inuit art and crafts, 121–23
Inuit Circumpolar Conference (ICC), 123
Iran, 90

"iron triangle" and African music, 84, 103
Italian Copyright Law of 1941, 231
ITC (International Trade Centre), 56

Jain, Jyotindra, 34, 63

Kani-Tropical Botanic Garden and Research
  Institute agreement, 20, 26–27, 32, 150,
  153*b*6.4, 195–97
Kente cloth from Ghana, 18, 126, 218
kettuvallom (Indian houseboat), 9, 69–70
khadi (Indian handloomed cloth), 70, 163
Khan, B. Zorina, 35, 86
KIRTADS (Erala Institute for Research, Training and Development of Scheduled Castes
  and Scheduled Tribes), 195
knowledge. *See* traditional knowledge
Korean animation industry, 11, 84, 87
Kumar, Ritu, 9, 68
Kuna in Panama and protection of indigenous
  crafts and culture, 18, 124
Kuyujani, 5, 41, 42
Kuyujani Originario
  founding of, 5, 41–42
  protecting indigenous rights, 46, 48–50
  protecting lands of Yekuana, 42–44

Lal-ji (Indian crafts dealer), 72
Larson, Robert, 163
Latin America
  See also specific countries and regions
  Andean Community's Decision 391, 139, 214
  crafts industry in, 18, 114, 123–26
  ICBG and royalties, 152
  indigenous ethnopolitcal movements in, 44–48
Layton, Ron, 83
LightYears IP, 11, 12, 80, 89
Limbe Botanic Garden (Cameroon), 142
Lisbon Agreement for the Protection of Appel-
  lations of Origin and Their International
  Registration, 227
live performances, 92, 223–24

Madrid Agreement for the Repression of False
  or Deceptive Indications of Source on
  Goods, 227
Mali, 13, 108
Maori rights. *See* New Zealand
Mashelkar, Anant, 168
Maskus, Keith, 85, 90
Mayacoba. *See* yellow beans and patent contro-
  versy
McIntire, John, 104

medicinal plants
  See also biopiracy; pharmaceuticals
  Ayahuasca, 25, 138, 169–71, 193–95
  commercialization of ethnobotanical knowl-
    edge, 134, 159–81
  commercial value of, 160
  Hoodia plant, 143–46, 146*b*6.2, 154–55
  neem products, 22, 161–66, 164*b*7.1, 213
  protection of, 192–97
  in Amazon Basin. *See* Amazon Basin
  in India, 66
  turmeric, 22–23, 166–68, 168*t*7.1, 212–13
Merck and Costa Rica's Instituto Nacional de
  Biodiversidad (INBio) agreement, 228
Mexican yellow beans and patent controversy,
  23–24, 174–76, 177
Meyer, Louise, 18, 126, 127
Miller, Loren, 169–70
Milpurrurru v. Indofurn (1994), 117, 187
misappropriation, 24–27, 183–206, 218
  See also copying and piracy
Model Provisions for National Laws on the Pro-
  tection of Expressions of Folklore Against
  Illicit Exploitation and Other Prejudicial
  Actions (UNESCO/WIPO), 29, 191–92,
  220–22, 232
Model Provisions on Protection Against Unfair
  Competition (WIPO), 226, 229
molas (Kuna dress), 18, 124
moral rights
  of performers, 224
  provided by copyright protection, 185, 219
  TRIPS Agreement requirement, 216, 233
Mould-Iddrissu, Betty, 126, 127
MP3.com, 111
Musicians' Association (Senegal), 15, 97, 99,
  102, 103, 104
  administration of, 110–11
  communication system of, 110
  copyright protection of, 105–6
  Declaration of the Association of Senegalese
    Musicians, 107–8
  increased influence of, 106–8
  training of, 108
music, protection of, 32–34, 217–18
  See also Africa Music Project; *specific culture,
    country, or region*
Myers, Paul, 78

National Indigenous Arts Advocacy Association
  (NIAAA), 191, 224
Native American crafts and folklore, 17–18, 118–21

copied in Asia, 113
Pueblo of Santo Domingo, 186–87
trademark protection of, 30, 217
neem trees and biopesticides, 22, 161–66, 213
chronology of commercialization of neem
biopesticide, 164*b*7.1
neighboring rights provided by copyright protection, 186
New Partnership for Africa's Development, 75, 85
New Zealand
patent procedures and Maori rights, 28–29,
216
trademark protection through "Maori Made
Mark," 225
Trade Marks Bill, 30, 217
NIAAA. *See* National Indigenous Arts Advocacy
Association
Nigeria and International Cooperative Biodiversity Groups, 154
Northern ATOs (alternative trading organizations), 10, 77–79
need for uniform standards, 80
Oxfam's decision to stop trading with, 81
possible impacts of, 87–88, 92

O'Hearn, Tracy, 122
Omnibus Trade and Competitiveness Act of
1988, 119
oral traditions and folklore, 176, 177, 184, 211, 218
copyright protection and, 185, 219
Guatemala's Cultural Heritage Protection
Law on, 192
organizations as protection mechanism, 125,
128
ownership issues, 32–34
See also copyright protection; patents; trademark protection
for genetic resources and traditional knowledge, 141
Indian traditional crafts, 60–64
individual vs. collective, 209–11
Oxfam, 78, 80, 81

packaging and trade dress, 225–26
Pakistan and basmati rice. *See* basmati rice and
patent controversy
Panama and protection of traditional knowledge, 18, 123–24, 125
Paris Convention, 226, 232
Patent and Trademark Office, U.S. (USPTO), 121
on Ayahuasca patent, 25, 170, 193–94
on basmati rice, 23, 171

on neem product patents, 22, 162, 166
patent approval process shortcomings, 24,
166, 176
trademark approval process and Native
American rights, 30, 217
on turmeric-based patents, 23, 167–68
patents, 28–29, 212–16, 227–28
Ayahuasca, controversy over, 25, 138, 169–71,
193–95
basmati rice, controversy over, 23, 171–74, 176
biopesticides from neem, controversy over,
22, 161–66, 164*b*7.1, 213
folklore and, 190–91
indigenous peoples' groups challenging, 138,
161
plant patents, eliminating as solution to
biopiracy, 177
recommendations for developing countries,
233
"technical" traditional knowledge and,
192–97
turmeric for treating wounds, controversy
over, 22–23, 166–68, 168*t*7.1, 212–13
yellow beans, controversy over, 23–24,
174–76, 177
paternity right of copyright protection, 219, 224
Pauktuutit (Inuit Women's Association of
Canada), 122–23
Penna, Frank J., 13, 84, 96, 103
performers' rights, 186, 223–24
Peru and protection of traditional knowledge,
124, 125, 138, 140*b*6.1
access to genetic resources, law governing, 139
union of artisans and, 125
pesticides made from neem trees, 22, 161–66,
213
chronology of commercialization of neem
biopesticide, 164*b*7.1
Pfizer, 145, 146*b*6.2
pharmaceuticals
See also medicinal plants
derived from genetic resources, 134
traditional medicine and, 84–85
Philippines
Constitution on recognition of indigenous
peoples' rights, 210
Executive Order 247 on Access to Genetic
Resources, 139
forgery of Native American goods in, 17, 120
Indigenous Peoples Rights Act of 1997, 139,
196, 210
traditional knowledge, protection of, 138

Phytopharm, 146*b*6.2, 154–55
piracy. *See* biopiracy; copying and piracy
P.J. Margo Private Ltd., 163, 164*b*7.1
plants
　See also medicinal plants
　patents for, eliminating as solution to
　　biopiracy, 177
Pod-Ners, 175–76
Policy Sciences Center, 229
prices and copies of handmade crafts, 113
Principles for Participating Institutions of
　botanic gardens and herbaria, 142
prior approval provisions
　for access to genetic resources, 138–41, 196,
　　214–15, 233
　Ethiopian folklore music, 189–90
　for expressions of folklore under Model Pro-
　　visions, 221
　for traditional knowledge use, 177, 178,
　　214–15, 233
　TRIPS and, 196, 214–15
prior use or art and patent approvals, 166, 168,
　169, 170, 176, 177, 194, 213
　searchable prior art, 215–16
Proctor, Larry, 175
public domain
　adding ethnobotanical knowledge to,
　　177–78
　folklore in, 186, 220
　payment for works in, 223
　traditional knowledge in, 31, 156
Pueblo of Santo Domingo, 3, 25, 186–87
Punja, Shobita, 2

radio stations' payments for African music,
　101–2, 105, 109, 110
Rafrache (African music band), 95, 102, 107
Reichman, Jerome, 225, 231
República Bolivariana de Venezuela. *See*
　Venezuela
research guidelines, 141–42, 155
　See also International Cooperative Biodiver-
　　sity Groups (ICBGs)
　survey of pharmaceutical companies on, 143
rice and controversy over basmati variety, 23,
　171–74, 173*t*7.2, 176
RiceTec, 171–73
Rio Declaration of 1992, 135
Roht-Arriaza, N., 209–10
Rome Convention, 223, 224
royalty collection. *See* collection societies
rubber exploitation of Yekuana, 38, 39

Santo Domingo Pueblo, 3, 25, 186–87
San traditional knowledge and Hoodia commer-
　cialization, 19, 144–46, 146*b*6.2, 150, 154–55
saris, 8–9, 58, 218
Schlatter, Sybille, 104, 105
Schmutter, Heinrich, 163
Schuler, Philip, 95
Seattle's Best Coffee, 83
secrecy
　See also trade secrets
　to protect intellectual property rights in
　　India, 67
　of tribal knowledge and folklore, 185, 186,
　　218, 229
Seigel, Seth, 89
Self-Employed Women's Association (SEWA), 63
Sen, Amartya, 2, 85
Senegal music industry, 13, 97–112
　See also Africa Music Project; African music
SERVV International, 10, 77, 78
Shiva, V., 211
Singh, Martand, 70
Soni, Shyam Lal, 72
South Africa and encrypted music sales, 111
South African Council for Scientific and Indus-
　trial Research, 145–46, 146*b*6.2
Southern ATOs (alternative trading organiza-
　tions), 10, 78, 79, 88
Sow, "Dou Dou," 103
Starbucks, 82–83
Stark, Pete, 83
stock investing and social responsibility, 82
sui generis protection of folklore, 29, 191–92,
　220–22, 232
supermarkets and fair trade products, 78, 83

taxes and African music, 34, 102
TBGRI. *See* Tropical Botanic Garden and
　Research Institute agreement with Kani
tea, 64, 90
technology
　See also e-commerce
　African music industry and, 15, 96–97, 109,
　　111–12
　biotechnology, 133–58
　See also biopiracy; bioprospecting agreements
Ten Thousand Villages, 10, 77, 78, 81, 89
territorial limitations of IP enforcement
　certification marks, 225
　patents, 228
　UNESCO-WIPO Model Provisions, 222
　unfair competition, 226

Thiam, Jean Louis, 103
Thiam, Kouraïchi, 97
Tobin, Brendan, 149
tourism
    African music and, 108
    Indian traditional crafts, effect on, 9, 69–70
trade dress, 225–26
Trademark Law Treaty Implementation Act of 1998, 217
trademark protection, 30, 64, 115–16, 216–17
    See also certificates of authenticity and certification marks
    Australia, 118, 191
    basmati rice, 171–74
    collective marks in, 211
    folklore, 190
    India, 64
    Inuit art and crafts, 122
    Native American art and crafts, 120–21, 217
    Peru, 124
    recommendations for developing countries, 233
    words from vernacular of indigenous people, 218
Trade-Related Aspects of Intellectual Property Rights Agreement. *See* TRIPS
trade secrets, 28, 156, 228–29, 234
traditional knowledge
    See also specific types (e.g., medicinal plants)
    bioprospecting agreements to protect, 137–38, 147–55
    commercial demand for, 84–85, 142–47, 144*t6.1*
    declarations, codes of conduct, research agreements, and other documents on use of, 141–42
    ethnobotanical knowledge, 159–81, 192–97
        putting into public domain, 177–78
    intellectual property rights to protect, 137–38
    intergovernmental agreements to protect, 107–9, 135–37
    Inuits and protection of, 122–23
    knowledge-sharing contracts for, 178
    Latin America countries and protection of, 123–26
    legal and policy framework to recognize, 134–42
    Maori and protection of, 216
    national laws to protect, 138–41
    Native Americans and protection of, 120–21

patent protection. *See* patents
    protection in developing countries, 30–34, 90, 212–32
    in public domain. *See* public domain
    regulation as destructive rather than protective force, 34–35
    San. *See* San traditional knowledge and Hoodia commercialization
    scope of, 207
Traidcraft plc, 81
Transfair, 78, 82–83
TRIPS (Agreement on Trade-Related Aspects of Intellectual Property Rights), 207–9
    on copyright, 218
    on geographical indications, 227
    harmonization with CBD, 137
    on individualization of rights, 210–11
    issues for developing countries from, 4, 13, 15, 28, 85–86, 95, 208–9
    See also costs as barrier in developing countries to enforcement of IP rights
    on moral rights, 216, 233
    on performers' rights, 223
    on plant patents, 194
    prior informed consent and, 196, 214–15
    scope of, 1, 3–4
    on secret information, 230
Tropical Botanic Garden and Research Institute (TBGRI) agreement with Kani, 20, 26–27, 32, 150, 153*b6.4*, 195–97
Tropical Disease Drug Development Program (Walter Reed Army Institute of Research), 154
tropical forest cultures. *See specific culture (e.g., Yekuana)*
Tunis Model Law on Copyright for Developing Countries (UNESCO/WIPO), 184, 219–20, 223
turmeric and medicinal uses, 22–23, 166–68, 168*t7.1*, 212–13
Tutuli Produce, 175

unfair competition, 226
    recommendations for developing countries, 234
United Nations Council on Trade and Development (UNCTAD), 214
United Nations Draft Declaration on the Rights of Indigenous Peoples, 135, 196
United Nations Educational, Scientific, and Cultural Organization (UNESCO), 53, 56, 184

Model Provisions on sui generis IP rights, 29, 191–92, 220–22, 232
Recommendation on the Safeguarding of Folklore, 184
report on folklore protection, 192
Tunis Model Law on Copyright for Developing Countries, 184, 219–20, 223
URMUL Rural Health Research and Development Trust, 63
Uruguayan tribe and Yerba Mate tea, 90
USPTO. *See* Patent and Trademark Office, U.S.

Venezuela
See also Yekuana
ABRAE as protected areas, 41
access to genetic resources, law governing, 139
Constitution of 1999 and indigenous rights, 43, 44, 211
debate over rights of indigenous people in, 43–44
Law on the Development and Protection of Craft Development, 125
new constitution and indigenous rights, 44
Prodesur and Conquest of the South program, 41
Vietnam
"Carpets" case involving copying of Australian aboriginal designs, 17, 117, 187
coffee crisis, 82
Visser, Coenraad J., 84, 103
Volkswagen (VW) America, 11–12, 35, 89

Walt Disney Co., 84
Walter Reed Army Institute of Research, Tropical Disease Drug Development Program, 154
wines and geographical indications, 227, 233
WIPO. *See* World Intellectual Property Organization
WIPO Copyright Treaty (WCT), 29–30, 222, 232
Wolfensohn, James D., 56
World Bank
African music, role in, 109–12
cultural industries, interest in, 56
culture programs of, criticism of, 96, 108
Development Economics Group on need for intervention in IP markets, 84
World Intellectual Property Organization (WIPO)
aid from, based on TRIPS, 209
Copyright Treaty. *See* WIPO Copyright Treaty (WCT)

Intergovernmental Committee on Intellectual Property and Genetic Resources, Traditional Knowledge and Folklore, 137–38, 184, 214, 216
Model Provisions on Protection Against Unfair Competition, 226, 229
Model Provisions on sui generis IP rights, 29, 191–92, 220–22, 232
Performances and Phonograms Treaty, 186, 223–24, 232
Portal of Traditional Knowledge, 28
Roundtable on Intellectual Property and Traditional Knowledge (1999), 123, 127
Tunis Model Law on Copyright for Developing Countries, 184, 219–20, 223
on types of protection, 114
world music market, 95
See also Africa Music Project; African music
World Summit on Sustainable Development (2002), 212
World Trade Organization (WTO)
See also TRIPS (Agreement on Trade-Related Aspects of Intellectual Property Rights)
aid from, 95, 209
copyright protection provided by, 219
on prior informed consent, 214
W.R. Grace's patents on biopesticides from neem trees in India, 22, 161–62, 163, 165, 166
chronology of commercialization of neem biopesticide, 164*b*7.1
Writer's Union (Senegal), 105, 107
WTO. *See* World Trade Organization

Yekuana, 3, 5–7, 37–51
Amazon Basin resources and, 39–42, 47
Aramare schools for, 42–43
changes to political and worldview consciousness of, 40–41, 48
Christian missionaries dealings with, 38, 39
Conquest of the South program and, 39
history of culture of, 37–39
intellectual property registration by, 50
protection of rights of, 42–44, 48–50, 229
restoration of culture of, 42–44, 49
rubber exploitation of, 38, 39
yellow beans and patent controversy, 23–24, 174–76, 177
Yerba Mate, 90
Yumbulul v. Reserve Bank of Australia (1991), 187, 189

Ziment, Irwin, 85
Zwonitzer, Mark, 32–33